ESSENTIAL PRACTICE

ESSENTIAL PRACTICE

Lectures on Kamalashīla's
Stages of Meditation in the Middle Way School

~

by Khenchen Thrangu Rinpoche

Translated by
Jules B. Levinson

Snow Lion Publications
Ithaca, New York ✦ Boulder, Colorado

Snow Lion Publications
P.O. Box 6483
Ithaca, NY 14851 USA
(607) 273-8519
www.snowlionpub.com

Printed in Canada on acid-free recycled paper.

ISBN 1-55939-181-2

Cataloging-in-Publication Data is available
from the Library of Congress

Text designed and typeset in Adobe Garamond
by Gopa & Ted2

This work is dedicated to the Seventeenth Gyalwang Karmapa,
Urgyen Drodül Trinley Dorje

~

Table of Contents

Introduction   1

Technical Note   4

Acknowledgments   5

PART 1: *First Treatise on the Stages of Meditation*   7

Chapter One: Kamalashīla, Compassion,
and the Mind of Awakening   9

Chapter Two: Practice   19

Chapter Three: Contemplation   31

Chapter Four: Calm Abiding   43

Chapter Five: Insight   55

Chapter Six: Certainty   65

Chapter Seven: Meditative Stabilization   77

Chapter Eight: The Ten Grounds of Bodhisattvas
and the Ground of a Buddha   89

PART 2: *Intermediate Treatise on the Stages of Meditation*   101

Chapter One: Compassion   103

Chapter Two: The Mind of Awakening
and the Causes of Calm Abiding   117

Chapter Three: The Causes of Insight   131

Chapter Four: The Selflessness of Persons   143

Chapter Five: The Selflessness of Phenomena   157

Chapter Six: The Six Transcendent Actions   171

Chapter Seven: The Fruit of Realization   187

Notes   199

Glossary   205

List of Works Cited   213

Introduction

I N THE SPRING OF 1988, the Ven. Thrangu Rinpoche traveled
from his home in Kathmandu, Nepal, to Boulder, Colorado,
where, at the invitation of the President and Faculty of the Nāropa Institute, he gave a series of lectures on the Indian master Kamalashīla's *First
Treatise on the Stages of Meditation in the Middle Way School*. He returned to
the Institute in the fall of 1989 and gave a second series of lectures, this time
focusing upon Kamalashīla's *Intermediate Treatise on the Stages of Meditation
in the Middle Way School*. A few words here may help readers to understand
the style of the instructions he gave then and the style of the translations I
have made now.

All sorts of people came to these talks. On any given evening, the listen-
ers would include students enrolled in the Nāropa Institute's program in
Buddhist Studies as well as students focusing upon other areas of the arts
and humanities, faculty representing the full range of the Institute's various
departments, numerous members of Boulder's sizeable Buddhist community, and the merely curious, carried in by serendipity. Some of those who
came to the lectures brought with them more than a few years of study and
practice in Buddhist communities; some may have known only that a fellow
with a big smile had come a long way to speak freely about wisdom. The
diverse audience provided a responsive canvas upon which to portray the
view, meditation, and conduct taught in the Great Vehicle (*mahāyāna*) of the
Buddhadharma.

Aiming to convey a clear and accessible account of Kamalashīla's treatises
that would prove handy to practitioners of the Buddhadharma, Thrangu
Rinpoche weaves many layers of scholastic expertise into an unruffled instruction. Rather than comment closely upon individual words and recalcitrant
passages, he focuses upon the themes of Kamalashīla's essays and brings them

into plain view. A reader of Kamalashīla's treatises will nevertheless find in these lectures the precision and guidance required for the navigation of a complex Buddhist treatise. Thrangu Rinpoche seems to hover gracefully just above the text, listening carefully to its melody, savoring the beauty and drama of its story, and then turning to us, his students, with whom he happily shares the meaning lifted lightly from an ancient heritage. As his translator on the occasion of these lectures, I marveled as the master worked his art, opening the palm fully, lavishing treasure upon the unsuspecting, beguiling all, disappointing none.

In translating these lectures, I have tried to remain faithful to Thrangu Rinpoche's tone and manner. I started from scratch by listening to the recordings that were made at the time and translating every word, aiming for accuracy and completeness. On the next round, I listened to the tapes again and looked hard at the English; wouldn't it be nice if the pleasure of listening to Thrangu Rinpoche were to come through? I hope that his many students will recognize the voice of their teacher in these translations. At minimum, readers will come away with a sense of how a veteran teacher of the Buddhadharma unfolds a passionate insight stage by stage.

Thrangu Rinpoche gave the first series of lectures one year after the death of Chögyam Trungpa, Rinpoche, the charismatic founder of the Nāropa Institute and a lifelong friend of Thrangu Rinpoche, alongside whom he had received ordination from the Sixteenth Gyalwang Karmapa, Ranjung Rigpe Dorje, at a young age. As a community, we stepped uncertainly into the void left by the death of our teacher. We found inspiration in the strength of heart and easy confidence, both in the Buddhadharma and in us, that Thrangu Rinpoche demonstrated on the occasion of these lectures; we look for words that will express our gratitude adequately but fail to find them.

In lecturing on Kamalashīla's treatises outlining the stages of meditation practiced in the Middle Way School, Thrangu Rinpoche remarked that "these treatises were composed newly in order to help the people of Tibet when the teachings of the Buddha were initially being established in Tibet. Now, because the teachings of the Buddha are beginning to flourish in America, I thought it would be helpful if I were to present these treatises, which are not like others." Some who study these instructions will be embarking freshly upon this noble journey. Others may feel that, after an extensive immersion in Buddhist teaching and Buddhist practice, they have at last come to the beginning of the path. Either way, a beginner's delight and a beginner's humility fit well with the accessible and authoritative portrait given here of a bodhisattva's view, meditation, and conduct. This record of a masterful teacher's instructions will help students old and new to determine what is essential to the practice of the Buddhadharma and thus to bring the Buddha's teachings into their own experience.

With devotion to the glorious lineages of genuine practice,
Jules B. Levinson
Boulder, Colorado
April 5, 2002

Technical Note:

In the transliteration of Sanskrit terms, I have departed from standard practice by replacing ś, ṣ, and c with sh, ṣh, and ch, respectively. Superscripted
Arabic numerals refer to notes that will be found at the end of Part 2. These
notes are numbered consecutively throughout the book. A glossary of
English, Tibetan, and Sanskrit equivalents will be found after the notes.

Acknowledgments

THIS VOLUME stands among the first offerings from the Light of Berotsana Translation Group, which Lama Chöying Wazi, Sangye Khandro, and I established in the spring of 1999. Over the coming years, we will offer many more volumes drawn from the literary and oral traditions of the Buddhadharma that have flourished among the Tibetan people. Please visit us at www.lightofberotsana.org if you would like to see where we are heading and how you may help us to go there. We offer our thanks to the Bodhi Foundation, the Rudolf Steiner Foundation, and Neal Greenberg for the vision and generosity that have made it possible for us to devote our energies to the work of translation.

Sidney Piburn and Steve Rhodes discovered many mistakes I had overlooked. Jessie Friedman untangled knotted sentences and led me to well wrought words. I thank all of them for diligent and creative labor. Thanks also to William Karelis and Lyle Weinstein for encouraging me to bring this work to completion and helping me to do so.

I made these translations using Nota Bene and its offspring. The many years of effort that Nota Bene's designers and programmers have put into creating a superlative family of tools for writers has made my task immeasurably easier and much more fun.

PART 1

*First Treatise on the Stages of Meditation
in the Middle Way School*

CHAPTER ONE

Kamalashīla, Compassion, and the Mind of Awakening

THIS EVENING I will say a few things about the Buddhadharma. I wish to thank all of you for regarding this as something important and for coming to hear what I have to say. I will begin by offering a supplication. Please listen with faith in the Buddha and the Dharma. After that I will begin to explain the text.

[TR chants]

This evening I will be speaking about the stages of meditation that were taught by the great Indian master Kamalashīla. In Tibet we have both Sūtra and Mantra. The stages of meditation that Kamalashīla explained in his text on that topic are mainly those of Sūtra.

In the seventh century, King Songtsen Gampo ruled in Tibet; later, Trisong Detsen ruled there also. Both caused the teachings of the Buddha to develop in Tibet. Trisong Detsen invited the Indian master Shāntarakshita, who has come to be known as the Bodhisattva Abbot, to come to Tibet. He accepted the king's invitation and established the Buddha's teachings newly in Tibet. Having disseminated the Buddha's teachings, while in Tibet Shāntarakshita entered nirvāṇa. Not long before dying, he said,

> I have planted the authentic Buddhadharma in Tibet. However, in the future there will be trouble for the Buddhadharma in Tibet. Generally, when there is trouble for the Buddhadharma, it comes from those who are not Buddhists, but that is not what will happen in Tibet. The trouble will come from someone who is a Buddhist but who will speak falsely. When trouble comes, you should invite my student Kamalashīla, who lives in India. He will quell the troublemaker, which will allow the authentic Buddhadharma to remain for a long time.

In that way, Shāntarakṣhita foretold what was to happen in the future.

Later, in accordance with the great Abbot Shāntarakṣhita's prophecy, a man named Hwa Shang Mahāyāna came from China to Tibet and taught dharma. The dharma that he taught was a little different from the dharma taught by the great master Shāntarakṣhita. Hwa Shang Mahāyāna said that just as black clouds cover space and the sun, so white clouds also cover space and the sun. Also, just as when a black dog bites, the bite causes pain and hardship, so when a white dog bites, the bite wounds and causes pain. The two dog bites are the same in that way. Similarly, both nonvirtuous thoughts and virtuous thoughts obstruct clear seeing. Therefore, we should remain without any thoughts at all. Hwa Shang Mahāyāna said that that was the main point.

When Hwa Shang Mahāyāna taught this slightly different dharma, everyone became confused. They did not know how to practice dharma. They did not know how to enter the paths. Thus, trouble arose. When the king realized that trouble had come to those who practiced dharma, he convened a meeting so as to determine what would remedy the situation. At the meeting, one of the great Abbot Shāntarakṣhita's students reminded the assembly of the prophecy that Shāntarakṣhita had given at the time of his death. Since things had come about as Shāntarakṣhita had foretold, the Tibetans invited Kamalashīla to come to Tibet, as Shāntarakṣhita had recommended.

When, having come to Tibet, Kamalashīla met Hwa Shang Mahāyāna for the first time, Kamalashīla thought, "If he has knowledge, we can meet in debate. If he is a fool, we cannot meet in debate." In order to see whether or not Hwa Shang Mahāyāna had knowledge, Kamalashīla circled Hwa Shang Mahāyāna's head three times with a stick, thereby posing the question, "From what cause do the three realms of cyclic existence arise?" Because Hwa Shang Mahāyāna had great knowledge and good qualities, he understood the gesture that Kamalashīla had made and withdrew his hands inside the sleeves of his robe, thereby replying, "The three realms of cyclic existence arise from the ignorance that conceives of the apprehended and the apprehender."

In dependence upon that, Kamalashīla knew that Hwa Shang Mahāyāna possessed knowledge and that they could meet in debate. Thereafter, people gathered for the debate. The king, a witness, Kamalashīla, and Hwa Shang Mahāyāna were sitting together, and the king placed one garland of flowers in the hands of Kamalashīla and another in the hands of Hwa Shang Mahāyāna. The king then said, "Two systems of dharma have arisen: the dharma of sudden realization and the dharma of gradual realization. Because of that, people have become confused about how to practice dharma. To clarify that confusion, please debate. When you have debated, the loser should, without pride, offer his garland of flowers to the victor. Then, whoever loses should leave Tibet and return to his own country."

Then they debated. Kamalashīla asked questions and defeated Hwa Shang Mahāyāna. Having lost, Hwa Shang Mahāyāna offered his garland of flowers to Kamalashīla, did not remain in Tibet, and returned to China. Beginning from then, the traditions of dharma taught by the great Abbot Shāntarakṣhita and by Kamalashīla have held sway in the snowy land of Tibet.

After that, King Trisong Detsen said the following to Kamalashīla: "You have seen the trouble that arose here. In order that the teachings of the Buddha not be afflicted similarly in the future, please compose newly a good treatise that is easy to understand and of great benefit." In dependence upon the king's request, Kamalashīla newly composed the threefold text known as the *Stages of Meditation*, which consists of the *First Treatise on the Stages of Meditation*, the *Intermediate Treatise on the Stages of Meditation*, and the *Final Treatise on the Stages of Meditation*.

Thus, these treatises were composed newly in order to help the people of Tibet when the teachings of the Buddha were initially being established in Tibet. Now, because the teachings of the Buddha are beginning to flourish in America, I thought it would be helpful if I were to present these treatises, which are not like others.

Kamalashīla returned to Tibet two more times. However, there are some who debate this. For instance, in the account of Kamalashīla's life given in the edition that I am using,[1] it is said that Kamalashīla did not return to Tibet again. Rather, the author of the introduction maintains that Hwa Shang Mahāyāna hired four Chinese men to kill Kamalashīla, and that indeed they succeeded in killing him. However, I think that Hwa Shang Mahāyāna was a great bodhisattva who taught dharma, and that he did not in any way arrange the murder of Kamalashīla.

Some people doubt that Kamalashīla returned to Tibet, and there is a basis for their doubt. When Kamalashīla left Tibet, he went to India. On his way to India, he came across the corpse of an Indian man who had succumbed to a terrible illness. Because the illness was contagious, no one dared come near the corpse. Kamalashīla wanted to help the people of the area. His consciousness moved to the corpse, walked the corpse to a distant place, and dumped it there. Then his consciousness came back to the place where he had left his own body. However, in the meantime, an Indian siddha named Padampa Sangye, who had a very ugly body, came across Kamalashīla's body, which was very handsome and completely free from illness. He thought, "This body of mine is not good. That fresh corpse is good and handsome. I would like my consciousness to transfer into that body." His consciousness then moved into the body of Kamalashīla and he walked off, leaving his own body. When Kamalashīla's consciousness returned, the only body around was the ugly corpse of the Indian siddha, into which the consciousness of Kamalashīla entered. Thus, the mind was Kamalashīla's but the body was not.

Kamalashīla came to Tibet twice in the body of Padampa Sangye. In that body, he disseminated the methods for practicing "the pacifier," also called "cutting."[2] This practice is included within the tradition of Sūtra rather than within the tradition of Mantra. Kamalashīla's *Stages of Meditation on the Middle Way* and the practice of pacification through cutting attachment are, in terms of their meaning, the same. Since the person who taught them is the same, it is not surprising that the meaning of these practices is the same.

The story that I have recounted to you is told in Karma Chakmay's *Mountain Dharma*. It does not accord well with the account given by the author of the Introduction to the edition of Kamalashīla's text that I am using. I believe that, in truth, the matter is probably as Karma Chakmay has reported it and, for that reason, I have presented it to you as he does.

Generally speaking, the *First Treatise on the Stages of Meditation* covers three topics: (1) the need for compassion, (2) the need for the mind of awakening, and (3) the need for bringing this into experience through practice. The first thing taught is the importance of compassion. The Buddha himself stressed the importance of compassion. In what sūtras did he express this? In the *Sūtra Compiling the Dharma Correctly*, in the *Sūtra Taught by Akshayamati*, and in the *Hill of the Gayā Head Sūtra*. The Buddha said, "Anyone who has one quality can become a buddha. What is that one quality? Compassion."

After that, the manner of cultivating compassion is taught. Knowing that compassion is important, we want to know the method for generating compassion in our continuum and the way to cultivate it. The way to do that is to consider sentient beings who are in pain. If we take many sentient beings to mind and consider their pain, great compassion will arise. For that reason, this treatise explains how to think about the pain that sentient beings experience.

What is the way taught here for considering sentient beings who are in pain? We consider the ways in which wanderers of the six types suffer. I understand that some of you have studied the Buddhadharma for a long time and that some of you have not studied the Buddhadharma very much. Those of you who have not studied the Buddhadharma will be astonished at this notion of six types of wanderers. However, if you study the Buddhadharma stage by stage, you will be able to understand the meaning. Therefore, I will speak about the six types of wanderers in accordance with the way that they are spoken of in the text.

First, sentient beings born in hells suffer greatly from heat, cold, and so forth. Similarly, sentient beings born as hungry ghosts suffer greatly from hunger and thirst. Also, sentient beings born as animals experience many sufferings such as eating one another, becoming angry with one another, harming one another, killing one another, and being used by human beings. If we think about such suffering, compassion for sentient beings who take birth as hell-beings, hungry ghosts, and animals will arise.

Similarly, human beings have many kinds of suffering. Some human beings are put into prisons. Some are destitute. Some are enslaved by others. Thus, they are not actually hell-beings, but their sufferings are like those of hell-beings; they are not actually hungry ghosts, but their sufferings are like those of hungry ghosts; and they are not actually animals, but their sufferings are like those of animals. We think in that way about the sufferings that human beings experience. Some human beings are wealthy and comfortable. However, that wealth and comfort does not last for a very long time. Not being able to enjoy wealth and comfort for a long time, in the end suffering comes to them too. When we think about the suffering that they experience, compassion arises.

The demigods suffer from continual jealousy of and warfare with the gods of the Desire Realm. As for the gods, though comfortable temporarily, later they fall down into painful situations and, at the time of falling, they suffer greatly. Similarly, even the gods of the Form Realm and the Formless Realm cannot just stay there. They fall down to the states of hell-beings, hungry ghosts, animals, humans, and so forth. When they fall, mentally they suffer greatly. Therefore, sentient beings born in the states of the six wanderers have nothing but suffering. If we think about that, compassion can arise.

In thinking about sentient beings who are suffering, we think, "If I had to undergo that suffering myself, I could not endure it." In that way, we generate compassion for others by imagining ourselves to be in their position. After that, we think about the suffering of our friends, relatives, and others who love us, and we cultivate compassion for them. When we can meditate well in that way, we think about ordinary people—those who are neither our friends nor our enemies—and cultivate compassion for them. When that goes well, we think about our enemies—those who harm us. Realizing that they too have suffering, we develop compassion for them. In that way, compassion is increased more and more greatly. When we can generate compassion for our enemies to the same degree that we can generate compassion for our friends, we must then cultivate such compassion for all sentient beings in all the ten directions.

Meditating in that way, the main thing is to develop compassion for all, as if they were equal, rather than for some but not for others. For instance, we may have compassion for human beings but not for non-human sentient beings. Or, we may have compassion for human beings included within "us" but not for human beings included within "them." Such compassion is not the genuine compassion that benefits everyone, both ourselves and others. If we have only partial compassion, then we will help some sentient beings but harm others. Compassion that accords with dharma is not like that. In the perspective of such compassion, all sentient beings are as if equal. If we have compassion for all sentient beings, that is the principal among all types of compassion, and it is superior compassion.

That is the first topic, the way to meditate so as to develop compassion. The second topic is the way to meditate so as to develop the mind of awakening. How do we do that? When we have developed compassion for all sentient beings, we feel that we must be of some use to others. If we help sentient beings with temporary things, generally it is useful and good. However, if we help people only with food, clothing, wealth, medicine, and so forth, it helps them only for the time being. When those things are used up, they suffer again. In light of that, what will really help? Enabling sentient beings to enter into the excellent dharma will really help because by way of the excellent dharma they can achieve the final fruition, the rank of a buddha, so that in the end they will not have to suffer at all. Such an attitude, which is the effect of compassion, thinks, "I must protect all sentient beings from suffering by establishing them in the rank of a buddha." That mind is the mind of awakening. If compassion arises in a genuine way, the mind of awakening will arise naturally.

There are two methods for cultivating that mind of awakening. What are the two? The first is that a guru, who is our spiritual friend and upon whom we rely, teaches the mind of awakening, speaks of its good qualities, and says, "It would be good if you were to give rise to the mind that aspires to supreme awakening. In fact, you must give rise to the mind that aspires to supreme awakening." Having thought about that, we give rise to a mind that aspires to supreme awakening. That is the first way of giving rise to the mind of awakening and it is a good way. The second way is to begin by giving rise to compassion. Then the mind of awakening will arise naturally. The first way is good, but the second way is stable and powerful. Therefore, the best way to give rise to the mind of awakening is in dependence upon great compassion.

That mind of awakening is important and beneficial. The Buddha himself explained this with an example. When a diamond is broken into pieces, it is still much better than ornaments of gold. Similarly, even if we are not actually able to put the mind of awakening into practice, due to having it as as our motivation, our virtue will surpass the virtue of hearers and solitary realizers. Therefore, the Buddha said, the mind of awakening is important.

Similarly, in another sūtra, the Buddha said that, although the merit of the mind of awakening has no form, if the merit of the mind of awakening did have form, it would fill all of space and would still exceed even that. The mind of awakening has that measure of benefit.

What minds of awakening are there? The mind of awakening has two aspects. What are the two aspects? There is the mind that aspires to awakening and the mind that enters into the activities that lead to awakening. The mind of aspiring to awakening thinks, "May I be able to accomplish the welfare of sentient beings. May I be able to establish all sentient beings in the rank of buddhahood." Making effort for the sake of that is the mind that enters into the activities that lead to awakening. Those are the two aspects.

That concludes the second topic. I will stop here this evening. If you have questions that you would like to ask, please ask them.

Q: It has been said by some scholars that Hwa Shang Mahāyāna did not leave Tibet. They say that he remained in Tibet and had something to do with the arising of the Great Completeness teachings. Could you comment on that?
A: Some people do say that; but to say that is to criticize the system of the Great Completeness, because it is to say that the system of the Great Completeness is like the system of Hwa Shang Mahāyāna. Those are words that refute the Great Completeness. Some say that Hwa Shang Mahāyāna lost

one of his boots when he left Tibet and that, through that condition, a little bit of his view is present in the Great Completeness teachings of the Nyingma. Actually, that is not so, and to say that it is so is to criticize the Great Completeness.

Q: You said that incomplete or partial compassion can harm other people. How is that?

A: Suppose that I have compassion for one group and do not have compassion for another group. If the two groups fall into disharmony, then I will take the side of the group for which I do have compassion and I will feel hatred for the group for which I do not have compassion. For instance, if I have compassion for my friend, and if there is someone who is harming my friend, I will feel hatred for that person. In dependence upon that hatred, I will initiate action that harms him or her. After I have harmed that person, he or she will harm me in return. Partial compassion is the cause in dependence upon which this arises.

Q: Are the six types of wanderers merely psychological states? You mentioned that in the human realm there are psychological states comparable to the hell-realm, hungry ghost realm, animal realm, and so forth. If they are not psychological states, where are the hell-realms and god-realms, and what are the beings there like?

A: The six types of wanderers are not just mind. Generally speaking, they have form. In Vasubandhu's *Treasury of Higher Knowledge* it is said that hell-beings and hungry ghosts are mostly under the ground of Jambudvīpa, which is to say, in the ground. The gods of the Desire Realm, the Form Realm, and the Formless Realm are in the sky. Therefore, it is probably like that. For instance, scientists say that within the earth there is fire. Some say that there are sentient beings there.

Q: Why is Hwa Shang Mahāyāna's doctrine false? Both black clouds and white clouds cover the sun. If we go to the bad migrations, they are painful. If we take birth in the upper realms, they provide only temporary happiness. Therefore, we must abandon all three realms of cyclic existence and achieve liberation. How does that differ from Hwa Shang Mahāyāna's tradition?

A: Generally, Hwa Shang Mahāyāna's thought is not some terrible thing. However, if we refute the value of virtue suited to the occasion, then people will not be able to practice virtue. If people are not able to practice virtue, meditation will not be able to increase to a higher level. In dependence upon that, saying that it is not good to refute the value of appropriate virtue, Kamalashīla refuted Hwa Shang Mahāyāna. Refuting the value of appropriate virtue does not lead to much good. It is in dependence upon our accumulation of virtue that our meditation increases to a higher level. In dependence upon our meditation increasing to a higher level, we achieve the rank of a buddha. Kamalashīla said that although the happiness of humans and gods is generally not very stable, to achieve liberation gradually it is important to have the body of a god or a human as our support. To achieve the lifetime of a god or a human, we need to practice virtue.

In Hwa Shang Mahāyāna's system, compassion is only a temporary virtue and must be destroyed. Kamalashīla held that we must cultivate both compassion and the mind of awakening. Hwa Shang Mahāyāna held that we must destroy both compassion and the mind of awakening. In his view, we must destroy everything. That was the point that they debated.

Q: I have heard that as human beings we have the unique ability to experience all of cyclic existence. Is there a connection between that and our ability to hear and practice the dharma? If not, what is it that makes birth as a human being an unusually opportune situation?

A: Kamalashīla's text explains that humans experience situations that are similar to those of bad migrations but are not identical to them. For instance, human beings who have been put into prison are not hell-beings but experience something similar to a hell. Also, human beings who are poor are not hungry ghosts but experience something like the poverty of hungry ghosts. However, it does not say that human beings experience the actual suffering that hell-beings or hungry ghosts experience. Thus, human beings experience something like the suffering of hell-beings but, compared to the suffering of actual hell-beings, human beings have little pain. Similarly human beings experience something like the suffering of hungry ghosts but, compared to the suffering of actual hungry ghosts, human beings have little pain. As human beings we have achieved the opportunity to practice dharma. Hell-beings and hungry ghosts have not achieved the opportunity to practice dharma. That is the difference between our situation and theirs.

Q: What about the sentient beings in the higher realms? What prevents them from hearing and practicing dharma?

A: They are extremely comfortable and are not able to feel discouragement with cyclic existence. Because they never feel discouraged with cyclic existence, they cannot generate the wish to enter into the dharma. In dependence upon that reason, they have no opportunity to practice the dharma.

CHAPTER TWO

Practice

IN ORDER TO LISTEN to the dharma, in accordance with our Buddhist tradition, we turn our minds toward supreme awakening. Generally, at all times and in all activities, as we discussed yesterday, we need compassion and the mind of awakening. In particular, when we are practicing dharma, or newly requesting dharma, or studying dharma, if we are motivated by the intention to accomplish supreme awakening, in the future our activity will serve as a cause of achieving buddhahood and as a cause of benefiting all sentient beings. That is why we need pure motivation. For that reason, please turn your minds towards supreme awakening and listen.

Yesterday I mentioned that the *First Treatise on the Stages of Meditation* covers three topics: (1) the need for compassion and the way to cultivate compassion, (2) the need for the mind of awakening, when we have grown accustomed to compassion, and the way to cultivate the mind of awakening, and (3) the way to bring the instructions into experience through practice. I spoke about the first two topics yesterday. Today I will speak about the way to practice.

First, in cultivating compassion we develop the motivation to protect sentient beings from suffering. Second, we must generate the mind of awakening, the motivation that is a wish to protect sentient beings from the suffering of cyclic existence by placing them in the rank of buddhahood. It is not sufficient just to generate the motivation. We must actually put it into practice. When we put it into practice, what must we do? We think, "How will I place all sentient beings in the rank of buddhahood?" We ordinary beings are not now able to establish sentient beings in the rank of buddhahood. What is the reason why we are not able to do that? It is because our minds are afflicted in various ways. To whatever extent our minds are afflicted, to that extent we are unable to help other sentient beings. Therefore, first we must abandon our afflictions and increase our good qualities and knowledge. For that reason, we must bring the teachings that we have received into experience.

What must we accomplish? We must accomplish the rank of a buddha. The Buddha said that if we practice well, we can achieve the rank of a great bodhisattva or buddha, and that if we do not take practice as the essence, we cannot achieve the rank of a buddha. Therefore, we must practice. Similarly, in the *King of Meditative Stabilizations Sūtra*, it is said that we must definitely practice. Why? If we practice, we can gain the rank of buddhahood. If we practice, gaining the rank of a buddha is not difficult. Therefore, we must practice.

What practices must we practice? Generosity, ethics, constancy,[3] exertion, stable contemplation,[4] and knowledge—the six transcendences. Similarly, immeasurable love, immeasurable compassion, immeasurable joy, immeasurable equanimity—the four immeasurables. Giving generously, speaking pleasantly, acting in accordance with the ways of the world, and furthering the welfare of trainees—the four bases for gathering students. And so forth. Conducting ourselves in accord with the conduct of bodhisattvas is the way to practice.

Since we must train both in the ways of the world and in the stable contemplations and knowledge that pass beyond the world, in brief a bodhisattva must train in method and knowledge. Also, the Buddha said that the rank of a buddha cannot be achieved either through method alone or through knowledge alone. Similarly, the Buddha said that if we have two qualities, the rank of a buddha can be achieved quickly. What are those two? Method and knowledge.

What is method? The five transcendences other than knowledge—transcendent generosity, transcendent ethics, and so forth—are method. The four bases for gathering students are method. Resources and wealth used for the benefit of sentient beings are method. All of those are called "method." If method is not affected by knowledge, there is the danger that method will become perverted. If it is affected by knowledge, method will be correct. Therefore, if the aspects of method—great resources, great wealth, great power, many activities, and so forth—are affected by knowledge, they will bring about a good result for everyone, both ourselves and others. For example, if poison is struck with a mantra, it becomes harmless. Similarly, if method is affected by the vitality of thoroughly pure knowledge, it becomes a cause of achieving the rank of a completely awakened buddha, who has destroyed the obstructions to awakening, who possesses all good qualities, and who has passed beyond misery. The Buddha said this in a sūtra.

Kamalashīla's treatises on the stages of meditation speak extensively about the need for both knowledge and method. What was the reason for speaking about this extensively? In propagating the dharma in Tibet, Hwa Shang Mahāyāna had said that knowledge alone was needed, and that method was not necessary. Thus, those who had been born in Tibet and had entered the Buddhist teachings regarded method as of little importance. They regarded method as something unimportant. In that way, they had gone on a wrong path. In order to protect them from that wrong path, Kamalashīla had come from India to Tibet. In Tibet, he had debated with Hwa Shang Mahāyāna. In debating Hwa Shang Mahāyāna, he defeated him. Therefore, on this occasion too, Kamalashīla said that without question and for many reasons knowledge and method must both be present, and that, if they are separated, by that the rank of liberation and omniscience will not be achieved.

The text tells a story about the eighth bodhisattva ground. Bodhisattvas who have achieved an eighth ground have become accustomed to meditative stabilization. They tend to abide in meditative stabilization. When they abide in meditative stabilization, the victorious, resplendent, and transcendent buddhas instruct them not to abide in meditative stabilization for such a long time. The buddhas rouse the bodhisattvas from meditative stabilization. If method were not needed, there would be no need for the buddhas to rouse from meditative stabilization the bodhisattvas who dwell upon an eighth ground. If knowledge alone were sufficient, those bodhisattvas would achieve the fruit of complete awakening from just that meditative stabilization. Kamalashīla therefore observes that the buddhas' rousing from meditative stabilization the bodhisattvas who dwell upon the eighth ground contradicts Hwa Shang Mahāyāna's thought that method is not needed.

Kamalashīla gave a citation from a sūtra to support his observation. In a sūtra, to a bodhisattva resting in meditative stabilization on an eighth ground, the Buddha said, "Son of noble family: you are able to rest in meditative stabilization. You can bear the ultimate. However, you do not now have all the good qualities of a buddha, such as the ten powers and the four fearlessnesses. You must now achieve those qualities of a buddha. Therefore, not remaining in meditative stabilization for a long time, you must undertake to exert yourself. You must develop further endurance. Do not cast those away. Similarly, many sentient beings have minds that are not peaceful, that have many types of afflictions, and various thoughts. They have much hardship. There are many who are like that. Think about them. You must further their welfare. Merely to rest in meditative stabilization is not sufficient. You must rise from meditative stabilization." The Buddha gave that command.

Furthermore, in the same sūtra, the Buddha said, "Son of noble family: the body of a buddha is immeasurable. The wisdom of a buddha is immeasurable. The pure lands of a buddha are immeasurable. The light of a buddha's body is immeasurable. The melodies of a buddha's speech are immeasurable. The activity of a buddha is immeasurable. You must definitely achieve those. You have now achieved nonconceptual meditative stabilization only. You have not achieved the other good qualities of a buddha in their entirety. The good qualities of a buddha are inconceivable, vast, immeasurable, and unparalleled. You must know that they are such and, knowing that, you must achieve them. Therefore, you must definitely rise from meditative stabilization." The Buddha gave that command.

In dependence upon the exhortations of the buddhas, the bodhisattvas dwelling upon an eighth ground arise from meditative stabilization and accumulate the collections of merit. In order to achieve the good qualities of a buddha, they exert themselves at developing endurance and becoming skilled in method. Exerting themselves in that way, they can achieve the ultimate, the rank of a buddha. Except for that, if the buddhas did not exhort the bodhisattvas dwelling upon an eighth ground to rise from meditative stabilization, the bodhisattvas would remain solely within meditative stabilization. Remaining within meditative stabilization, they would not achieve the rank of a buddha. If they were not to achieve the rank of a buddha, they would not be able to further the welfare of sentient beings in the way that a buddha can. The Buddha spoke about this in a sūtra. His statements there contradict those of Hwa Shang Mahāyāna.

In a sūtra known as the *The Extensive Collection of All Qualities*, the Buddha spoke to Shrī Mañjughosha. When he spoke to Shrī Mañjughosha, he said that, if we abandon dharma, that is a great obstruction that will bring immediate retribution. Some people think that some of what the Buddha said is good and that other things that the Buddha said are not good. In that way, they abandon dharma. If we abandon dharma in that way, it is the same as deprecating the Buddha. For instance, thinking that the factor of knowledge is good and that the factor of method is not good serves as deprecation. Therefore, students ought to value both method and knowledge and keep them together, rather than thinking that one is good, the other bad, and separating them.

In another sūtra, the Buddha put questions to his regent, the protector

Maitreya. The six transcendences are for the sake of achieving buddhahood. Some people think that practitioners need only transcendent knowledge and do not need the other transcendences. That is mistaken. Why is that a mistake? The Buddha asked, "Maitreya, what do you think? When I was the king in Kāshika, I protected the life of a pigeon. When I protected the life of that pigeon, I cut flesh from my body and gave my flesh to a hawk who wanted to eat the pigeon. Was this a stupid thing to do? Between knowledge and method, this was done on account of method. Was this, therefore, the work of an idiot?" To which Maitreya replied, "Not at all. This was truly appropriate." Similarly, the Buddha asked, "If we accumulate the virtues of the six transcendences in their entirety—if we accumulate virtue that possesses all six transcendences—will that harm our achievement of buddhahood?" Maitreya replied, "It will do no harm." What was the need for asking those questions? The Buddha asked those questions in order to demonstrate the need to practice knowledge and method together. The exchange between the Buddha and Maitreya refutes Hwa Shang Mahāyāna.

In that way, both knowledge and method are necessary. Therefore, they must both be taught. For that reason, here, the way of bringing knowledge into experience is taught from the point of view of two aspects, those being knowledge and method. The Buddha said that nirvāṇa must be achieved in dependence upon authentic knowledge. Why is that? There are two obstacles to achieving nirvāṇa: superimpositions and deprecations. To regard as existent something that does not exist is superimposition. To regard as nonexistent something that does exist is deprecation. Abandoning the two extremes of superimposition and deprecation, practitioners can achieve the rank of buddhahood. The two extremes must be abandoned by way of knowledge.

What do we need to do in order to generate knowledge? In our Buddhist tradition, we speak of three aspects of knowledge. The three aspects of knowledge are the knowledge that arises from hearing, the knowledge that arises from contemplation, and the knowledge that arises from meditation. We must generate those three. From among those three, when we engage in meditation initially, we need to generate the knowledge that arises from hearing first. What is the reason for that? It is because we do not know how to generate knowledge. We need to rely upon the instructions of someone who does know how to generate knowledge. Who can teach those instructions? The Buddha can teach them. Therefore, we rely upon the words of the completely awakened Buddha and upon the treatises that comment upon his thought. Moreover, we hear those from the mouths of our own gurus, who are our spiritual friends. Because we ourselves must know their meaning, we must generate the knowledge that arises from hearing.

The Buddha spoke about this in the *King of Meditative Stabilizations Sūtra*. In that sūtra he said that the selflessness of all phenomena must be realized. How is that selflessness to be realized? First, our own individual knowledge analyzes and investigates well. After that, we meditate. That is how nirvāṇa must be achieved. Through other causes, the rank of a buddha will not be achieved.

Similarly, in another scripture, the Buddha spoke about emptiness by saying that nonproduction is true and that phenomena such as production are not true. Similarly, in a *Sūtra on Transcendent Knowledge*, speaking to Subhūti, the Buddha said, "Subhūti, form is empty of form's own entity." That is to say, emptiness is the entity of form itself. Similarly, consciousness is empty of consciousness. In that way, the Buddha taught the meaning of emptiness. The knowledge of hearing must be generated through hearing such words of the Buddha and treatises that comment upon his thought.

After that, we need to generate the knowledge that arises from contemplation. What knowledge arises from contemplation? We ourselves must investigate and analyze with reasoning. The Buddha himself said that, when it comes to bringing into our own experience the instructions that I, the Buddha, have given, both monks and the learned must investigate and analyze well. We should not merely think "The Buddha said so" and practice without investigating and analyzing. He compared the way that monks and scholars should analyze his teachings with the way that someone intending to purchase gold will analyze gold carefully to ensure that it is genuine. First, to see whether or not it is good, we will burn it in fire. When we burn it, does the color change? If the color does not change, externally the gold is good but internally there may be a flaw. To see whether or not the gold is flawed internally, we cut it and look inside. Even if the gold is not grossly flawed internally, there may still be random flaws here and there. For that reason, we polish the gold. If after investigating and analyzing the gold in these three ways—burning, cutting, and polishing—we think that the gold is good, we will want to purchase it, but we will not do so merely due to believing some other person who says that the gold is good. Like that example, the Buddha said, we should not enter into practice just thinking, "The Buddha said that." Rather, he said, we have to enter through investigating and analyzing with reasoning.

Having heard the sūtras spoken by the Buddha, we must analyze with the knowledge that arises from contemplation. Having analyzed, we can then truly place our confidence in what the Buddha said. We can then feel confident and think, "It is actually true." Therefore, after generating the knowledge that arises from hearing, we must generate the knowledge that arises from contemplation. At the point of discussing the knowledge that arises from contemplation, Kamalashīla speaks about emptiness. In order to know whether what is said about emptiness is true or not, we must analyze by way of two reasonings. So, at this point, two reasonings are taught.

The first reasoning is an analysis of causes. If these things were not emptiness, then they would first have to arise from causes. There would first have to be causes. They would have to arise from causes. If they arose from causes, they would be things. Because [we think] they are things, we analyze whether or not they arise from causes. This is called, "analysis of causes." Generally, in the context of treatises, this reasoning is one taught by the master Chandrakīrti in his *Entrance into (Nāgārjuna's) "Treatise on the Middle."* How do these things arise from causes? If these things actually exist, how do they arise? Do they arise in dependence upon causes or not?

Some people think that causes are not necessary. They think that things do not need causes and can exist without them. This is mistaken. Think about it. If you plant a seed in a flowerpot, a flower will grow. It will not grow from this table in front of me now. What is the reason for that? The causes for a flower are present in a flowerpot, and for that reason a flower can grow there. The causes for a flower are not present on the surface of this table, and for that reason a flower cannot grow there. If things arose in the absence of causes, a flower would have to be able to grow from the surface of this table even though the causes for a flower are not present there. Or, as we know, flowers bloom in the summer but not in the winter. What is the reason for that? In the summer, the causes and conditions for the growth of flowers are complete. In the winter, they are not. In dependence upon that, flowers grow in the summer but not in the winter. If causes were not necessary, flowers would grow in the winter also. They would grow at all times.

Some think that things arise in dependence upon causes. Some religious traditions maintain that things arise in dependence upon causes. For instance, some non-Buddhist traditions say that a permanent cause, a god such as Maheshvara or Viṣṇu creates things.[5] They say that such a god has existed without change from the very first until now. They say that this permanent god makes this entire world. If the god were permanent, there would be no change in the entity of that god. If there were no change in the entity of that god, then that god would always be complete. If that god were complete, then flowers ought to grow in the winter as well as in the summer, and they ought to grow from this table as well as in a flowerpot. Why? Because the causes for the arising of flowers are present in that god. If we ask them why flowers do not grow from the top of the table or in the winter, they say that it is because the concordant conditions are not entirely complete. That entails that the god is impermanent: sometimes the god makes flowers, and sometimes the god does not make flowers. Because of that, the god is impermanent.

Some say that things arise in dependence upon impermanent causes. However, things do not arise from impermanent causes. Impermanence involves the gradual change of past, present, and future. That which has passed cannot produce effects. That is because the past has already passed; it is not a thing.[6] Similarly, the future does not produce effects. That is because the future has not yet arisen. The future is that which will come later. It does not exist now. It is not a thing and not a cause. Because it is not a cause, an effect will not come from it. Thus, neither the past nor the future produce effects.

If something arises now, the present must produce it. The present is a thing. Because the present is a thing, it must be able to produce effects. However, if we say that the present produces its effect now, both the cause and its effect exist now. If the effect already exists now, it does not need to arise from a cause. If the cause exists now but its effect does not, the cause will no longer exist at the moment when its effect comes into existence. When it no longer exists, it cannot produce anything. Therefore, impermanent causes do not produce effects.

If we examine, we see that (1) effects do not arise in the absence of causes, (2) permanent causes do not produce effects, (3) impermanent causes do not produce effects, (4) the past does not produce effects, (5) the future does not produce effects, and (6) the present does not produce effects. Therefore, because causes do not produce effects, we can know that they are emptiness.

In that way, causes do not produce effects. They are emptiness. However, merely conventionally, in dependence upon causes, effects merely arise. In the context of dependent relationship, they merely appear, merely dawn, and are called "the conventional." Their nonestablishment when analyzed with reasoning is called "the ultimate."

This is the reasoning that analyzes causes. Who set this reasoning out? Chandrakīrti set it out. However, Chandrakīrti did not make it up himself. The Buddha taught it briefly in the *Rice Seedling Sūtra*. Then Chandrakīrti taught it extensively. It is also taught here, in Kamalashīla's *Stages of Meditation in the Middle Way School*, as a method for realizing emptiness.

Tonight I have presented the first of the two reasonings set forth by Kamalashīla. Tomorrow evening I will present the second reasoning. I think it will become clear then. If there are any points about which you feel doubt or that you do not understand, please ask questions.

Q: Many teachings from different masters are similar and noncontradictory. When we choose the Buddhist path, does that exclude all other paths? Can the Christian path and the Buddhist path be taken simultaneously?

A: Generally there are many traditions of dharma. Jesus had a kind heart and vast activity. He was a great and unusual being. The completely awakened Buddha was an actual buddha. Both are extremely good. When we practice a religion, it is acceptable to practice points that are common to different traditions. Where the traditions diverge, there are contradictions. What is the reason for that? The dharma spoken by Jesus is good but Jesus did not say, "If you practice this dharma, you will achieve the rank of a buddha." He instructed people to do good, to love, and to have compassion. If we practice the dharma that he spoke, we achieve the results of which he spoke. If we practice the dharma that the Buddha spoke, we achieve the results of which the Buddha spoke. The results are a little different. Where there is agreement, it is acceptable to practice the two traditions together. Where there is disagreement, practicing both traditions doesn't work. Why not? Individual results are achieved individually. Jesus did not teach anything bad. He taught good things and vast activity arose. The same is true of the Buddha and his teaching. If we practice the individual methods of which they spoke, we achieve the individual results of which they spoke.

Q: Does the Buddhist path exclude all others? If you receive the vows of refuge, does that exclude practice of all other traditions?

A: Receiving the vows of refuge does not require us to abandon all other traditions of dharma. Nor can we say that we do not abandon any other traditions. We abandon whatever contradicts the Buddhist tradition. We do not abandon that which does not contradict the Buddhist tradition, such as excellent action. We cannot say unequivocally that we have abandoned all other traditions of dharma when we have gone for refuge to the Buddhadharma. Nor can we say unequivocally that we have not abandoned other traditions of dharma. That depends upon their individual, internal meanings. Where there is contradiction, one or the other has to be abandoned. When there is no contradiction, neither has to be abandoned.

Q: My notes on the four ways of gathering students are not complete. Please tell me again what they are.

A: If a teacher thinks that the excellent dharma will link another person to a good result, then, in order to establish an accord with his or her mind, there are four things that he or she can do. The first is to give gifts of things that the student needs. The second is to speak pleasantly. He or she says things that the student can endure hearing rather than things that the student cannot endure hearing. The teacher speaks to the student in a way that the student finds pleasant rather than in a way that makes the student depressed or angry. The third is to act in a way that accords somewhat with the student's way of doing things. In order to draw the student to the dharma, the teacher accords slightly with the ways of the student. This is called "according with the ways of the world." Fourth, the teacher must not act in a way that contradicts the dharma. If we are to draw others to the dharma, our own behavior must accord with the dharma rather than contradict it. These four are the four ways of gathering students. They are methods that enable students to enter into the dharma correctly.

Q: I'm not sure whether the analysis of which you were speaking this evening goes with knowledge or with method. Would you explain that?

A: Investigation and analysis are mainly the practice of knowledge. Knowledge includes the knowledge that arises from hearing, the knowledge that arises from contemplation, and the knowledge that arises from meditation. This evening I spoke about the first two kinds of knowledge, i.e., those that arise from hearing and contemplation.

Q: Does that mean that method refers to the earlier practices of the immeasurables and the transcendences, and that knowledge comes subsequently?

A: Not exactly. Method and knowledge are to be practiced together. Method accompanies knowledge and knowledge accompanies method—that is how we are to bring these teachings into our own experience.

Q: Is it accurate to say that method is what is involved with the practice of meditation and knowledge is what is involved with analysis? Are they separated in that way?

A: No. Method mainly means conduct, and knowledge mainly applies to meditation.

Q: I got a little lost in the analysis of causes. Flowers do not grow from tables and they don't grow in the winter. Things do have causes but, if you look at them, they don't come from permanent or impermanent causes. The point seems to be that if you take a line of analysis to an extreme, it falls apart. Then you talked about Chandrakīrti's discussion of the conventional. I'm not sure how the teaching of the conventional relates to the analysis that leads to the discovery of emptiness.

A: How do we come to realize that, ultimately, all things are emptiness? First, we think, "This is real." Then we investigate and analyze with reasoning. We do not find the well-established thing that we took to be so real. Therefore, ultimately it is emptiness. However, it appears as a mere conventionality. There is conventional appearance. That conventional existence depends upon other things. For example, when I am on this side of a river, the mountain on the far side of the river is the mountain over there and the mountain on the near side of the river is the mountain over here. When I have crossed to the other side of the river, the mountain that was over there is now here and the mountain that was nearby is now the mountain over there. Which one is really over there and which one is really over here? There is neither stability nor definiteness to that. Therefore, neither mountain is either here or there. In dependence upon the mountain that is further away, the closer mountain is said to be over here. In dependence upon the mountain that is closer, the mountain that is further away is said to be over there. These are merely conventions.

For instance, if you compare these two sticks of incense, this one is long and this one is short.[7] So, *this* one is long, right? Now, *this* one is long and *this* one is short.[8] So is this one long or short?[9] Who can say? When you put it with the longer one, it is short. When you put it with the shorter one, it is long. Actually it is neither long nor short. However, in relation to other things, it may be either long or short.

Q: You explained that knowledge without method is a problem. That makes sense. You also said that method without knowledge is a problem too. I don't think that I understand that. Please explain that point.

A: Method without knowledge does not see ultimate reality directly. Method alone will not enable us to achieve the rank of a buddha.

CHAPTER THREE

Contemplation

IN THE BUDDHIST TRADITION, when we listen to the dharma, motivation is of the greatest importance. The reason for that is that if our motivation is pure, the actions of our body and speech will naturally become pure. If our motivation is not pure, our actions will naturally become impure. Therefore, pure motivation and the correction of our motivation are important. What is the pure motivation that we need? The mind that aspires to supreme awakening for the sake of all sentient beings is the supreme among all motivations; therefore, please rouse that aspiration and listen.

In the first section of Kamalashīla's *Stages of Meditation*, there are three topics: compassion, the mind of awakening, and practice. From among those three, this evening I will be discussing practice. The discussion of practice involves two topics: method and knowledge. Currently we are considering knowledge, which is presented in terms of the knowledge that arises from hearing, the knowledge that arises from contemplation, and the knowledge that arises from meditation. I spoke previously about the knowledge that arises from hearing; this evening I will continue speaking about the knowledge that arises from contemplation. Here, that is explained by way of two reasonings: (1) an analysis into causation, which I described last night, and (2) the reasoning of freedom from one and many, which I will describe to you now.

Kamalashīla sets forth the reasoning of freedom from one and many in accordance with the intention of the *Sūtra on the Descent into Laṅka*. He analyzes the things that we perceive directly by categorizing them into two groups: (1) those that have form, which is to say, things that can serve as objects for sense consciousness, and (2) those that do not have form, which is to say, consciousnesses, which are present internally in the aspect of mind. In general, the Buddhist treatises speak of the outer—the apprehended, that which is composed of particles, matter—and the inner—consciousness, luminous and knowing in nature. Here, Kamalashila speaks of those two groups as that which has form and that which does not have form.

Let us first examine things that have form and that are composed of particles. The text speaks of "vases and so forth." It means vases, pillars, buildings, mountains, caves, and so on. We are to analyze the external forms that can serve as objects for sense consciousness. They are not truly established as single, indivisible entities. Rather, they are all just particles that have been gathered into a lump. Therefore, the fully awakened Buddha spoke of the "aggregate of form." He called them "aggregates" because they are not truly established as one thing. Rather, because they are a lump into which many things have been gathered, he called them "aggregates of form."

It is helpful to illustrate this point in terms of some particular thing. For instance, this is my hand.[10] I think, "This is my hand." Also, if I show it to other people, they will say, "That is a hand. It is one hand." In the context of mere conventionalities, it does the work of a hand. It writes letters, puts things here and there, and so on. It does all the things that a hand is supposed to do. Is it truly one thing? No, it is not. There is a thumb, an index finger, a middle finger, a ring finger, and a little finger. Distinguishing the many, individual things, we can then ask, is the thumb the hand? No, it is a thumb. Is the index finger the hand? No, it is the index finger. Is the middle finger the hand? No, it is the middle finger. Similarly, there is the skin outside and the flesh, bone, and blood inside. There are many things there. What, then, is the hand? My mind considers the gathering of many things—thumb, fingers, flesh, skin, and so on—to be a hand. Except for that, there is no hand that is truly one thing.

We may think that even though a hand is not truly one thing, perhaps a finger is one thing. That is not so either. A finger is composed of one section up to the first joint, a second section up to the second joint, a third section up to the third joint, a fingernail, and so on—it is many things gathered together.

Then we may think that even though a finger is not truly one thing, perhaps one section of a finger is one thing. It is not. There is the outside, the inside, and everything in between. Continuing to probe in this way, in the end we arrive at tiny particles. Thus, a finger is only a lump in which many, many tiny particles are gathered together.

Thus, a hand is not truly one thing, a finger is not truly one thing, a section of a finger is not truly one thing, and a fingernail is not truly one thing.

In each case, many things gathered together are conceived to be one thing. Nothing is truly one thing.

When we analyze in this way, we arrive in the end at particles. We may wonder whether or not one particle may truly be a single thing. At this point, we are considering particles so tiny that they cannot be separated into pieces. However, they can still be divided mentally. When examined mentally, there is an eastern portion and a western portion. That makes two parts. If even this tiny particle has parts, then partless things just do not occur. Everything is multiple in nature; nothing whatsoever is truly one. What, then, are things such as forms? They are all like dreams. There are no things that are truly established.

This teaches that external forms are emptiness. We may think that, even though external forms are emptiness, mind, which has no form, is truly one. However, when investigated, mind too turns out to have no entityness. For instance, an external form may have many colors: blue, yellow, red, white, and so on. Thus, it is not truly established as one, for it is many things rather than one thing. Once it is many, the consciousness that apprehends it is also many. For instance, my hand is not truly established as one because it is a composite of many things, such as the thumb, the index finger, the middle finger, the ring finger, the little finger, and so forth. The mind that apprehends the hand is also not one solid lump. There is the apprehension of the thumb, the apprehension of the index finger, the apprehension of the middle finger, and so on. Thus, the mind too is multiple in nature; there is no mind that is truly established as single. Therefore, the Buddha said,

External forms do not exist.
Our own minds appear as the external.

First, the Buddha said that external forms do not exist. All are empty. While not existing, they appear. In that case, where do appearances appear? Blue and so forth are not outside; our own mind appears externally.

How can we understand that internal mind appears as external things? For example, when we go to sleep at night, we can dream many things: mountains, valleys, companions, horses, elephants, and so on. The appearances in our dreams look like real elephants, mountains, and water, and we go along thinking that they are real. In fact, they are not separate from our own minds. We are sleeping in our bedrooms. There are no elephants in our bedrooms; no horses, no mountains, and no buildings. Our minds can dawn in the aspect of external objects. Like the elephants and so on in that example, so now these appearances too dawn as appearances of our minds.

Therefore, internal mind dawns as many things. Internal mind is multiple; it is not established as one. In dependence upon that reason, an external form is not truly one thing, and internal mind is not truly one thing.

We may think that, even though an internal or external thing is not truly one thing, it may truly be many things. However, true multiplicity does not occur. Why not? If there were one, there could be many. Starting with one, there could be two, three, four, five, and six. If one does not exist, there is no way whatsoever to get to many.

Therefore, neither external form nor internal mind is truly established. Everything is false. However, like the appearances in dreams, internal mind appears despite being false and, like illusions, external forms dawn despite their entity not being established. Such was said by the Buddha. Therefore, one does not exist and many do not exist. Why do neither one nor many exist? Because they are empty entities. Because all things are not established ultimately, one and many do not exist.

Such is said in the *Descent into Laṅka Sūtra*, where forms are compared to the forms that appear in a mirror. The forms that appear in a mirror are neither one nor many. The likenesses of form that appear in a mirror are neither one with the mirror nor separate from the mirror. Thus, they are neither the same as nor other than the mirror. Despite being neither one nor many, do those likenesses of form nevertheless appear in the mirror? They do. Like this example, all things are seen in the minds of ordinary beings. We do see them; are they true? They are not true. What is the truth? The Buddha said that the ultimate—all phenomena not being established by way of their own entity, emptiness—is the truth.

In dependence upon reasoning, we can show that things are emptiness. Last night, through analyzing causes, we showed how things are an emptiness that is the nonestablishment by way of entity. This evening, analyzing whether things are one entity or different entities, we showed from another point of view that things are emptiness. In dependence upon these demonstrations of emptiness, we may think that karma—cause and effect—does not exist. We may think that, since phenomena are emptiness, there are neither virtuous nor evil actions. We may think that there are neither causes nor effects. Are these the implications of emptiness? No. Why not? It is because things are emptiness that change occurs. It is because of emptiness that it is suitable for effects to arise from causes. It is because all phenomena are emptiness that it is beneficial to accumulate virtuous karma and disadvantageous to accumulate evil karma. If phenomena were not emptiness, things would be concrete and truly established, and effects would therefore not arise from causes. Last night we discussed the impossibility of things arising from existent causes, causelessly, from permanent causes, or from impermanent causes. From whatever point of view we look at it, if causes were truly established, they would have no effects. Because of being empty, all of that can happen. Therefore, "conventional truth" does not in any way entail the absence of karma—cause and effect.

For example, sometimes a likeness of the moon appears in water. When we see a likeness of the moon in the water, the moon is not actually there. Seeing the moon there is false. Because of being false, the moon can appear in the water. If the moon in the water were the actual thing, how could it appear in the water? It could not, could it? If the moon in the water were truly the moon, it would not appear in the water. It is because the moon that appears in the water is false that it can appear in the water. It is because of not being true that a moon can appear in the water. Like the moon in the water, whatever appears to us—causes, effects, everything—dawns through the power of not being truly established.

Generally, there are many reasonings. However, here, in Kamalashila's *First Treatise on the Stages of Meditation in the Middle Way School,* in the context of the knowledge that arises from contemplation, these two reasonings are taught. They allow the definite knowledge that all phenomena are emptiness to arise in our minds. Analyzing with these two reasonings, we come to think, "All phenomena are emptiness, aren't they?" When we have not trained in the books, if someone were to say, "My hand is emptiness," who would believe that? No one would. Everyone would scoff at that. When these two Middle Way reasonings have been grasped, if someone were to say, "My hand is emptiness," we would think, "Oh, that's so, that's true." Therefore, these two reasonings prove all phenomena to be emptiness.

This is how knowledge arises from contemplation. Why must we generate the knowledge that arises from contemplation? Merely hearing these explanations does not generate conviction and definite knowledge. In order to generate distinctive and definite knowledge, we must investigate and analyze by way of reasoning. Because we must investigate and analyze, these two reasonings are taught. When these two reasonings have been taught and definite knowledge has arisen, what then? Definite knowledge alone will not link us to a good result. It is necessary to meditate. Until then, we may feel convinced that phenomena are emptiness, but we will not be able to see that they are emptiness in direct perception. Why not? Because of predispositions to which we have become accustomed from time without beginning. What antidote to those predispositions do we require? Familiarity with emptiness. To become accustomed to emptiness, we must meditate. In that sense, we must generate the knowledge that arises from meditation.[11]

When we meditate, we can really understand the meaning. Why? If we were to meditate consistently upon something that is *not* true, the appearance of it would probably arise. For instance, if we were to meditate for a month or a year upon a horn growing from our own heads, the image of just such a horn could come to be present upon our heads. That image is not true; it is just something that we have imagined in meditation. Emptiness is not like that. In meditating upon a horn growing from our heads, we would be mistaking what is not for what is. When we meditate upon emptiness, we familiarize with what is already so. Therefore, the apprehension of emptiness can gradually become ever more clear and stable.

For these reasons, we must meditate. How must we meditate? In general, there are two types of meditation: calm abiding and insight. With which of those two do we begin? We do not begin by meditating upon emptiness. We must first understand emptiness, but when we meditate, we must first cultivate calm abiding. Why? Initially, our minds are not stable. Many thoughts arise. We cannot meditate. Therefore, in order to calm those many thoughts, we must first cultivate calm abiding. For example, when water is shaken or stirred, the likeness of a form cannot appear in it. When water becomes still, a likeness of the moon can appear in it. Therefore, if a likeness of the moon is desired, the water must first become still. Similarly, we do not meditate upon emptiness at first. First, we must cultivate calm abiding. Why must we cultivate calm abiding? This is done in order to stabilize our minds.

When our minds are still, whatever we meditate upon will appear clearly. That is to say, when the mind is still, it is possible to accomplish what we have set out to do. Therefore, we must cultivate calm abiding. What do we need in order to cultivate calm abiding? Kamalashila enumerates four causes. First, he says, "Do not look to desire, and abide well in ethics."[12] "Do not look to desire" means that if we make all sorts of astonishing plans, thinking "In the future I will do great and wonderful things: I will establish a hugely successful business and I will become immensely wealthy," then our minds are not still. For that reason, we do not indulge in extreme desire. Rather, we think, "Now I will meditate well."

What does it mean to "abide well in ethics?" Generally, there are many ethics. Here, Kamalashila does not speak specifically of, for instance, the ethics of a monk. He means, rather, that we should not behave recklessly and indiscriminately. Instead of carrying on in a completely unregulated way, we act in a simple way. We govern ourselves well. That is called "abiding well in ethics."

Kamalashila then speaks of a third factor that will enable us to cultivate calm abiding: "having the nature of taking on suffering voluntarily."[13] That means that we are able to bear the difficulty of meditation as well as the time that it takes. When it becomes a little difficult to meditate, we do not think, "I have been meditating for such a long time. It is so hard to continue. Despite all this meditation, nothing whatsoever has come of it." Rather, we are able to bear the difficulties of meditation. Finally, Kamalashila names a fourth quality that we will need: exertion. Kamalashila says that if we have these four, we will be able to accomplish meditation quickly.

This explains, in a general way, four causes or roots from which good meditation can grow. Tomorrow evening I will speak about the way to meditate: how to arrange our bodies, where to reside, and so on. This evening I will stop here. If you have any questions, please ask them because they will probably be helpful to everyone.

Q: Since all things have a nature of emptiness, what is the cause of emptiness and how does a mind perceive this phenomenon, emptiness?
A: Emptiness does not need a cause. Why not? Suppose that, having gone to sleep, I were to dream of a large elephant. That elephant would not be established. I would be mistaken about that elephant. What is the cause of that elephant's absence? There is no cause of that elephant's absence. Except for the fact that there is no elephant, there is no reason why there is no elephant. From the first, it is absent, right? When I see an elephant in my dream, I am mistaken. Since seeing an elephant is a mistake, there is no elephant. Therefore, there is no particular cause for the elephant not existing.

As for your second question, this evening I have spoken to you about the prerequisities for successful meditation. Later I will explain the way to meditate. Then you will hear about the way that a mind sees emptiness.

Q: Are we one world? Also, what does "all sentient beings" include?
A: Generally we do not limit our discussions to this world. We say, "equal

to the limits of space." That means that we are concerned about all sentient beings wherever they may be.

"All sentient beings" means that we are not thinking only about human beings. We are thinking about animals also and, in the context of the Buddhadharma, we are thinking about the six types of sentient beings who go from lifetime to lifetime. For instance, to speak about those sentient beings that we can see, there are the sentient beings that live on dry land, those that live in water, those that fly in the air, and so on. In brief, "sentient being" means the presence of a feeling mind. For instance, this book has no feeling.[14] Something unlike that, where a feeling mind is present, is a sentient being.

Q: Then what is the responsibility of the individual to the nonsentient matter of this world? If we have the responsibility of compassion to sentient beings, I would think that we have some responsibility toward the nonsentient world too.

A: If we were to take care of the water, the trees, the air, and so on, that would certainly be a good thing to do. However, the Buddhadharma does not specifically teach that we must take up that responsibility. The Buddhadharma teaches the methods for well being and the absence of suffering where mind is present. There is certainly no contradiction between bringing happiness to the minds of sentient beings and taking care of the planet, but in the Buddhadharma it is not said that we must without fail do that.

Q: When you say that things are not one, you give as your reason the fact that they are many. Then, you say that things are not many because they are not one. That's not fair! How can you say that?

A: From the point of view that one does not exist and many do not exist, it is not possible to speak either of one or of many. However, now we are speaking of them. One does not exist, but we see as if there were one. Because we see in that way, it is then said that one is not established. Similarly, many do not exist but we see as if there were many. We are mistaken. That misleading many is a many that does not exist. For instance, suppose that, when someone dreams of an elephant, we were to say that there is no elephant in the dream. If there is no elephant whatsoever, how can we say that there is no elephant? We can say that. There is no elephant in the dream, but in the dream an elephant was observed. In dependence upon that, we can say, "You dreamed of an elephant, but there was no elephant."

Q: Could you not just say that things are not one because they are many and, for that reason, there is no true essence. Why do you need to say that things are not really many?

A: Let's consider the example of the hand again. First, my hand is not one. There are various parts, and we can count them. We see that a hand is many. Because we see multiple elements, we then set that seeing of many parts as the sign proving that the hand is many. We see that it is many. After mulling that over, we think, "Okay, it is not one but it is many, isn't it?" No, it is not many either. If initially there were one, there would then be a basis from which to build up to many. Because there is no basis upon which to build, many do not exist either. In this way, the matter is settled decisively with reasoning. Then we ascertain definitively that neither one nor many are present.

Too concise? Okay, let's try again. To prove that one does not exist, we investigate, for instance, a hand, and count the parts: one, two, three, four, five. It is a fivefold thing. It is many things, not one. Initially, the hand is apprehended as one. The apprehension of one is refuted. What is the apprehension of one that is to be refuted? The appearance for my mind—that is what I refute. How does it look then? We think, "Well, it is not one, but it is many, isn't it?" But thinking about this again, we realize that many does not work either. If there were one, there could be many: one, two, three, four, up to a lot. However, we cannot get to one. How could there be many? Reasoning settles it decisively. In fact, one does not exist, and many do not exist; then, all things are emptiness. The two branches of this reasoning are taught as methods enabling us to understand this.

In sum, to prove that things are not truly established as one, we introduce many. When many is introduced, we think, "It is many, not one." After many has been introduced, the conception of many remains, and the nonexistence of many has to be introduced.

Q: You said that it is because the moon is not in the water, you can see it there. It struck me that if the moon were in the water, you would see it pretty well. I think you meant that the way you are seeing it depends on the fact that the moon is in the sky and the light reflects from it. When you say that the reason we can see things at all is that they are not there, do you mean that the process of perception itself depends on the fact that what you are perceiving is not there?

A: Let me give you a second example. Suppose that I were to go to sleep in a tiny room and dream of an elephant. If that elephant were truly established, how could it fit in that tiny room? It would not fit, would it? It is through the power of not being truly established that an elephant can appear in the tiny room where I am sleeping, right?

Q: You spoke about consciousness as "that which does not have form." Is consciousness subject to the same analysis as form?
A: When "that which does not have form" looks at a form, various appearances dawn. Therefore, mind too is multiple rather than single. That is how consciousness is analyzed in the context of searching for truly established one and truly established many.

Q: Are eye consciousnesses that arise during meditation conventional minds?
A: Well, we have been talking about the knowledge that arises from contemplation of what we have heard. The way in which appearances arise from meditation is a little different. I will talk about that later.

Q: I do not understand how we can see the reflection of a moon without there being a real moon, or how we can dream of an elephant without prior experience of an elephant. How else can we account for the perceptions that we do have?
A: Right now we are considering examples for the forms that appear on various occasions rather than examples for the causes of those appearances. For instance, in giving the appearance of the moon in the water as an example, we are not giving it as an example for the appearance of a moon in the sky. We are asking about the moon appearing in the water: "There is a moon in the water. Is it really there? Is it true or not?" We are not yet asking, "From where does the moon in the water come?" Similarly, when giving the elephant appearing in a dream as an example, we are analyzing whether or not the elephant appearing within the dream is itself truly established; we are not giving examples for the predispositions that are the cause of that appearance.

Q: How is it that we perceive what we perceive? If what we perceive is actually emptiness, how is it that we agree in our perceptions?
A: It is possible for common appearances to dawn. For instance, now we see the likeness of electric lights in this glass of water.[15] A likeness of the lights dawns there, but the lightbulbs themselves do not actually go into the water. This likeness of the electric lights is false. They are not there. Nevertheless,

we all see this. We see the same thing, don't we? It arises in dependence upon the same causes and conditions.

Q: We also agree that there are lightbulbs in the room, and yet the nature of the lightbulbs themselves would be emptiness.

A: Yes, and in speaking of the likeness, I was giving an example of that. Like the false image appearing in the glass, the electric lights themselves are emptiness. If we analyze with reasoning that which is emptiness, it can dawn as emptiness. Then we can have confidence that they are emptiness. Even though they are emptiness, we can all see them.

CHAPTER FOUR

Calm Abiding

IN OUR BUDDHIST TRADITION, we have both Sūtra and Mantra. In the context of Sūtra, we speak of the causal vehicle of defining characteristics. When calling this the causal vehicle of defining characteristics, we do not take the result as principal; rather, we emphasize causes. The result must be achieved, and when causes bring about transformation, then the result can arrive in a genuine manner. In dependence upon that, presently, in the context of causes, if we first modify our motivation into something good, then conduct of body and speech also will naturally become good. Therefore, at all times and in all aspects, motivation must be regarded as important. Now, on the occasion of listening to dharma, as I mentioned to you yesterday, it is necessary to develop pure motivation, the mind intent upon supreme awakening. Thus, please refresh such a mind intent upon supreme awakening and listen.

In the first of his three treatises known as the *Stages of Meditation*, Kamalashīla discusses compassion, the mind of awakening, and practice. We have already considered the first two, bringing us to the third, practice. In discussing practice, Kamalashīla presents both method and knowledge; we have considered method already, bringing us to knowledge. Knowledge arises in dependence upon hearing, contemplation, and meditation, and we are now concerned with the third, meditation. Meditation consists in calm abiding and insight; we have come to the discussion of calm abiding. Yesterday, we mentioned four causes for the arising of calm abiding. Today, we will look at the portions of the treatise that teach the way in which calm abiding is brought into experience.

With these four supports for calm abiding well established, the question of where to meditate arises. The treatise explains that we should meditate in a place pleasing to the mind. Generally, for people such as ourselves, this means a place where there is little disturbance from others in the daytime—that is to say, where there are not many people going back and forth—and not much noise at night, meaning not much screeching of animals and human beings. The place should also be clean and pleasant. That is the sort of place in which we should meditate.

When it is time to meditate, place before you a representation of the form of the Buddha, the forms of bodhisattvas, or the supports for the body, speech, and mind of the awakened ones as a support for our faith. Then, in order to accumulate the collection of merit, offer prostrations, acknowledge your ill deeds, rejoice in the merit of others, and so forth, and in that way accumulate the collection of merit by way of the seven branches. Make great compassion for all sentient beings manifest, such that you are meditating not for the sake of your own comfort, for the sake of temporary happiness, or in order to achieve happiness and well being for yourself alone. In that way, generate a mind of compassion in your continuum, in the hope that your meditation will be of benefit to all sentient beings.

Having established a pure motivation, arrange the posture of your body. On this occasion, we are instructed to straighten our bodies and sit on a comfortable seat. That is to say, when cultivating meditative stabilization, we should sit comfortably. According to the quintessential, uncommon instructions of the Kagyü, we may sit in the posture known as the Seven Qualities of Vairochana or in that known as the Five Qualities of Stable Contemplation; either one will do. These postures have great purpose. Therefore, in this treatise, it is said that our seat should be comfortable, which means that we do not have to sit in the vajra posture. If we sit comfortably, meditative stabilization can be accomplished easily. In this way, all the instructions for the essential points of the body are given.

The treatise has spoken of the place where we should stay and the posture of our bodies. It then teaches the methods for placing the mind. Generally, we must place our minds upon a thing. That is to say, generally speaking, if we were to place our minds upon a non-thing, due to the power of familiarization from time without beginning, it would be a little difficult. In order to lead our minds there gradually, first our minds are placed upon a thing. Things come in two varieties: those that have form and those that do not have form. In the beginning it is best to place the mind upon the five aggregates, or the eighteen elements, or some other aspect in which all things are included, and merely to observe them in a natural manner. Here, that is said to be the way to begin to practice meditative equipoise.

Gradual methods of leading the mind to meditative stabilization are given also in the context of quintessential instructions. For instance, the Ninth Karmapa, Wangchuk Dorje, composed three treatises giving instruction in the practice of Mahāmudrā: the *Ocean of Definitive Meaning, Dispelling the Darkness of Ignorance,* and *Pointing a Finger at the Dharmakāya.* Within those, in order to lead gradually to calm abiding, first our minds are held to something external, beginning with something impure, such as a pebble or a piece of wood. We place a small stone or a small piece of wood in front of ourselves, and the mind is held there, merely not forgetting the object. Or, we may place a small, colored drop in front of ourselves—blue, white, red, and so on—and meditate upon that, not forgetting it, such that our minds become focused and undistracted. Afterward, our minds are held to something pure, such as the body of the Tathāgata. We place a small representation of the body of a buddha in front of ourselves, and the mind is held to the body of that buddha merely without forgetting it. Later, holding the mind a little bit internally, we will hold the mind to the inhalation and exhalation of breath. Such methods for training in meditative stabilization are taught. However, on this occasion, it is said that we hold our minds to a mere coarse thing.

It is said that, when we meditate in that way, there will be obstacles to the cultivation of meditative stabilization. For instance, all sorts of thoughts—desire, hatred, bewilderment, pride, envy, and so on—will arise. When those thoughts arise, our minds wander away. Here, this treatise does not explain extensively the steps we should take when our minds wander into such thoughts. Rather, it mentions only briefly that meditation upon ugliness serves as the antidote to desire, that meditation upon love serves as the antidote to hatred, that meditation upon dependent relationship serves as the antidote to bewilderment, and so forth. Meditation of that sort gradually causes hatred, pride, desire, and so on to diminish. The treatise recommends these contemplative practices as effective techniques that we must know and understand; however, fearing that a thorough discussion of these topics would result in an excessively lengthy book, Kamalashīla has only mentioned them here. If we want to read about these topics in detail, we should look at the chapter on stable contemplation in the *Ornament for Precious Liberation* composed by Gampopa. There, in the section describing the cultivation of calm abiding, Gampopa explains extensively the way in which to meditate upon ugliness as the antidote to desire, upon love as the antidote to hatred, upon dependent relationship as the antidote to bewilderment, and so on. If you read there, I think you will gradually come to understand this way of working with obstacles and training the mind.

Even if the particular antidotes to particular obstacles are not explained extensively in this treatise, the antidote to all of them is explained in a general way. How so? When such distractions arise, they arise because we do not like meditative stabilization and we do like distraction. As an antidote, we must come to like meditative stabilization and dislike distraction. What method will serve to reverse my preference for distraction? Thinking about the good qualities of meditative stabilization, we reflect that meditative stabilization is necessary and beneficial; that it is helpful to all—both ourselves and others; that, except for meditative stabilization, nothing will protect us from suffering; that, in dependence upon meditative stabilization, happiness will arise in our minds and bodies; that, in dependence upon meditative stabilization, all afflictions will be pacified, the rank of a buddha will be achieved, all good qualities will be generated, and so on. When we contemplate in that way, joy and delight in meditative stabilization will arise. As for distraction, whether we are distracted by desire, by hatred, or by something else, that distraction will obstruct meditative stabilization and prevent us from achieving meditative stabilization, in dependence upon which good qualities will not arise in us. Not only will good qualities not arise, but also we will experience various aspects of suffering in different states of cyclic existence and our own afflictions will increase. Then, in dependence upon the increase of our afflictions, various aspects of suffering will arise. Thinking correctly about those faults, we come to dislike distraction, whereupon distraction diminishes, and we come to like meditative stabilization, whereupon exertion at meditative stabilization increases. Therefore, from that point of view it is said that we must pacify distraction.

The treatise speaks now of the obstacles that harm meditative stabilization in particular: laxity and excitement. The treatise teaches the methods for abandoning those two. Sometimes lethargy, sleepiness, and laxity arise. Or, our attention becomes hazy. Or, we actually fall asleep. In those ways, our minds become lax. What must we do when our minds become lax? "Cultivate discrimination of appearances."[16] Set the mind such that all appears lucidly. This will help with laxity and sluggishness. That is one method. Second, think of the good qualities of a buddha in general, and also think of yourself achieving the rank of a buddha. Remember that meditative stabilization causes us to achieve the good qualities of a buddha. When we think of the good qualities of meditative stabilization and of buddhas, our minds become more lucid, and laxity and lethargy diminish as well. Those are the methods for dispelling laxity.

How does excitement come about? We remember happiness, good things, and joy that we have experienced in the past. Then our minds become wild. When wildness arises, our minds seem to be more lucid. We must loosen that apparently enhanced lucidity. How can we do that? By meditating upon impermanence, remembering the suffering of cyclic existence, and in that way generating a little discouragement with cyclic existence. When we do that, we separate from wildness, which does us no good.

Laxity and excitement are not merely afflictions; they are the principal obstacles to meditative stabilization. Because they are principal among obstacles to the actual practice of meditation, the methods for overcoming these two are taught here in an easy way.

When laxity and excitement arise, there are two types of instructions that can be applied: (1) those requiring effort and (2) those that are effortless. When do we apply the instructions that require effort? We must be able to recognize laxity and excitement as soon as they arise. Having recognized laxity, we must make the effort of applying the methods for abandoning laxity until laxity has been abandoned. Or, if wildness arises, we must make the effort of applying the methods for abandoning wildness until wildness has been abandoned. When do we apply the instruction of effortlessness? When we have separated from laxity and excitement and rest correctly in the equipoise of meditative stabilization, if we were again to make effort, that would cause the mind not to rest in meditative stabilization. Therefore, at that time, we make no effort whatsoever. When mind rests well, free from laxity and excitement, we must meditate in an effortless, relaxed way. Those are the two ways of overcoming laxity and excitement: with effort and effortlessly.

In a sūtra, the Buddha, who had destroyed the two obstructions, taken possession of all good qualities, and passed beyond the extremes of existence and peace, taught the nine methods for the mind's abiding that compose the path of calm abiding. "Placing the mind" is the first of those nine methods for the mind's abiding. "Placing" means setting the mind in equipoise such that it does not fall under the power of distraction. We set the mind and make it stable for a brief period of time. "Continually placing" is the second of the nine. When the first step is going well, then we can lengthen the period of time so that the mind abides not merely briefly but for a while. "Repeatedly placing" is the third of the nine. When placing the mind continually, distractions intervene. Occasionally mind wanders. When the mind wanders, we understand that and reflect, "I have become distracted. I have slipped into that thought." Dropping that thought, we again set the mind back in meditative stabilization. For that reason, the third method is called "repeatedly placing."

"Close placement" is the fourth of the nine mental abidings. In the third mental abiding, we abandon distractions and place our minds again. The fourth mental abiding, "close placement," serves as a method for lengthening the period of nondistraction. Recognizing that we have slipped into distraction, we sustain meditation by way of mindfulness and conscientiousness. In that way, we set our minds in equipoise. This is called "close placement." "Taming" is the fifth mental abiding. What method for taming the mind do we need? We need a technique that will enable our minds to abide in meditative stabilization. Great delight and great joy in meditative stabilization is the technique. When we think of the good qualities of meditative stabilization, we can abandon distraction in a gentle manner, without difficulty or hardship. We will be able to meditate joyfully and with delight. Generating joy and delight in our minds is called "taming." "Pacifying" is the sixth mental abiding. When we generate joy, some distraction will arise. As a method for abandoning that distraction, we must know the faults of distraction. Knowing distraction to be faulty and seeing the disadvantages of distraction, we will not enjoy distraction. If we can see distraction as an opponent and even become a little angry with distraction, then we will not enjoy distraction and it will not come around very much. That is called "pacifying," the sixth of the nine mental abidings.

"Thoroughly pacifying" is the seventh mental abiding. When laxity and sleepiness arise, then, through applying the practices explained previously, we thoroughly pacify laxity and sleepiness. When they arise, we must rely vigorously upon the antidotes. "Making one-pointed" is the eighth mental abiding. In dependence upon the methods for the mind's abiding, the mind abides in a stable way; that is the stage called "making one-pointed." When the mind abides in a stable way without relying upon any antidotes at all, we place our minds loosely and gently. We do not apply antidotes or make any effort. We rest freely in a natural state. "Evenly placing" is the ninth mental abiding. When the mind abides in the way just described, we cultivate neither joy nor sorrow. Neither do we repair it with an antidote. Rather, we rest in equanimity. That is called "evenly placing." In dependence upon those nine methods for the mind's abiding, the mind is caused to abide.

In order to meditate well, we must consider the faults that may prevent meditative stabilization. When they are gathered into groups, there are six principal types of faults. They make for flawed meditative stabilization or they prevent abiding in meditative stabilization. How must we abandon them? The Buddha himself spoke of eight applications or techniques that will cause us to abandon the six types of faults. He said that we must rely upon those. When we rely upon them serially, what fault comes first? First comes laziness. Laziness means having no interest in meditation, not liking meditation, or finding meditation to be difficult. We do not want to meditate. We cannot engage in meditation. Upon what must we rely as the antidote to laziness? Here, it is said that we must rely upon a fourfold antidote. First, we must generate faith. What faith must we generate? We need faith in the good qualities of meditative stabilization. We need conviction that meditative stabilization has good qualities. I think that meditators in the West do have great conviction and great faith in meditative stabilization. If that sort of conviction is present, laziness will not be much of a problem. Second, we must generate longing. When, in dependence upon faith there is great conviction, we feel that, come what may, we must cultivate meditative stabilization. Such faith, longing, and aspiration are necessary because they motivate us actually to take the instructions in hand. "Taking the instructions in hand" means not merely wanting to meditate; it requires exertion. First, we must be able to engage in meditative stabilization. After that, we must be able to sustain meditative stabilization. After that, when faults and obstacles arise, we must be able to abandon them. For all of those, we will need exertion. What result arises in dependence upon faith, longing, and exertion? A thoroughly refined body and mind. When we exert ourselves well, then body and mind become serviceable. When our bodies become serviceable, we can rest in the equipoise of meditative stabilization for however long we wish. When our minds become serviceable, then we can meditate for however long we wish. That serviceability of body and mind is called thorough refinement. Such thorough refinement is in some sense the result of abandoning laziness. These four antidotes abandon laziness, the first of the six faults.

Forgetting the object of observation is the second fault. Upon what instruction should I meditate? How should I meditate? When should I meditate? When I meditate, what faults will there be and when will they arise? Upon what methods for abandoning those faults should I rely and when should I rely upon them? Sometimes, mind wanders and we forget the instructions as well as the object of observation. Thus, forgetting is the second fault. What do we need as the antidote to the second fault? Among the eight applications that cause us to abandon the six faults, we need the fifth. Mindfulness is the fifth. Always making our minds one-pointedly undistracted, looking for faults that arise when we cultivate meditative stabilization, asking whether or not meditative stabilization and the methods of meditative stabilization have been forgotten, and in that way causing our minds not to forget the object of observation—that is the role of mindfulness, the antidote that abandons the second fault, forgetting the object of observation.

Laxity and excitement are the third and fourth faults. Previously, the treatise has spoken about them several times. Laxity and excitement are the principal obstacles to meditative stabilization. Awareness serves as the antidote to laxity and excitement. Generally, mindfulness and awareness are quite similar. However, mindfulness prevents forgetfulness, and awareness inspects: Am I meditating? Am I wandering? How's my work going? Awareness inspects the details, and it does so concurrently rather than subsequently. In this way it serves as the antidote to the third and fourth faults.

Not making effort is the fifth fault. This refers to not making the effort to correct a fault when one arises. Intention is the antidote to not making effort. Intention is the seventh among the eight applications that cause us to abandon the six faults. Intention regards the practice of meditative stabilization as important and considers it utterly necessary to abandon the fault that has arisen. It is intention that makes the effort to apply the techniques that will abandon that fault. Thus, intention, the seventh among the eight applications, serves as the antidote to not making effort, the fifth among the six faults.

Making effort is the sixth fault. When the mind abides in a stable manner, if we make great effort, the mind will become agitated again. For example, if we continually stir calm water to the right and to the left, then the water swirls and swirls but never becomes still and calm. Similarly, if we continually try to fix our minds, even when they already abide, they will always move. What serves as the antidote to this fault? Equanimity. Here, equanimity means resting in a relaxed way, not considering anything to be terribly important. When the mind is already still and our meditative stabilization is already free from faults, it is important to relax in equanimity.

In this way, it is taught that six faults afflict meditative stabilization and that we should rely upon eight applications that serve as antidotes to those faults and enable us to abandon them.

I will stop here tonight. If you have questions, please ask them and I will give an answer.

Q: How do we know when to exert ourselves and when to apply an antidote?
A: We investigate our meditative stabilization. Is there a fault? If there is a fault, then we must make effort in order to abandon it. If there is no fault, then there is no need to make that effort. Rather, we must relax in equanimity.

Q: If lethargy is the obstacle, how do we recognize it?
A: We must catch lethargy at the beginning. For instance, if we are falling asleep. Just as our minds begin to sink, we must apply the methods for abandoning laxity. Similarly, just as our minds begin to scatter, we must apply the methods for abandoning excitement. Thus, we must destroy them at the outset.

Q: How do we distinguish between lethargy and equanimity?
A: Lethargy refers to thoroughly unclear states of mind. Probably we are falling asleep. We do not want to meditate. Even just sitting there is difficult, and we feel depressed. As for equanimity, when meditative stabilization shines forth clearly and brightly, then relax and meditate continuously.

Q: What about just spacing out? There is a sense of ease, and we are not absorbed in thoughts, but the element of clarity is missing.
A: This seems to be a more subtle type of laxity. We can tell the difference between this and equanimity because, here, we feel bored. We do not feel joy in or take delight in the practice of meditation. Equanimity does not involve investigation of our meditative stabilization. Rather, we practice continuously and joyfully, taking delight in the practice.

Q: How does the contemplation of dependent arising serve as an antidote to bewilderment?
A: Bewilderment refers to not understanding correctly the mode of abiding of phenomena. In dependence upon that, we do not understand virtuous and evil actions or the way in which the misleading appearances of cyclic existence arise. Also, we do not understand emptiness correctly. Bewilderment refers to that. Meditation upon the twelve branches of dependent relationship is taught as a method for dispelling that lack of understanding.

From what does this world of cyclic existence initially arise? It arises from our ignorance. In dependence upon ignorance, we accumulate conditioned actions. In dependence upon actions, the consciousness that accumulates the actions due to which we go to other births arises. In dependence upon consciousness, this body of ours is gradually established. If we meditate upon the twelve branches of dependent relationship according to its stages, then dependent relationship enables us to understand former and later births, and to place our confidence knowledgeably in actions that serve as causes and the results of those actions, as well as in the emptiness of all phenomena, and so forth. Therefore, meditation upon dependent relationship is taught as the antidote to bewilderment.

Q: I have studied the presentation of faults and their antidotes, and I have tried to apply that to the practice of meditation. I found it confusing and cumbersome: what fault is present now? Which antidote shall I apply? In the end, it seemed easier to label everything "thinking." Is that a problem? Should I try to work more with faults and antidotes? Is there a way to apply that scheme that is less cumbersome.

A: There is no flaw in your procedure. It is not necessary to interrogate ourselves continually. "Is there a fault? Is it this one or that one? Should I apply this antidote or that one?" There is no need to meditate that way. If we practice meditation regularly, we become familiar with the faults that tend to detract from our own practice of meditative stabilization. Knowing our own habits, we can consider which antidote will most likely help us, study it well, and be ready to apply that technique to our own practice. For instance, if laziness affects my practice, then I can reflect that I need to rely upon the antidotes to laziness, join them to my own practice, and in that way purify my practice of meditation. Constantly interrogating ourselves by looking for faults and scavenging for antidotes—there's no need to meditate that way.

Q: Recently you said that it is necessary to abandon excessive desire in order to meditate properly. Can excessive desire for fruition in our practice be an obstacle?

A: When this treatise characterizes excessive desire as an obstacle to the practice of calm abiding, it means that the ambition to accomplish great things in business, politics, and so on can interfere with the practice of meditative stabilization. Desire to achieve the fruition of meditation is not considered to be an obstacle to the practice of meditation. Rather, that desire is considered to be a worthy aspiration and an important cause of actually accomplishing the practice.

Q: What I mean is that I have the feeling that I am pushing too hard.

A: I don't really see that as a problem. Exerting ourselves and having a strong wish to practice is commendable.

Q: What shall I do with the sense of difficulty?
A: Inspiration and a strong wish to practice are important. If you have those, the difficulties will pass.

CHAPTER FIVE

Insight

I N ORDER TO LISTEN to the dharma, please rouse thoroughly pure motivation, the mind turned toward supreme awakening, and listen.

The *Stages of Meditation in the Middle Way School* composed by the master Kamalashila has three parts: (1) the need to cultivate compassion, (2) the need to cultivate the mind of awakening, and (3) practice of the excellent dharma as the essence. The third of those, practice of the excellent dharma as the essence, teaches that we must practice both method and knowledge. Knowledge has three components: the knowledge that arises in dependence upon hearing, contemplation, and meditation. The knowledge that arises in dependence upon meditation also has two aspects: calm abiding and insight. Today, we will consider the way to cultivate the meditative stabilization of insight. This involves the ways in which to meditate upon (1) the teaching that external things are not established, (2) the teaching that even the mere internal mind is not established, and (3) the realization of those as emptiness.

What was taught previously? It was taught that we must meditate upon the meaning of emptiness. Why must we meditate upon emptiness? We must definitely and without fail meditate upon emptiness. At the root, we meditate upon emptiness in order to abandon perverse, bad predispositions, the bad predispositions for afflictions. Generally speaking, there are many types of meditation. In some meditations, such as the meditative absorption in which there is no discrimination, a meditation that is cultivated by non-Buddhists, the mind stops. When the mind stops in that way, afflictions do not arise for as long as we remain in meditative equipoise. Afflictions do not arise and bad thoughts do not arise. However, except for thought and affliction stopping for the duration of this meditative stabilization, the seeds of affliction have not been destroyed. In dependence upon the seeds of affliction not having been destroyed, when the meditator rises from such meditative stabilization, afflictions arise once again. What is the reason for their arising again? They arise in dependence upon the root of affliction not having been abandoned. Therefore, we must abandon the root of affliction.

What is the root of affliction? Our afflictions—desire, hatred, bewilderment, pride, envy, and so on—serve as the causes for the arising of various types of suffering and as conditions that prevent liberation from cyclic existence. Even if we identify them and think, "I will annihilate this affliction, desire," we are not able to annihilate them. What must we do? If we conceive all things to exist truly, then, in dependence upon that, desire, hatred, and other afflictions will arise. What will prevent them from arising? If we know that all things lack inherent existence and are emptiness, we will know that the objects of desire, hatred, and so on do not exist. Through investigating and analyzing all things, we realize them to be emptiness. In dependence upon realizing things to be emptiness, all afflictions together with their seeds will be stopped from the root. In dependence upon that reason, when afflictions are abandoned in this way, they do not arise again. That is to say, when afflictions are abandoned by way of our having meditated upon emptiness, they have been abandoned from the root. Because their root has been cut, they do not arise again in any way.

In order to realize emptiness, we must stop believing in visible forms and so on. To stop that, we need to know with certainty that forms are emptiness; that is to say, we need to know for sure that these things lack inherent establishment. Ascertaining that requires us to overcome our doubts; we will have to go beyond just wondering whether or not things are established. If we do not go further than wondering and doubting, we will not come to certain knowledge of emptiness. For that reason, we will have to abandon our doubts. How shall we do that? We cannot extract doubt in the way that we remove a thorn from our hand. To abandon doubt, we will need meditative stabilization and knowledge. First, we will need the meditative stabilization of calm abiding so that our minds abide in a stable manner. After our minds have come to abide in a stable manner, knowledge must correctly investigate and analyze the object that calm abiding observes. If meditative stabilization and knowledge are present, we can leave doubt behind, and certainty can be born.

Here, mistaking a rope for a snake is given as an example. When I mistake a rope for a snake, I become afraid, thinking, "A snake has come into my house, and now I'm in danger." Mistaking a rope for a snake exemplifies well the misleading appearances of cyclic existence. It accords well with the misleading appearances of cyclic existence. The misleading appearances of cyclic existence are, in fact, not established. Similarly, the snake is not established in the rope. Nevertheless, when we fear the rope that we have mistaken for a snake, we cannot stop being afraid no matter what we do, even if we have a rifle or a knife in our hand. Those methods cannot abolish our fear, but neither do we need them. Why not? For instance, if we shine a light on that rope, illuminate it, and investigate it well, we will know, "This is not a snake. It is a rope." Certain knowledge will arise. When I have seen the rope directly, then, even if someone else says to me, "It is a snake," and goes on to tell me a story—"There is a snake. Really, there is. Yesterday the snake came in through there."—I will not become confused. I will have confidence that the supposed snake is really a rope, that there is nothing to fear, and that there is no danger. Similarly, all phenomena are emptiness. Having investigated and analyzed with correct reasoning, I can know them to be emptiness. In dependence upon my knowing that, my afflictions are abandoned. Even if a bad advisor tells me that all phenomena are not emptiness and gives me a slew of reasons why they are not emptiness, that will not change my mind at all because I will have given rise to conviction from the depths. For that reason, I will have no doubt whatsoever and afflictions will not arise.

With regard to such certainty, if meditative stabilization and knowledge do not combine together, doubt and affliction cannot be annihilated. For example, in darkness, I will not know where my stuff is. Similarly, without meditative stabilization and knowledge, we cannot know emptiness. Therefore, we need meditative stabilization and knowledge. This treatise illustrates the need for meditative stabilization and knowledge with an example. In this example, our bad thoughts are compared to an illness. What must we do in order to abandon these bad thoughts, which are like illnesses? With the hand of meditative stabilization, we take hold of knowledge, which resembles a weapon, such as a knife, and grip it firmly. The knife-like weapon of knowledge performs careful surgery upon our minds and removes the internal illness. We must without fail dispel this illness, and we need both the hand of meditative stabilization and the weapon of knowledge if we are to accomplish that. In the absence of the meditative stabilization and knowledge, the illness within our minds cannot be removed.

Therefore, the afflictive obstructions must be abandoned. The abandonment of the afflictive obstructions is not a negligible suppression; abandoning them entails cutting them from the root. To cut them from the root, we will need both calm abiding and insight. When we have both calm abiding and the knowledge of insight, then those afflictions cannot remain at all. For example, when the sun shines, darkness cannot remain. Similarly, when we see reality's mode of abiding clearly, ignorance and the afflictions will naturally vanish. That vanishing will not be a negligible vanishing. Rather, ignorance and afflictions will be uprooted, never to arise again. Their destruction will be complete.

When we see such an emptiness, there is nothing to be seen that will surpass this and there is no road more distinguished. There is nothing other than this that we must view and there is nothing more distinguished than this that we must know. We must realize things to be empty in this way. When we realize things to be empty in this way, generally speaking, we realize all things to lack establishment, to lack existence, and to be emptiness. Having realized things to be emptiness, do we conceive that emptiness to be nonexistence? No, conceiving nonexistence does not occur either. After the conception of things as existing has been abandoned, the conception of their nonexistence will naturally be pacified. What is the reason for that? If even one thing were to exist, its nonexistence, which depends upon its existence, would be possible. Because not even one thing has ever been found to be established at all, the nonexistence of things is naturally not established. In this sense, when a yogin views with the eye of knowledge, all things in the three times—past, future, and present—are not observed. Since things are not present to begin with, an absence of things that trounces them is not present either. Therefore, elaborations are pacified, afflictions are abandoned, and a peace that is both flawless and fully endowed comes to pass.

When the sphere of reality that is free from elaborations is realized, two types of obstructions are abandoned. What are those two obstructions? Afflictive obstructions and obstructions to omniscience. What are the afflictive obstructions? Generally, the term "affliction" means extremely painful and extremely difficult. What is the cause of such pain and difficulty? Afflictions such as desire, hatred, bewilderment, and pride. Realization of emptiness abandons them. There is also a second obstruction that is not an affliction. What is that? It is called the obstruction to omniscience. The mere presence of afflictions produces various types of suffering, but the mere presence of obstructions to omniscience in us does not produce suffering. Still, the obstructions to omniscience do gradually serve as the causes for the arising of afflictions. What are obstructions to omniscience? Confusion. Even though all things lack inherent establishment and are emptiness, we conceive of them as not emptiness. For instance, we think that mountains, enclosures, and houses really do exist. We think also that our bodies and so forth really do exist. Such conceptions will serve as the causes of afflictions arising in the future, and they are called obstructions to omniscience. These two obstructions serve as the roots of all the suffering of cyclic existence. How can we abandon those two? In dependence upon thoroughly pure calm abiding and thoroughly pure insight, thoroughly pure knowledge arises and abandons the two obstructions from the root.

Our tradition speaks of two approaches to meditation: the analytical meditation of the scholar and the placement meditation of the simple person. Which of those two does Kamalashīla teach here? The analytical meditation of the scholar. The analytical meditation of the scholar initially emphasizes knowledge. First, we must generate knowledge correctly. In dependence upon what will knowledge be generated? It will be generated in dependence upon investigation and analysis. In dependence upon the distinctive certainty that arises in us through investigation and analysis, knowledge arises. We meditate with certainty as our basis, and we come to accurate and authentic knowledge. That is the analytical meditation of the scholar.

The analytical meditation of the scholar is extremely stable and also correct. However, if we consider the length of the journey, it is the longer way. In our actual application of the tradition of meditation, which is that of the Vajrayāna, we practice the placement meditation of the simple person. Meditation in the style of a simple person means placement meditation that is free from elaboration. Looking at the entity of the mind, and resting evenly, we meditate. This can be an exceptionally short and good path, one that is convenient and free from hardship. On the other hand, if this has not been introduced well, our meditation will be a fool's meditation. Without that good introduction, no matter how hard we work, maybe not much comes of it. Maybe the fruit eludes us. Therefore, in our Vajrayāna tradition, we practice both. We connect one to the other, and that leads to something good.

The Buddhist teachings that flourished in Tibet are called the Vajra Vehicle of Secret Mantra, but those are not the only teachings that we have and use. How so? When we study, we study the topics treated in the sūtras. For instance, we study the Middle Way, the Higher Knowledge, Valid Cognition, and so forth. We inquire from the point of view of dependently related conventionalities and also from the point of view of the ultimate. What is emptiness? What is knowledge? When we meditate, what should appear for analytical meditation? What is the reason for cultivating calm abiding? What is the reason for cultivating insight? What are the diverse types of afflictions that are to be abandoned? What obstructs omniscience? How do we rely upon antidotes as methods for abandoning the afflictive obstructions? In what way do those antidotes and the afflictions oppose one another? How, in dependence upon that opposition, do the antidotes destroy the afflictions? How do antidotes suppress the afflictions? How do antidotes sever afflictions from the root? Study causes us to understand these points clearly and with certainty.

In dependence upon ascertaining those meanings, there is no danger of taking a mistaken path and no danger of not realizing the path. We ascertain the entire path clearly. Afterwards, if we then also practice the analytical meditation of a scholar, the path will be long: investigate, analyze, then, based upon that, meditate. If we practice in that way, realization can only arise slowly. In dependence upon that reason, when we actually meditate, we practice the placement meditation of a simple person. When we practice such placement meditation, the path will be shorter and also stable. Everything will go as it should. In dependence upon that, this path is called "the path that is the union of Sūtra and Mantra."

When we meditate, it is not absolutely necessary for us to meditate in the way that Kamalashīla has explained in his *Stages of Meditation*. However, we must without fail know the stages of meditation that Kamalashīla has taught. If we know these stages of meditation, our path will not be obstructed and we will not take a mistaken path, because these instructions are correct. Therefore, we must without fail study these stages of meditation, know them, and ascertain them.

If you have any questions or doubts, please ask questions.

Q: I have heard some instructions on the Middle Way School and emptiness, and intellectually I understand that everything is interdependent and empty, but that is not really my experience. To think, in our daily lives, that everything is empty, would be an overlay imposed upon our sense perceptions and our experience. How can we apply this knowledge? Should we try to remember that things are empty when, for instance, we find ourselves becoming angry?
A: Even if we have understood emptiness by way of the words, primarily we need definite knowledge of the meaning. Were the Buddha himself to come here, stand before us, and say, "All things are truly established," we would think, "In the end, they are not truly established." We need that degree of certainty. When we have become that sure, will everything suddenly vanish into emptiness, as if we were drunk on beer? Will hatred and bewilderment disappear immediately? No, that cannot happen. Why not? In previous lifetimes we have become accustomed to bad predispositions. That condition has led to the afflictions, suffering, and obstacles of the present lifetime. However, if

we generate outstanding certainty in the Middle Way, then we will understand clearly when we are meditating well and when we are not. We will not have to ask others; we will know this ourselves: "Now my meditation is going well. This is it. There is no mistake here." If we meditate well, then afflictions will gradually decrease and work will be free from hardship. This will happen gradually, not all at once.

Q: Please explain the two obstructions once again.

A: Generally, the Tibetan word *drip pa*, here translated as "obstruction," is to be understood as indicating blockage and inability to see. What is obstructed? Seeing reality's mode of abiding is obstructed. Achieving the rank of a buddha is obstructed. Cut short, stopped.

When obstructions are categorized, two are posited, and there is purpose in that. Those that prevent liberation are the afflictive obstructions. Those that prevent omniscience are the obstructions to omniscience. The afflictive obstructions prevent liberation in that that they prevent liberation from cyclic existence. What is said about this inability to achieve liberation from cyclic existence? The afflictions of desire, hatred, and bewilderment resemble roots, and the conception of a self of persons is *their* root. Twenty proximate afflictions are enumerated as branches. The presence of these root and proximate afflictions is called the afflictive obstructions. Those afflictions accumulate actions. In dependence upon the accumulation of actions, we are born in cyclic existence. Therefore, they are called afflictive obstructions.

Obstructions to omniscience do not endanger us greatly in the way that afflictions such as desire and hatred do. Conceiving that all things do exist, conceiving that they do not exist, conceiving that external objects do exist, conceiving that internal mind does exist, and so forth—these are called obstructions to omniscience. Adhering strongly to these appearances is called an obstruction to omniscience. When we adhere strongly to appearances, then we think, "It must be this way," or "Yes, I think it is like that," or "If it is not like that, then it is no good at all." Why are these called obstructions to omniscience? They obstruct seeing reality's mode of abiding. They block the accomplishment of the two aspects of a buddha's omniscience, the knowledge of the modes and the knowledge of the varieties. In dependence upon that reason, they are called obstructions to omniscience.

In dependence upon what, mainly, are those two obstructions abandoned? In dependence upon realizing the selflessness of persons, the afflictive obstructions are abandoned. In dependence upon seeing all other phenomena as selfless, the obstructions to omniscience are abandoned. In dependence upon seeing all phenomena as emptiness, both obstructions are abandoned.

Q: I have heard that there are different kinds of emptinesses. How can we make categories in nonexistence?

A: It is not emptiness itself that is being divided into categories. Categories are set forth not from the side of the quality itself; they are set forth from the side of phenomena that possess that quality. Some people think, "External things are emptiness, but I doubt that internal things are emptiness." Some people think, "Internal things are emptiness, but I doubt that external things are emptiness." Therefore, the sūtras and treatises speak of the emptiness of the external, the emptiness of the internal, and the emptiness of the external and the internal. Others think, "These things are emptiness, but east, south, west, and north are not emptiness." Therefore, the sūtras and treatises speak of the emptiness of the great. Again, some think, "These things are emptiness, but emptiness itself is not emptiness." For them, the sūtras and treatises speak of the emptiness of emptiness. And so on. For the sake of cutting through the doubts of individuals, the emptiness of each of these appearances is taught, individually, separately, and specifically. In dependence upon that reason, the sūtras and treatises speak of the sixteen emptinesses, the eighteen emptinesses, and the twenty emptinesses.

For instance, previously someone said, "There is no sense in the lists given in the *Heart Sūtra*. What need is there to say, 'There is no eye, no ear, no nose, no tongue'? Why not just say, 'There is no head'? That would be easier." It is not like that. For the sake of cutting through the individual doubts that we may have, all of the particulars are stated specifically. Therefore, the sixteen emptinesses and so forth are stated.

Q: When you spoke about placement meditation, you mentioned the importance of being introduced correctly to this type of meditation. Please explain more about that.

A: Here we speak of being guided by the experience of someone who possesses realization. When practicing the analytical meditation of a scholar, we investigate and analyze external things. When practicing the placement meditation of a simple person, we set external things aside temporarily. They are emptiness, of course, but for the time being we set them aside. When we have not investigated and analyzed the internal mind—when we have not looked at it—it seems solid and powerful, extraordinarily imposing, and out of control. However, suppose that we were actually to look correctly and decisively. My mind seems hard and powerful but when I look for it, I cannot find it anywhere. It is not outside the body. It is not inside the body. It is not somewhere in between. I ask, "Where is my mind?," and I look everywhere for it, but no matter where I look, I cannot find it and I cannot see it, not at all. Why not? Because I've closed my eyes and do not see what is in fact present? No. Mind is not present. That is to say, empty of inherent existence, mind's entity is neither to be seen nor to be found. For instance, when I become filled with hatred, really strong and violent hatred, and look for that hatred—how did it arise and where?—that hatred cannot be found. I think that I know where and how this hatred rises up, but it is not to be seen. That apparently palpable and immediate hatred is not to be found demonstrates directly that hatred is actually emptiness. We do not need to rely upon reasoned investigation and analysis. Meditation that rests evenly upon that meaning is called the placement meditation of a simple person.

Q: If self is empty, who or what renounces ignorance and attains awakening?
A: When we mistake a rope for a snake, there is no snake in the rope. In the absence of a snake, why does fear arise? Why do we mistake the rope for a snake? How do we initially mistake the rope for the snake? For what reason do we mistakenly impose the presence of a snake upon its absence? How do we realize that there is no snake there? Initially, we mistake the rope for a snake and later we do not mistake the rope for a snake, but the entity of the rope has not changed in the interim. When we mistake it for a snake, it is a rope. Later, when we realize that it is a rope, it is still a rope, just as it was previously.

Similarly, we have made a mistake. It is not that an existent self must achieve buddhahood. Rather, we must separate from the mistake that we have made. Suffering arises in dependence upon that mistake.

Q: Who separates from that mistake?
A: First come appearances as five aggregates. Those five aggregates are mistakenly taken to be one thing, in dependence upon which continuity arises. The continuity is not understood to be emptiness, in dependence upon which all the misleading appearances of cyclic existence arise. When these five aggregates, naturally dawning, are realized to be empty of inherent existence, the mistake is turned back and the continuity of the five aggregates is severed.

The essence of the Sugata is present in mind. The Buddha spoke of this with an example. Suppose gold were buried under earth and many filthy things were poured onto it. Then the gold remained covered by this filth for thousands or even tens of millions of years. Many people need this gold but they do not know that gold is present there. The gold cannot say, "I am here." If a clairvoyant god were to come there, then he or she would say, "There is gold underneath this earth. Don't you need gold? If you dig here, gold will come forth from underneath." Then, the people dig and bring forth gold.

Similarly, there is ignorance in our minds. Not seeing the ignorance that is present in our minds, we fool ourselves and cause ourselves a lot of trouble. However, the Buddha comes here and says, "You are causing yourselves a lot of trouble. The roots of all the trouble that you are causing yourselves are in your minds." Having been introduced to the source of our troubles, we understand that flaws are present in our minds. Recognizing that, if we eradicate those flaws, we will enjoy ease and comfort, we understand also that, if we practice meditation, we will achieve happiness.

Q: If we have compassion for others, we want to free them from pain, but the truth often hurts. What shall we do?

A: Generally speaking, compassion is a method for separating sentient beings from suffering. Nevertheless, compassion needs to be guided by knowledge. Not much benefit will come from dumb compassion. There will not be much benefit for us, and there will not be much benefit for others. Therefore, knowledge is necessary. Knowledge looks for a way in which we can actually be of help. Will there be much benefit or only a little? We need to apply compassion intelligently.

For instance, there is a story of a king who was guarded by a brave monkey. One night, a thief came into the king's palace and arrived at the king's residence. The king was sleeping, and while he slept, a bug bit him on the head. Seeing the bug biting the king, the monkey raised his sword and whacked the bug. Of course, when he hit the bug with his sword, he also hit the king in the head. Meanwhile, the thief, busy stealing the king's goods, watched the monkey smack the bug and the king. Horrified, he shouted, "Ha! He's killing the king!"

If you have knowledge, you will be able to help even your enemies. If you do not have knowledge, you will treat even your friends as if they were enemies and will not be able to help them, like the monkey who killed the bug but hit the king in the head with his sword. Therefore, if you have no knowledge, compassion will be of little benefit to anyone.

CHAPTER SIX

Certainty

I WOULD LIKE TO SAY a few words about rousing the mind of awakening, the mind that is directed toward supreme awakening. This is the Tibetan way of practicing the excellent dharma. What is the reason for this tradition? Generally, in the Buddhist way, if we repair our motivation at the start, our conduct can become pure and correct. If we do not repair our motivation at the start, our conduct cannot become pure and correct. For that reason, we need pure motivation. What pure motivation do we need? Generally, we should undertake activity that benefits ourselves and others rather than activity that harms ourselves and others. If we cherish others more than ourselves, that will serve as a cause of what benefits both others and ourselves. Therefore, let us exert ourselves at activity that benefits others. Moreover, let us distinguish between temporary and final benefit. If you have the aspiration and intention to achieve supreme awakening, from which final benefit arises vastly, such that you think, "I will place all sentient beings in the rank of a completely pure and masterful buddha, who has destroyed the two obstructions, who possesses all good qualities, and who has passed beyond the two extremes," that will serve as thoroughly pure motivation. That motivation, the aspiration and intention to achieve supreme awakening, is extremely important at all times and in all activities, whether we are working, practicing, or studying. In particular, if we have thoroughly pure motivation when we are listening to dharma, then listening to dharma and, subsequently, bringing dharma into experience will become the real thing. Please listen with the aspiration and intention to achieve supreme awakening.

From among the three principal divisions of Kamalashīla's *Stages of Meditation in the Middle Way School*—compassion, the mind of awakening, and bringing the instructions into experience through practice—we are considering the third, bringing the instructions into experience through practice. Practice is discussed in terms of method and knowledge; we are considering knowledge. Knowledge is discussed in terms of hearing, contemplation, and meditation; we are considering meditation. Meditation is discussed in terms of calm abiding and insight; we are considering insight. As for the way to enter into insight, first, external things are shown to be emptiness. After that, internal mind is shown to be emptiness. After that, all phenomena are shown to be emptiness. All phenomena are not conceived as merely nonexistent; rather, all are shown to be emptiness. I have explained these points already. Such meditation upon phenomena as emptiness must be done with certain knowledge. If we meditate with certainty, that will abandon doubt. In dependence upon abandoning doubt, afflictive obstructions will be abandoned. Moreover, it is not merely afflictive obstructions that will be abandoned; obstructions to omniscience will be abandoned too. That is what I will explain today.

Generally, seeing things is seeing perversely. That perverse misunderstanding pervades all things. In dependence upon seeing all things as emptiness, that misunderstanding is abandoned and, therefore, the obstructions to omniscience are abandoned. When the obstructions to omniscience are abandoned, it is as if the sun had been freed from clouds. When clouds obstruct the sun, the sun is not seen clearly. When the sun is freed from clouds, the sun becomes clear and bright. Similarly, when obstructions to omniscience are abandoned, wisdom becomes clear and bright.

How does wisdom that is like the sun in a sky free from clouds dawn? It is described as yogic direct perception. Between ordinary beings—those born in dependence upon their individual karma—and yogins, here we are considering yogins. Their wisdom is not speculation from an inferential point of view, as is the case with ordinary beings. Neither is it pensive and lacking in clarity. Rather, it sees directly, for which reason it is called yogic direct perception. When we ordinary beings think about a thing, there is something in the way, obstruction, due to which we do not see clearly and directly. When those obstructions—the afflictive obstructions and the obstructions to omniscience—have been dispelled, then knowledge arises as yogic direct perception. When yogic direct perception arises, how does it see? It sees phenomena in a conventional context and it also sees reality in an ultimate context. In the conventional context, wisdom sees the shapes, colors, and defining characteristics of whatever things exist in worldly realms, individually and without mixing them, just as they are. This wisdom knows the varieties of phenomena. Similarly, in the context of reality, wisdom sees the meaning of emptiness directly; this wisdom knows the mode of all phenomena. In dependence upon release from the afflictive obstructions and the obstructions to omniscience, the wisdoms knowing the modes and the varieties actually arise.

Someone in whom those two wisdoms are present is a buddha. For what reason must those two wisdoms be present? In dependence upon having abandoned the two obstructions, a buddha possesses these two wisdoms. For that reason, a buddha is called by the name "All Knowing." What does "all" mean here? In the conventional context, a buddha knows all and everything that exists in the worldly realms. However, a buddha knows not only the appearances that are conventional but also the mode of abiding that is ultimate. Therefore, a buddha knows all, with nothing left incomplete. A buddha's directly-perceiving knowledge and good qualities set him or her apart. From what do the distinctive good qualities of a buddha arise? They arise from the power of abandoning the two obstructions. In dependence upon what does the capacity to abandon the two obstructions arise? Obstructions are mistakes; in dependence upon seeing reality's mode of abiding just as it is, we part way with mistakes. Then, like the sun free from clouds, the wisdoms that know the modes and the varieties are born naturally. Therefore, the sole path proceeding to finality must be traversed in dependence upon settling the view and practicing meditation in this way. In brief, the wisdom that knows all arises in dependence upon separation from the two obstructions, and separation from the two obstructions arises in dependence upon realization of the mode of abiding. In dependence upon separation from the obstructions, the wisdoms of a buddha arise.

Although Buddhists do have such a path, non-Buddhists such as the Forders do not. It is not only non-Buddhists who do not have such a path; even among Buddhists, hearers and so forth cannot abandon the obstructions to omniscience. Why are they unable to abandon the obstructions to omniscience? They do not have a path that realizes the mode of abiding of reality unerringly. Therefore, the rank of a completely enlightened buddha cannot be achieved by a hearer's path. The wisdom that realizes the modes and the wisdom that realizes the varieties cannot arise by way of a hearer's path. In dependence upon that reason, the Buddha said that hearers realize that all phenomena arise from conditions and are aggregations but do not know reality's mode of abiding. Definitively speaking, they have not achieved the rank of nirvāṇa but, while not having achieved nirvāṇa, they give rise to the notion that they have achieved nirvāṇa. However, they have not actually achieved nirvāṇa. Why not? They have not realized the selflessness of phenomena.

Therefore, the Buddha said, we should not enter the paths of hearers. Rather, we must achieve final paths. In that case, if hearers do not realize reality's mode of abiding just as it is and do not actually achieve the rank of nirvāṇa, for what reason did the Buddha teach the paths of hearers? The Buddha did not teach the paths of hearers to sentient beings who were to be tamed within thinking that hearers achieve the final nirvāṇa. He taught these paths in order that those who were to be tamed enter gradually. Were he to teach them the paths of emptiness from the first, they would not be able to enter directly. In order to enter gradually, he thought, first they must realize this path and achieve its fruit. The Buddha taught these paths in order for these students gradually to realize the final mode of abiding. How did he teach? Initially, he did not show all phenomena to be emptiness. Rather, he taught that the five aggregates are established in the entities of phenomena but that a self of persons is not present there. He spoke these teachings so as to place these students in higher paths, the paths of the Great Vehicle.

The Buddha's efforts were not exhausted with teaching the dharma of hearers. After that, he taught that all phenomena—these three realms—are only mind. That is to say, he taught also the tenets of the Mind Only School. From there, he went further in order for students to enter in stages into the meaning of emptiness, which is final. In dependence upon that reason, realization of all phenomena as mind only is not realization of the suchness that is the actual ultimate. Why not? The Buddha himself spoke to this point in a sūtra. "Some bodhisattvas realize all these sentient beings traveling among the three realms to be mind only. Will this suffice? No, it will not. It is necessary to realize that mind too has neither a limit nor a middle. In what way does mind lack both a limit and a middle? In the beginning, mind is not born. At the end, mind does not fall apart." Birth is a limit. Falling apart is a limit. What is there between birth and death? Abiding, which is called a middle. We may think that, if mind is not born and does not fall apart, then it abides. However, there is no abiding either. Mind has neither limit nor middle.

How does such meditation become pure? When a bodhisattva first generates compassion and, at the end, makes good aspirational prayers, his or her path becomes pure. Even when a bodhisattva abides in cyclic existence for the sake of sentient beings, through the force of pure aspirational prayers, the faults of cyclic existence do not sully him or her. Not only that, but also the vision of reality and the liberating activities of a bodhisattva arise effortlessly and spontaneously.

If all phenomena are emptiness, then who are the yogins who see all phenomena? Someone asked that question yesterday. The answer is given here. If we were to say that there is no such yogin, then, generally speaking, that would be true. In the context of the ultimate, there is no independent self or yogin who realizes reality's mode of abiding or who manifestly and completely becomes a buddha. There is no one who sees and no seeing. Not at all. However, there is both reality—the quality itself, ultimate truth—and that which possesses the quality, the conventional that is misleading. In the context of the conventional, the mere figure of objects, such as forms, and the mere consciousnesses that know those objects do arise. In dependence upon conventional appearances, we say that we saw someone or that someone did or said something; we designate such things conventionally. There is no self, but such conventional designations are suitable.

For the ultimate, no phenomena are established. However, in the context of the conventional, there is the knowledge of the yogin and also the knowledge of the ordinary person; those are taught in the context of the conventional that is misleading. For that reason, the Buddha himself spoke of two truths. The conventional is misleading, but in its own context it is true. The ultimate is simply true. In dependence upon that reason, the Buddha spoke of two truths. In the ultimate, there is no achieving of the fruit and no cultivation of the path, for all phenomena are emptiness. In the sphere of the conventional, we must achieve the fruit. In order to achieve this fruit, we must abandon the afflictions. In order to abandon the afflictions, we must cultivate the path. There are many paths: the paths of hearers, the paths of solitary realizers, the paths of bodhisattvas, the paths of ordinary beings, the paths of buddhas, and so on.

Such distinctions arise in the context of the conventional. If they did not exist even as mere conventions, there would be no reason to distinguish hearers, solitary realizers, bodhisattvas, buddhas, and ordinary beings from one another. Within a conventional context, we may then distinguish the conventionally false from the conventionally true by distinguishing what does not occur even conventionally from what does. In brief, if the causes do not exist, neither will the effects; for instance, the horns of a rabbit do not exist even conventionally. When considered in the context of the ultimate, what appears conventionally is not true. Therefore, it is said that these conventions are like illusions, like reflections, and like echoes.

How do conventional appearances arise? They arise through a process of *dependent relationship*. In this context, the Buddha spoke about the *twelve branches of dependent relationship.*[17] What is the root of cyclic existence? *Ignorance,* or, more literally, not knowing. What is it that we do not know? We do not know the truth about reality. Not knowing the truth about reality, we are mistaken. Through the power of that mistake, this cyclic existence arises. Therefore, ignorance is the root of the misleading appearances of cyclic existence. What does ignorance do? It makes us confused. It is then followed by *conditioned action,* the second from among the twelve branches of dependent relationship. Conditioned action is like accomplishing work; we accomplish the work of ignorance. What work does ignorance do? Having become confused by ignorance, sometimes we accumulate virtuous actions; these serve as causes for achieving the support for a lifetime as a god or human being. Sometimes we accumulate non-virtuous actions; these serve as causes for taking birth as a hell being, a hungry ghost, or an animal. Therefore, the second from among the twelve branches of dependent relationship is called conditioned action.

The third from among the twelve branches of dependent relationship is called *consciousness.* Whether I accumulate virtuous karmas or ill deeds, the potency of the predispositions established by the actions that I have accumulated is placed with consciousness. Predisposition means a degree of familiarity; it indicates that to which the mind has become accustomed. Because predispositions are present with consciousness, later they do something like rising up again. Temporarily, they are placed with consciousness. In the future, the predispositions will rise, as if they were welling up or standing up. The phase during which predispositions are placed with consciousness—the third from among the twelve branches of dependent relationship—is called consciousness.

How do the predispositions that have been placed in the medium of consciousness rise later? In a later lifetime, after the body that has served as the support for this previous lifetime has been cast away, predispositions rise again serially and I then take hold of the body of the later lifetime. At this point, we are considering *name and form,* the fourth from among the twelve branches of dependent relationship. In that fourth stage, I have the aggregates that are the bases for a name. Feelings, discriminations, compositional factors, and consciousnesses are the aggregates that are the bases for a name. I also have a form. That form is the body that I take up as the support for this lifetime. It comes to me due to craving, which arises due to predispositions upon which the power of actions has been imprinted. This composite of aggregates, called name and form, marks the beginning of a lifetime and is identified as the fourth from among the twelve branches of dependent relationship. Since the eye, the eye consciousness, and so forth have yet to develop fully, we have mere form and merely the aggregates that are the bases for a name. For that reason, this phase is called name and form. This refers to the time when we dwell in the wombs of our mothers.

In dependence upon name and form, the *six sense fields* arise. These six—eye, ear, nose, tongue, body, and mental—constitute the fifth from among the twelve branches of dependent relationship. They have the aspect of subjects that possess objects.

In dependence upon the six sense fields—or, through the power of the six sense fields—which serve as causes, there is *contact* with objects. The eye sees forms. The ear hears sounds. The nose experiences smells. And so on. Thus, there is contact. From among the twelve branches of dependent relationship, contact is the sixth.

What arises subsequently in dependence upon contact? *Feeling*. Some are good feelings. Some are bad feelings. In dependence upon the meeting of object and subject, the experience of feeling will arise without fail. Among the twelve branches of dependent relationship, feeling is the seventh.

The process does not rest with the mere experience of feeling. If we experience a good feeling, then comes the *craving* of wanting, which thinks, "I need that." If we experience a bad feeling, then comes the craving for destruction, which thinks, "I do not need that. I will demolish it." Either way, there is craving, the eighth among the twelve branches of dependent relationship. That arises in the mind without fail.

In dependence upon craving, there follows *grasping*. Grasping is not mere craving; it goes further than merely to contemplate mentally. While thinking, "I must achieve it. I must accomplish it. I must do it," we act. That is called grasping. By way of grasping, we again accumulate actions.

In dependence upon accumulating actions through grasping, there follows *existence*. When the predisposition that has accumulated an action is again placed in the continuum of the mind, the cause for going to or being born in a later lifetime has been established. The element that will go to the later lifetime and that takes up the aggregates of the later lifetime has now been set up. Existence refers to the predisposition.

In dependence upon existence, there follows *birth*, which is the eleventh among the twelve branches of dependent relationship. Birth is followed by *aging and death*, the twelfth among the twelve branches of dependent relationship. Having taken birth again, we continue to revolve in cyclic existence.

Since ignorance, the root of cyclic existence, has yet to be extinguished, it arises again. In that way, we revolve from lifetime to lifetime. From the previous birth to the present; from the present to the subsequent birth; from the subsequent birth to the one that will follow. In stages, and without severance of the continuum of births, we go from birth to birth. These are called conventional, dependently related appearances. What must we realize in order to sever the continuum of conventional, dependently related appearances? When we realize the truth about reality, ignorance falls away. When ignorance falls away, then conditioned action, consciousness, name and form, and so on naturally cease.

How do conventional appearances, which are like echoes, illusions, and dreams, arise? They arise by way of the twelve branches of dependent relationship. What is the the method that will stop them? When we see the truth about reality, the continuum of the twelve branches of dependent relationship will be severed.

I will stop here this evening. If you have questions, please ask them.

Q: If cyclic existence arises in dependence upon causes and conditions, and if nirvāṇa does not depend upon causes and conditions, how can we achieve liberation from cyclic existence and achieve nirvāṇa? That seems to suggest that something that is caused produces something that is uncaused. How can that be? Similarly, if it is possible to achieve omniscience, is something finite producing something infinite? How will we make the transition from limited to unlimited knowledge?

A: Generally, the abiding nature and the manner of appearance are different. The ultimate is the abiding nature. Cyclic existence is the manner of appearance. For example, when we mistake a rope for a snake, there is a conceptual mind that thinks, "It is a snake." The mind that thinks it is a snake is mistaken. In dependence upon thinking that it is a snake, fear arises. In this case, snake is a mistake and rope is actual. True enough, but if we wonder how a mind apprehending it as a rope can arise from a mind apprehending it as a snake, there is no way to make sense of that. Nevertheless, the apprehension of it as a snake is a mistake and rope is the actual thing—the truth. Therefore, if we investigate and analyze, we can realize the rope. In that way, the mind apprehending snake will be abandoned. Similarly, the misleading appearances of cyclic existence are mistakes. They have causes and effects.

Nevertheless, they are mistakes. So long as we are mistaken, we are not realizing their abiding nature.

We may wonder how nirvāṇa can arise from the misleading appearances
of cyclic existence. Still, it can. How? We realize the abiding nature. In
dependence upon realizing the abiding nature, the mistake falls away.

Q: Do cyclic existence and nirvāṇa both exist from the start?
A: Cyclic existence and nirvāṇa are both present from time without beginning. Nirvāṇa is present as the factor that is true. Cyclic existence is present
as the factor that is mistaken. They differ in that one is true and the other is
not, but they do not differ in regard to time. For example, consider a rope
that we have mistaken for a snake. The rope itself is just as present when we
mistake it for a snake as it is later when we realize it to be a rope. However,
the two occasions differ in regard to realizing or not realizing the snake to be
a rope. Initially, when we mistake a rope for a snake, the rope is present.
Later, when we know the rope to be a rope, the mistake has fallen away. The
rope has not changed. The difference is that, previously, we had not realized
the rope to be a rope.

Q: Is it therefore possible for us to realize nirvāṇa now?
A: It is not possible for us to experience nirvāṇa now. Why not? From the
object's side, the mistake and the abiding nature can abide together. For
example, while we mistake a rope for a snake, the entity of the rope does not
change. Nevertheless, from the subject's side, there is contradiction. So long
as we have not overcome the apprehension of the snake, the mind apprehending the rope cannot arise. Similarly, until the mistake falls away, it is not
possible to realize nirvāṇa.

Q: What is the difference between conceptual and non-conceptual minds?
A: There is some difference between conceptual and non-conceptual minds.
A non-conceptual mind can see directly. A conceptual mind investigates and
analyzes an object that is hidden from its view; it cannot see directly. For
instance, there is a difference between an eye consciousness and a mental
consciousness. When a mental consciousness considers something, it looks at
an unclear image. In the language of valid cognition, we describe this image
as a meaning generality. An eye consciousness, however, sees directly. Thus,
conceptual and non-conceptual differ significantly in clarity.

Q: If we were to experience non-conceptual direct perception, would we feel certain about our experience?
A: Direct perception does not necessarily involve certainty.

Q: How do we know that we are not merely conceptualizing emptiness? For instance, if I see an object and consider it to be empty, how will I know that I am not merely thinking that it is empty?
A: At present, we do not know emptiness directly. In the future, we will see it through the power of meditative stabilization. For instance, right now, if we look with our eyes, we are not able to see Marpa House.[18] However, if we turn our minds to it, a mental consciousness can think about Marpa House even though it cannot see Marpa House in direct perception. Later, when we go there, we will be able to see Marpa House in direct perception. Similarly, at present we think about emptiness. We consider emptiness, but we do not see emptiness in direct perception. Later, when we have cultivated meditative stabilization and brought forth its potential, yogic direct perception will see emptiness directly.

Q: I have heard that a bodhisattva's compassion is the experience of dependent arising in the sense that a bodhisattva realizes the interconnections shared by all things, such as that all sentient beings have been our mothers. Is it true that a bodhisattva's compassion is the experience of dependent relationship in a positive sense? If so, does that positive side of dependent arising have any connection to the dependent relationship that a bodhisattva has done away with?
A: Because all things arise dependently, dependent relationship and emptiness are said to be undifferentiable. The dependent relationship that we are discussing tonight is a particular type of dependent relationship. Still, it has a relationship with emptiness and, of course, with dependent relationship or dependent arising in a more general sense. How does this cyclic existence arise? In dependence upon ignorance, conditioned action arises. In dependence upon conditioned action, consciousness arises. In dependence upon consciousness, name and form arise. And so on. Thus, the dependent arising of cyclic existence is a particular instance of the dependent arising or all things.

Q: Does that mean that taking a narrow view of the more general and more pervasive dependent arising is the ignorance that is the root of the dependent arising of cyclic existence?

A: Dependent arising and dependent relationship refer to the relationship between cause and effect. For instance, what is the relationship between ignorance, which is a cause, and its effect? In dependence upon ignorance, conditioned action follows.

CHAPTER SEVEN

Meditative Stabilization

A S WE ARE NOW to receive the excellent dharma, then all of us must prepare ourselves for our roles. Mine is to explain the dharma, and yours is to listen. Generally, the reason for entering the dharma is to achieve the final fruit ourselves and, similarly, to enable all sentient beings, who are to be tamed by dharma, to be joined to the good results that arise by way of the excellent dharma. Therefore, first of all, we need thoroughly pure motivation. Here, that means the aspiration to achieve supreme awakening for the sake of all sentient beings. To generate that aspiration, we resolve, "For the sake of all sentient beings, I will achieve the rank of a buddha." This pure motivation has two aspects: furthering the welfare of sentient beings and achieving the rank of a buddha ourselves in order to further their welfare. To achieve the rank of a buddha, we need to understand the nature of the excellent dharma and to practice meditative stabilization. Therefore, please listen to the excellent dharma with pure motivation to practice meditation and to understand the nature of meditation.

I have explained many topics from within this treatise on the stages of meditation according to the Middle Way School. This evening I will speak about how to practice meditative stabilization. Ultimately, all phenomena lack establishment. However, as mere conventions, the relationships between actions, cause and effect, are infallible. We need to understand this union of the two truths accurately. That is to say, we need to realize the union of (1) the infallibility of the dependent relationships between conventional phenomena and (2) the emptiness that is the ultimate truth. If realizing emptiness to be the ultimate truth were to lead us to contempt for actions consisting in causes and effects, which are true conventionally, we would not be traveling on a genuine path. If confidence in actions consisting in causes and effects uninformed by realization of the emptiness that is the ultimate truth were to leave us conceiving that, ultimately, things do truly exist, we would not be traveling on a genuine path. The existence of things conventionally does not interfere with or refute their nonexistence ultimately, and their nonexistence ultimately does not lead to a nihilistic view of actions that do exist conventionally. In dependence upon the conventional, we realize the emptiness that is ultimate; in dependence upon the ultimate being emptiness, the dependent relationships between conventional phenomena are infallible. On this point, we need confidence.

Someone who has realized this is called a *yogin*. Someone who has not realized this is called an ordinary being.[19] That is the difference between an ordinary being and a yogin. In the Tibetan word for *yogin, nal jor ba,*[20] *nal* names the genuine abiding nature, *jor* means "connect," and *ba* indicates a person who does this. Since it is mind that connects to the genuine abiding nature of things, here *jor* also has the sense of "know" and "understand." Thus, *yogin* signifies someone who joins his mind precisely and appropriately to the abiding nature of things. A *yogin* understands and realizes the genuine meaning, which is the truth.

What does it mean to say that those who have not realized the genuine abiding nature of things are ordinary beings? Ordinary beings have individual actions and individual appearances. They cannot realize the ultimate truth. Neither can they realize the mode of abiding of conventional truths. Ordinary beings are mistaken in various ways and, in dependence upon those various mistakes, are ignorant in various ways. In dependence upon the various aspects of ignorance, ordinary beings accumulate various, dissimilar actions. Individually, they have mistaken appearances. Individually, they accumulate actions. Individually, they experience the effects of those actions and are born into those situations. Therefore, they are called ordinary beings.

In the *Sūtra Compiling the Dharma Correctly*, the Buddha spoke of a magician who emanated an illusory being. That emanated illusory being underwent various types of suffering, such as illness, being struck by weapons, and so on. In order to liberate that illusory being from suffering, the magician then created devices that would work on his behalf. Even though he produced those devices, he nevertheless knew that the emanated being was not in pain. Moreover, the magician felt no attachment to the emanated being. Similarly, the three existences—the Desire Realm, Form Realm, and Formless Realm—are like emanations, and those who are learned in complete awakening know that. For the sake of the sentient beings who travel from lifetime to lifetime within the three realms, and in order to protect them from suffering, buddhas and bodhisattvas exert themselves at creating a variety of devices. Nevertheless, they know that all those travelers in cyclic existence lack inherent existence.

We must meditate in that way. When we meditate in that way, what faults will arise? Sometimes laxity will arise. Sometimes excitement will arise. When they arise, we must dispel them by relying on the instructions that were given previously, along with the instruction in the cultivation of calm abiding. Starting from the point of their having been dispelled, a genuine calm abiding free from laxity and excitement will arise. Moreover, genuine insight will arise at this same juncture. We have become capable of entering into calm abiding and insight equally. In this way we arrive at the genuine path.

Entering initially into that genuine path, we must intensify our admiration to whatever extent our exertion will permit. Because we must intensify our admiration, first we develop certainty, in dependence upon which we cultivate meditative stabilization. These, the grounds of a beginner, are called the grounds of conduct through admiration. How does a beginner meditate? A beginner meditates by abiding on the grounds of conduct through admiration.

What has been taught up to this point is the main practice of meditative stabilization. That is to say, thus far the treatise has presented the way in which beginners—bodhisattvas who abide on the grounds of conduct through admiration—cultivate the meditative stabilization of equipoise when bringing these teachings into experience. Following that, the treatise teaches the way in which to generate the meditative stabilization of subsequent attainment.

After resting in equipoise, we rise from meditative stabilization. That means that our minds rise from meditative stabilization, for the body remains in the posture of meditation. While continuing to sit upon our cushions, we must investigate and analyze. In what way? First, we must reflect that, during meditation, all these phenomena ultimately have no entity of their own. All phenomena are emptiness. Nevertheless, conventionally, the dependent relationship of phenomena, which means the dependence of effects upon the actions that are their causes, is infallible. Moreover, in a sūtra, the Buddha, who had destroyed the two obstructions, who possessed all good qualities, and who had passed beyond the two extremes, said that, during the equipoise of meditative stabilization, when the most excellent knowledge investigates and individually realizes forms, feelings, discriminations, compositional factors, and consciousnesses, it knows them to be devoid of birth. However, because forms and so forth exist for consciousnesses that conceal suchness, childish ordinary beings have not realized such an emptiness. Rather, they adhere strongly to things and, due to the power of that adherence to things, they wander everywhere in cyclic existence, not even knowing where they are going. As they wander, they experience manifold suffering. For such beings, the Buddha said, we should feel compassion.

Having aroused great compassion for all sentient beings, we reflect in the following way: Because all sentient beings wander in cyclic existence, I meditate upon reality's abiding nature. Through meditating on the abiding nature, I will achieve the rank of a buddha. Having achieved the rank of a buddha, I will enable all sentient beings to understand the truth of reality and in that way stop them from wandering in misery. We cultivate compassion in that way.

After cultivating compassion, we make offerings to all buddhas and bodhisattvas. We supplicate them. We make good aspirational prayers. Similarly, having arisen from meditative stabilization, we must accumulate the collections of merit and wisdom through generosity, ethics and so forth. In a sūtra, the Buddha taught that because method and knowledge are united, we must give birth to great compassion. Having given birth to great compassion, if we come to have ethics, meditative stabilization, and knowledge, we will achieve the rank of a buddha.

The Buddha taught that we must generate a surpassing intention to benefit all sentient beings. We must want to help all sentient beings. In what way must we accomplish that? Bodhisattvas must realize the five aggregates to be like illusions. Despite realizing them to be like illusions, we do not cast away those illusory aggregates. Why not? For the sake of all sentient beings, who are to be tamed by the dharma, we do not cast away the aggregates, which are like illusions. The eighteen elements are like poisonous snakes. We must realize them to be like roots that produce suffering. Despite the need to realize them as such, we do not throw them away. For the sake of all sentient beings, who are to be tamed by the dharma, we let them be. Similarly, we must realize all of the twelve sense fields[21] to be like empty villages. Nevertheless, we do not abandon the sense fields. We must realize the aggregate of form to be like a ball of foam. Just as a ball of foam has no essence at all, the aggregate of form has no essence. It is like an accumulation of bubbles. We must realize it to be such but we do not cast it away. Why not? In the future, we must accomplish a Tathāgata's Form Body. That Form Body, like all forms, has no essence, and we realize it to be without essence, but we do not cast it away. Rather, in order to benefit all sentient beings, who are to be tamed by the dharma, we must accomplish the body of a Tathāgata. Similarly, all feelings are like bubbles in water. Discriminations are like mirages. Compositional factors are like plantain trees. Consciousnesses are like illusions. We must realize the aggregates to be like those things, but we are not to abandon the aggregates. For the sake of all sentient beings, who are to be tamed by the dharma, we must use the aggregates to further the welfare of sentient beings.

In that way, we bring these teachings into experience mainly through the methods of meditative equipoise and subsequent attainment. How will we traverse the paths in dependence upon the practices of meditative equipoise and subsequent attainment? As explained previously, first there are the grounds of conduct through admiration, which are twofold: the paths of accumulation and the paths of preparation. Beginners abide on paths of accumulation, which are called that because the conduct of subsequent attainment consists mainly in accumulating the collection of merit through generosity, ethics, and so forth.

When paths of accumulation are presented in fine detail, there are twelve. A beginner, who has just embarked upon the paths of accumulation, has a small path of accumulation. When our meditation has increased slightly, we achieve a middling path of accumulation. When it has increased significantly, we achieve a great path of accumulation. Thus, in general, paths of accumulation are threefold. However, each of those has four parts. The first, a small path of accumulation, is composed of the four close placements of mindfulness: close placement of mindfulness upon the body, close placement of mindfulness upon feeling, close placement of mindfulness upon mind, and close placement of mindfulness upon phenomena. Without our attention wavering, we recognize that, ultimately, all four—body, feeling, mind, and phenomena—lack true establishment. However, conventionally, the infallible relationship between actions and their effects applies also to the body, to feeling, to mind, and to phenomena. In that way, on the small paths of accumulation, we cultivate four close placements of mindfulness.

In dependence upon the increase of a small path of accumulation, a middling path of accumulation is achieved. What do we cultivate at the time of a middling path of accumulation? We cultivate the four genuine abandonments. The four genuine abandonments emphasize the relationship between actions and their effects. First, we do not newly generate non-virtue that we have not generated previously. Second, we abandon non-virtue that we *have* previously generated. Thus, two of the four genuine abandonments pertain to non-virtue. Third, we *do* newly generate virtue that we have not previously generated. Fourth, we cause the virtue that we have generated previously to increase to ever higher levels. Those are the four genuine abandonments that arise at the time of the middling path of accumulation.

At the time of a great path of accumulation, we achieve four legs of magical emanation. Magical emanations are of many types; to understand *legs* of magical emanation, we have to understand that magical emanations must be achieved in dependence upon meditative stabilization. Therefore, the four legs of magical emanation refer mainly to four aspects of meditative stabilization that we achieve at this time. *Aspiration* to meditative stabilization is the first of those. We develop great admiration for meditative stabilization. In dependence upon admiration for meditative stabilization, we make effort at meditative stabilization. In dependence upon that *exertion*, we have the *intention* to stabilize in meditation, which means the intention to abide genuinely in meditative stabilization. *Analysis* is the fourth. Analysis has the aspect of knowledge. Aspiration, exertion, and intention have the aspect of calm abiding; analysis has the aspect of insight, for it has the certainty and knowledge that arise from investigating and analyzing reality's abiding nature. Those are the four legs of magical emanation. Thus, a path of accumulation has twelve aspects, which we traverse in that manner.

Such paths of accumulation increase gradually by means of conduct through admiration. In dependence upon that gradual increase, all good qualities gradually develop. We traverse the paths of accumulation gradually, and at their limit, when our meditation becomes stable, we go to a path of preparation. The paths of preparation prepare us to see the truth of reality in direct perception on the path of seeing. For that reason, they are called "paths of preparation."

A path of preparation has four aspects. Generally, we may speak of external appearances and internal consciousnesses. When realization of external appearances as emptiness begins, we have reached the first of the four paths of preparation, known as "heat." Because it is the sign that the wisdom of a sublime person, which resembles fire, will soon arise, it is called "heat."

In dependence upon the increase of that path, we reach the path of preparation known as "peak." The appearance for this meditative stabilization surpasses that of the previous path in clarity. It resembles a peak in our realization of external things as emptiness, and for that reason this path is called "peak."

This is followed by the third path of preparation, called "forbearance." Here, we not only realize all appearances of external things as emptiness but also begin to realize internal consciousnesses too as emptiness. Because we can bear such realization of emptiness, this path is called "forbearance."

The increase of "forbearance" brings the fourth among the four paths of preparation, called "supreme mundane quality." Why is this path called "supreme?" There are the paths of conduct through admiration and the path of seeing, which sees reality in direct perception. The paths of conduct through admiration are called paths of ordinary beings. Seeing reality in direct perception is called the path of a sublime person. The fourth of the four paths of preparation is the supreme among all the paths of conduct through admiration. No path of an ordinary being goes beyond it. For that reason, this path is called the "supreme mundane quality." Here, we realize internal mind to be emptiness. Not long thereafter, the wisdom of a path of seeing will be born. That wisdom will directly see all phenomena as emptiness and selflessness; it will see reality's abiding nature in direct perception.

Seeing the truth of reality in direct perception is called the "path of seeing." At that point, we have achieved the first ground of a sublime person. Why is this path called the path of seeing? Having come to the end of inferential meditation upon reality's abiding nature, we see directly. Because we see directly, this path is called the path of seeing. It is also called "the ground of a sublime person." Among the ten grounds of a sublime person, this is the first one, and it has the name Very Joyful. Why is it called Very Joyful? At this time, we see the truth of reality, which we have not seen previously. In dependence upon seeing the truth of reality, we know that we will soon have the ability to protect sentient beings from suffering, and we achieve confidence that we will accomplish the rank of a buddha without difficulty. Therefore, great joy arises in the mind of that bodhisattva. For that reason, the first ground is called Very Joyful.

This evening I have spoken about the paths of accumulation, preparation, and seeing. Tomorrow I will start with the path of meditation and continue from there. If you have any questions, please ask them.

Q: Please explain the example of the magician again.
A: In that example, initially the magician emanates an illusory being. Then, he may exert himself at liberating that illusory being from suffering. The

magician does not consider the illusory being to be a human being, knows that the illusion does not suffer, and understands that there is no need to make effort at the methods for liberating the illusory being from suffering. Nevertheless, the magician displays the aspects of rescuing the illusion. Similarly, all the buddhas and bodhisattvas exert themselves to protect sentient beings from suffering and to further the welfare of sentient beings, but they do not regard those sentient beings as truly or substantially established. Neither do they determine the suffering of sentient beings to be present in reality. That is the meaning of the example.

Q: I do not understand how to harmonize the ultimate and the relative. On the one hand, we have heard that the world is our mind's projection. On the other hand, we see things that look real and solid, such as birds flying in the sky. How can we join those?

A: To understand the relationship between the two truths, we will need a good example, and the one you have used will not do. For example, consider a rope that is mistaken for a snake. The rope and the snake can coexist in that appearing to be a snake can coexist with being a rope. Someone may think, "It is a snake." In fact, he or she will see it as a snake. When that person sees the rope as a snake, is there a snake in that rope? No, not in the slightest degree. Consider the object itself: is it a snake or a rope? It is 100 percent rope. Does the person see a rope? No, he or she sees a snake, 100 percent. In that sense, the snake and the rope coexist. For a mistaken consciousness that conceals the rope, there is the appearance of a snake. For the knowledge that has abandoned the apprehension of the snake, there is no snake. If you use that example to look at the two truths, you will be able to understand the relationship between them.

Q: Ultimately, it is neither a rope nor a snake. It depends upon how you see it. If you think it is a snake, and it is actually a rope, is it a rope or a snake?

A: In the circumstance I have described, the object is a rope. What does the person see? An appearance as a snake. Similarly, emptiness—the ultimate— is the object, but the subject sees suchness dressed up as something else. That explanation works.

Q: Last night you spoke about the paths of hearers and bodhisattvas. You mentioned solitary realizers. What are the paths and realizations of solitary realizers?

A: Generally speaking, three vehicles have been taught: those of hearers, solitary realizers, and bodhisattvas. However, for the most part, solitary realizers are included within hearers. Why? First, they seek principally their own welfare. Similarly, when they meditate and when they practice, they do not enter into the conduct of bodhisattvas and they do not realize the selflessness of phenomena to any significant degree. For those reasons, they are included within hearers.

If they are included within hearers, for what reason are solitary realizers explained separately? Solitary realizers have slightly greater knowledge than hearers. They rely upon having heard a buddha's speech in a previous lifetime and, in the lifetime in which they achieve liberation, they do not depend upon a buddha's speech. They take birth in isolated places. Under their own power, they go to a charnel ground, see the bones of human beings who have died, and understand that to be impermanence and suffering. They recognize that the bones arose in dependence upon death. They understand that the appearances of this lifetime are impermanent. They reflect that, in the end, this will come to all of us. Examining carefully and looking for the source of the appearances of this lifetime, they understand that, initially, these appearances arise in dependence upon ignorance. Knowing that this ignorance can be abandoned in dependence upon realization of selflessness, they meditate alone. The fruit that they achieve ultimately is called the rank of a solitary realizer.

It is said that they realize external things to be mere emptiness. However, they have not realized a view that accords with Mind Only. They realize that these external particles merely do not exist. They realize that mere external things do not exist. They realize these appearances to be partless in nature, which is to say, emptiness, but they do not realize all appearances to be mind's appearances. They do not encompass the view that recognizes all appearances for the eight consciousnesses as dawning from the consciousness that is the basis for all. They see in a general way that things merely dawn from the mind and that external things are merely not established. Therefore, they are mostly included within hearers.

Q: What do the words existence, appearance, and reality mean?
A: "Manner of appearance" gives a name to the appearances that dawn for us. For example, when we mistake a rope for a snake, the rope appears as a snake; the appearance as a snake is the manner of appearance. Still, even though we mistake the rope for a snake, there is nothing other than a rope there; that

rope is the "manner of abiding" of what appears to be a snake. As for existence and nonexistence, when we mistake a rope for a snake, what exists? A rope exists. What does not exist? A snake does not exist.

Q: But ultimately the rope does not exist.
A: In speaking of the rope and the snake, I have given an example. Applying the example to other things, we can say that, ultimately, there are no things at all, and that, conventionally, things do appear. But conventional things do not exist ultimately.

Q: What is wrong with the word "existence?" Why is it a mistake to say that appearances exist or that emptiness exists?
A: If emptiness were to exist, that would be a problem. Emptiness is emptiness; it isn't anything at all. If appearances were to exist, there would be a slight problem: they appear but they do not exist.

Q: This word, "existence," is losing all meaning. It is supposed to be the core of delusion, but what is it?
A: What don't you understand?

Q: What is the difference between appearing and existing?
A: That is what I have been talking about: the snake appears but does not exist. Where there appears to be a snake there is, in fact, a rope.

Q: What would it be like if we were walking down the street with the understanding that phenomena are empty and that mind is empty? What would that experience be?
A: When we watch television, we may see someone being killed, and we may see a thief stealing gold. However, we do not think that what we have seen has really happened. To have realized emptiness and then to wander through the world of phenomena would be like that. No worries, no suffering.

Q: If all things are emptiness, why teach the dharma?
A: For example, there are shows on television, right? They are emptiness, aren't they? There's nothing there. Nevertheless, there are twenty-five channels, all showing different things. Why? Why show them?

Q: Are these things the play of emptiness?

A: Ha ha. I suppose so. These things are emptiness, but not all sentient beings have realized emptiness. Therefore, it is necessary to teach the Buddha-dharma.

CHAPTER EIGHT

The Ten Grounds of Bodhisattvas and the Ground of a Buddha

IN ORDER TO LISTEN to the excellent dharma, we need pure motivation. The pure motivation that we require is the aspiration to achieve supreme awakening for the sake of all sentient beings. Inspired as we may be to accomplish the happiness and benefit of all sentient beings, we nevertheless do not presently have the ability to do so. Because we lack that ability now, we resolve to accomplish the rank of a buddha. To achieve that, we will need to bring the excellent dharma into our experience. To do so, we listen now to the excellent dharma. Reflecting in that way, please rouse your aspiration and listen.

Kamalashila's *Stages of Meditation* begins with the cultivation of compassion, continues with the cultivation of the mind of awakening, and concludes with a presentation of bringing these instructions into experience through practice. Among those three, we have reached the third, which has two parts: how to accomplish these instructions and the result of having accomplished them. We have reached the second of those two. When we traverse this graduated path, we begin with the grounds of conduct through admiration, which include the paths of accumulation and preparation. These bring a practitioner to the paths of seeing, which are followed by the paths of meditation. At the end of the paths of meditation, a practitioner achieves the rank of a completely awakened buddha, who has destroyed the two obstructions, who possesses all good qualities, and who has passed beyond the extremes of existence and peace, which is the ultimate accomplishment. We have considered the presentations of the paths of accumulation, preparation, and seeing. This evening I will speak about the way in which a practitioner travels the paths of meditation and achieves the rank of a buddha.

Generally speaking, there are ordinary beings and sublime persons. Having gone beyond the paths of ordinary beings, we achieve the grounds of a sublime person. Beginning with the first ground, Very Joyful, and continuing through the tenth ground, Cloud of Dharma, for bodhisattvas there are ten grounds. To achieve the rank of a buddha, bodhisattvas must traverse these ten grounds stage by stage in a most gradual manner.

Very Joyful is the name of the first of those ten grounds. How do we traverse the ground known as Very Joyful? A bodhisattva who achieves the first ground, Very Joyful, newly sees the truth of reality, which he or she has not seen previously. For that reason, this ground is called the path of seeing. What objects does it abandon? A bodhisattva's path of seeing abandons the acquired afflictive obstructions and the acquired obstructions to omniscience. Following that, he or she traverses the paths of meditation.

The remaining nine grounds compose the paths of meditation. What objects are abandoned on those grounds? Generally, bodhisattvas on the paths of meditation abandon sixteen afflictions. What are those sixteen? The first is the view of the transitory collection as a self. Next come the two extreme views: the extreme view that conceives things as existent and the extreme view that conceives things as non-existent. In addition to those, there are desire, hatred, pride, and ignorance. Sentient beings who inhabit the Desire Realm have all six of those afflictions: the view of the transitory, the extreme views, desire, hatred, pride, and ignorance. The meditative stabilizations of sentient beings who inhabit the Form Realm and the Formless Realm have already subdued hatred; temporarily, those sentient beings have no hatred. Therefore, in the Form and Formless Realms, only five afflictions are present. The six afflictions present in the Desire Realm together with the five that are present in each of the two upper realms adds up to a total of sixteen afflictions; these sixteen afflictions are abandoned by paths of meditation. The afflictions that are abandoned by paths of meditation can be divided into coarse, middling, and subtle levels of affliction. Each of those three can be divided again into coarse, middling, and subtle levels. That yields nine cycles of afflictions to be abandoned gradually by paths of meditation.

In what conduct do we engage during periods of subsequent attainment as we traverse the ten grounds? In stages, we accomplish the ten transcendent actions. Generally, a bodhisattva accomplishes all ten transcendent actions on each ground, but on the first ground, the emphasis falls on transcendent generosity. Why? At the first ground, a bodhisattva newly realizes the abiding nature of the sphere of reality. In dependence upon that realization, a bodhisattva ceases to regard his or her own welfare as principal. With great compassion for others, whose afflictions are to be subdued by the dharma, bodhisattvas devote themselves to furthering the welfare of others. Thus, among the ten transcendences, transcendent generosity predominates.

What is the difference between the first ground and the second ground? Bodhisattvas who abide on the first ground have mastered the meaning of emptiness and the meaning of reality. However, they make subtle mistakes in regard to matters of conduct. For as long as bodhisattvas cannot abandon those slight downfalls and subtle mistakes, they remain on the first ground. When they can abandon those subtle mistakes, they are said to have reached the second ground. What good qualities are completed on the second ground? Because bodhisattvas do not then stumble even in subtle matters, on the second ground transcendent ethics predominates, and that bodhisattva can accomplish such ethics genuinely and accurately. Therefore, Stainless is the name of the ground on which such a bodhisattva abides. In what way are stains absent? Because that bodhisattva is free from the stains of inappropriate ethics and bad conduct, the second ground is called Stainless.

When do bodhisattvas cross from the second ground to the third ground? On the second ground, bodhisattvas have the ability to abandon even mere subtle stains that would otherwise mar their ethics. However, on the second ground, they do not have the ability to enter into all and every meditative stabilization. Also, on the second ground, when bodhisattvas hear the excellent dharma from their spiritual friends, from completely awakened buddhas, and so on, they do not have the ability to retain in their minds whatever dharma they hear. So long as they lack these abilities, they remain on the second ground. When they generate the good qualities of being able to enter into each and every transmundane meditative stabilization and to retain all the meanings that they have heard, they are said to have reached the third ground. On that third ground, because they can retain in their minds whatever genuine dharma they have heard and can enter thoroughly into all meditative stabilizations, they can bear all suffering. Therefore, transcendent constancy predominates in the practice of bodhisattvas who abide on the third ground. In dependence upon that practice and meditative stabilization, wisdom shines forth brilliantly and without limit. Therefore, the third ground is called Luminous.

How do bodhisattvas cross from the third ground to the fourth ground? On the third ground, they have achieved genuine meditative stabilization. However, they are not able to enter the meditative stabilizations or pure paths on which the rank of a buddha is achieved whenever and as frequently as they would like. So long as they lack that ability, they remain on the third ground. When they have abandoned that fault, they have reached the fourth ground. Bodhisattvas who abide on the fourth ground enter into such meditative stabilizations again and again. Moreover, such bodhisattvas can undertake with great exertion the paths of awakening that lie beyond the objects of body, speech, and mind. Because of the exertion of which they are capable, bodhisattvas who abide on the fourth ground complete the practice of transcendent exertion. In dependence upon that great exertion, on this ground their rays of light have the power to abandon and exhaust all afflictions. For that reason, the fourth ground is named the Radiant.

How do bodhisattvas ascend from the fourth ground, Radiant, to the fifth ground, Difficult Training? Bodhisattvas who abide on the fourth ground bring the qualities of awakening into experience uninterruptedly. In so doing, they fully intend to turn back from cyclic existence and to approach nirvāṇa. Bodhisattvas who abide on the fourth ground cannot reverse directions, approach cyclic existence, and turn back from nirvāṇa. They lack the means that would enable them to refrain from accomplishing the rank of nirvāṇa in order to further the welfare of sentient beings. So long as bodhisattvas lack that ability, they remain on the fourth ground. When they have become accustomed to approaching cyclic existence and turning back from nirvāṇa—when they do not strive to accomplish the rank of nirvāṇa because of wishing to further the welfare of sentient beings—they have reached the fifth ground. It is extremely difficult to train in such a mind. For the time being, we do *not* want to achieve the rank of a buddha and we do *not* want to abandon cyclic existence. Because it is so difficult to train in that way, the fifth ground is called Difficult Training. Also, bodhisattvas who abide on the fifth ground cultivate strong meditative stabilization. Thus, on this ground, transcendent stable contemplation predominates.

Bodhisattvas who abide on the fifth ground take up a difficult training: liking cyclic existence and disliking nirvāṇa. It is terribly difficult to train in not abandoning cyclic existence and not accomplishing nirvāṇa. Because the work is difficult, there is some sadness in their minds. That sadness makes it hard to rest in equipoise upon the meaning of emptiness, reality, and signlessness. Generally speaking, of course, bodhisattvas who abide on the fifth ground do rest in equipoise upon the meaning of signlessness, but not in the joyful way that bodhisattvas who abide on the sixth ground rest in meditative equipoise upon the meaning of signlessness, emptiness, and reality. Until bodhisattvas resolve this problem, they remain on the fifth ground. When they have abandoned that fault and can rest in equipoise upon signlessness without difficulty, they have reached the sixth ground. On the sixth ground, through meditating upon the meaning of dependently related arising, bodhisattvas engage mainly in transcendent knowledge and thus emphasize transcendent knowledge. In dependence upon that emphasis, transcendent knowledge arises manifestly and the qualities of a buddha will become manifest. On the sixth ground, the causes of achieving the rank of a buddha become manifest in the sense that bodhisattvas realize clearly the paths that will lead to the rank of a buddha; for that reason, the sixth ground is called Manifest.

How do bodhisattvas progress from the sixth ground to the seventh ground? On the sixth ground, bodhisattvas achieve signlessness. However, bodhisattvas who abide on the sixth ground are not able to rest in equipoise upon signlessness without intervals. So long as they must occasionally rise from equipoise, bodhisattvas remain on the sixth ground. When bodhisattvas can rest in equipoise without intervals, they have reached the seventh ground. On the seventh ground, bodhisattvas master signlessness. There, having stopped all signs and all that possess signs, bodhisattvas complete transcendent method. In dependence upon completing transcendent method on the seventh ground, bodhisattvas achieve spontaneity on the eighth ground. Because the seventh ground is related with the path of spontaneity, the seventh ground is called Gone Afar. From what have bodhisattvas gone far away? They have gone a long way from signs. In what sense? Having abandoned all signs, they have gone far away from signs and come close to the path of spontaneity. For that reason, the seventh ground is called Gone Afar.

Bodhisattvas who abide on the seventh ground can rest in equipoise upon signlessness and have come close to spontaneity, but they are not able to enter into spontaneity itself. So long as they are not able to enter, bodhisattvas remain on the seventh ground. When bodhisattvas are able to enter into spontaneity itself, they have reached the eighth ground. Bodhisattvas who abide on the eighth ground enter effortlessly and spontaneously into all classes of virtue; therefore, all their wishes come about spontaneously and without effort, established from their mere aspiration. For that reason, on the eighth ground, from among the ten transcendences, transcendent aspirational prayer is completed. Because those bodhisattvas have completed transcendent aspirational prayer, in their minds there are no signs. Moreover, they have neither striving nor movement. Therefore, the eighth ground is called Immovable.

How do bodhisattvas cross the boundary separating the eighth ground from the ninth ground? On the eighth ground, bodhisattvas abide in spontaneity and signlessness. Nevertheless, they have not achieved command over enumerations and etymologies of names in all their categories and fine distinctions. So long as they remain unable to teach in that manner, bodhisattvas remain on the eighth ground. When able to teach them, bodhisattvas have reached the ninth ground. What enables bodhisattvas to teach them? On the ninth ground, bodhisattvas achieve the four individual correct knowledges, by means of which the power of knowledge increases ever higher. Because their knowledge has become powerful, from among the ten transcendences, bodhisattvas abiding on the ninth ground achieve transcendent power. In dependence upon achieving transcendent power and by way of the four individual correct knowledges, these bodhisattvas have become skilled in teaching the dharma. They can teach whatever needs to be taught—words, meaning, doctrine, and so on—flawlessly and skillfully. Because bodhisattvas abiding on the ninth ground have achieved remarkable intelligence and knowledge, the ninth ground is called Good Intelligence.

How do bodhisattvas who abide on the ninth ground achieve the tenth ground? On the ninth ground, bodhisattvas abide in the four individual correct knowledges. However, while abiding on the ninth ground, bodhisattvas cannot display the field, retinue, and emanations of a buddha. Moreover, those bodhisattvas cannot display the qualities of a buddha in their entirety. Also, bodhisattvas who abide on the ninth ground can thoroughly ripen sentient beings but cannot do so in the way that a buddha can. So long as bodhisattvas can neither display a similitude of a buddha's qualities nor ripen sentient beings in the manner of which a buddha is capable, they remain on the ninth ground. When bodhisattvas can display the field, retinue, and emanations of a buddha and can also ripen sentient beings thoroughly in the way that buddhas do, that ability is called the tenth ground. Internally, the difference between a bodhisattva's tenth ground and the ground of a buddha is great; however, externally, as for taming those who are to be tamed, bodhisattvas who abide on the tenth ground can display the deeds of a buddha, ripen students, and teach the excellent dharma in just the way that a buddha accomplishes those deeds. Therefore, bodhisattvas who abide on the tenth ground achieve great wisdom resembling a buddha's wisdom. In dependence upon that reason, from among the ten transcendences, bodhisattvas abiding on the tenth ground achieve transcendent wisdom. In dependence upon achieving transcendent wisdom, bodhisattvas cause a rain of the excellent dharma to fall upon all who are to be tamed, filling their minds. Therefore, the tenth ground is named Cloud of Dharma, which causes a rain of dharma to fall.

The bodhisattvas who abide on the ten grounds achieve ever increasing good qualities as they progress from the first ground to the tenth ground. On the first ground, a bodhisattva achieves one hundred sets of twelve good qualities. On the second ground, a bodhisattva achieves one thousand sets of twelve good qualities. On the third ground, a bodhisattva achieves one hundred thousand sets of twelve good qualities. Kamalashīla has not written about them here because, he says, describing them at this point would make this treatise too long.

Bodhisattvas who abide on the tenth ground have achieved power over emanations. This power enables them to affect others just as a buddha does. However, bodhisattvas on the tenth ground do not have a buddha's good qualities of abandonment and realization internally. For that reason, bodhisattvas of the tenth ground cannot know all objects of knowledge just as they are in the precise way that a buddha knows them. Why not? A buddha has destroyed the passions, which are afflictive obstructions, and the impediments, which obstruct omniscience; a bodhisattva has not. There are subtle afflictive obstructions that a bodhisattva has yet to abandon. Similarly, there are subtle obstructions to omniscience that a bodhisattva has yet to abandon. When bodhisattvas who abide at the end of the ten grounds give rise to the vajra-like meditative stabilization, which serves as the antidote to those subtle obstructions, they abandon the most subtle afflictive obstructions and obstructions to omniscience. In dependence upon that reason, prior to giving rise to the vajra-like meditative stabilization and abandoning the afflictive obstructions and the obstructions to omniscience, bodhisattvas remain on the tenth ground. When they have abandoned those obstructions completely and given rise in their entirety to the wisdoms that know the modes and varieties of phenomena, they are known as buddhas.

Following the vajra-like meditative stabilization, bodhisattvas achieve the rank of a buddha. What are the qualities of a buddha? A buddha's qualities are inconceivable and inexpressible. Therefore, Kamalashīla writes that someone such as himself cannot know all the good qualities of a buddha. However, it is possible to describe the rank of a buddha as the flawless and fully endowed welfare of oneself and others. The Tibetan equivalent for the Sanskrit term *buddha* is *sang gyay*. *Sang*, which means "cleanse," refers to flawless and fully endowed abandonment of all that is to be abandoned: the phenomena of cyclic existence, which are faulty. *Gyay*, which means "expand," refers to the perfection of good qualities and wisdom. Thus, abandonment and realization describe the good qualities of a buddha in a general way. In dependence upon such shedding of all flaws and perfection of all good qualities, the welfare of ourselves and others is accomplished.

How is our own flawless and fully endowed welfare accomplished? That comes by way of a buddha's Body of Truth. Having completed all the good qualities of abandonment and realization, the entity of a buddha's mind has become the entity of the excellent dharma. A buddha's mind has become the distinctive and superior wisdom that cannot be differentiated from the sphere of reality, for which reason it is called the Body of Truth. It is our own flawless and fully endowed welfare.

The body that is the flawless and fully endowed welfare of others brings benefit to disciples by placing them in the ultimate fruition. We may divide disciples into the pure and the impure. In this context, bodhisattvas who abide on the grounds of sublime persons are pure disciples. The activity of a buddha enables pure disciples to train in paths in which they have yet to train and to raise to a higher level the paths in which they have trained. What, specifically, enables them to train in this way? A buddha's Body of Complete Resources. In dependence upon possession of the Body of Truth, a Body of Complete Resources appears effortlessly and spontaneously for the perspective of all pure disciples. What are the "resources" to which the name refers? The ability to accomplish the activity of a buddha. What resources does a buddha need? A buddha's activity, which benefits disciples. When such resources are complete, a buddha accomplishes the activity of placing students in genuine paths and, in the end, placing bodhisattvas who abide on the grounds in the rank of a buddha. For that reason, this body is called the Body of Complete Resources.

Impure disciples are not able to meet with the Body of Complete Resources. For them, in dependence upon the convergence of the aspirational prayers and noble heart of a buddha and the power of the disciples' merit, a buddha's Supreme Emanation Body is emanated. That body has the thirty-two major and eighty minor good marks. For instance, consider the aspect of our teacher Shākyamuni, who turned the wheel of dharma in stages and placed disciples in the paths that lead to liberation and omniscience. His life illustrates the activity of a Supreme Emanation Body. Thus, the rank of a buddha is to be understood in terms of these three bodies.

Having written about these topics, Kamalashīla then concludes his first presentation of the stages of meditation in the Middle Way School with an aspirational prayer that, through the merit of his having composed this treatise, those of weak intelligence will achieve great intelligence.

If you have any questions, please ask them.

Q: Is it necessary to understand our own unique obstacles before we can bring these teachings into experience?

A: When beginners enter into these practices, initially they do not need to understand the particular obstructions that are to be abandoned. As they travel gradually along these paths, they will need to know the objects that are to be abandoned and the fruition that is to be achieved. Otherwise, knowing neither the path nor the destination, they will wander around more or less lost.

Q: Developing knowledge requires bodhisattvas to understand dependent relationship. Do bodhisattvas see that what arises for them is the fruition of their action?

A: Bodhisattvas do generate powerful wisdom, but ever so gradually. They listen to the words that were spoken by the Buddha and to the treatises that comment upon his words. Having listened, they contemplate and meditate upon the meaning of those words. In dependence upon such hearing, contemplation, and meditation, knowledge arises gradually. In dependence upon knowledge arising, bodhisattvas begin to understand dependent relationship. In dependence upon realization of dependent relationship, bodhisattvas gradually come to understand the presentation of actions, which is to say, of causes and effects. However, this does not mean that from the first they must understand the dependent relationships between causes and effects. Knowledge increases gradually. Accordingly, understanding of dependent relationship increases gradually.

Q: Is karma ever circumvented? Is it possible to awaken completely without having purified all of our karma?

A: No, it is not possible to awaken fully without purifying our karma. However, as we traverse the paths of a bodhisattva and begin to awaken, our karma will naturally be purified.

Q: The treatise teaches that a bodhisattva develops transcendent constancy on the third ground. Does a bodhisattva become increasingly sensitive to ever more subtle forms of suffering? If so, how does that lead to realization of emptiness?

A: Constancy means the capacity to exert ourselves at the cultivation of meditative stabilization and at the work of furthering the welfare of sentient beings. That constancy entails fearlessness in the face of difficult work. However, a bodhisattva's constancy does not involve subtle forms of personal suffering, for bodhisattvas who abide on any of the ten grounds have already seen all phenomena to be emptiness. They do not suffer on their own account. But of course they see vividly the suffering that other sentient beings experience.

Q: How does a bodhisattva's practice of "sending and taking" lead to realization of emptiness?

A: In practicing "sending and taking," we must understand that the happiness and suffering of those wandering from lifetime to lifetime depends upon their individual actions. Therefore, we cannot simply suffer in place of others or give our happiness to them. However, things do change. Slowly, very slowly.

We practice "sending and taking" in order to change our own thought. We cherish ourselves and we do not cherish others to the same degree. We practice "sending and taking" in order to turn that around. Through this practice, we become accustomed to cherishing others more than we cherish ourselves.

In dependence upon meditation in which we imagine taking the suffering of others upon ourselves and giving our happiness to others, certainty arises in our minds. When certainty arises, although we do not directly take the suffering of other sentient beings upon ourselves, in dependence upon teaching the excellent dharma and the paths, we will become able to dispel the suffering of others gradually. At present, the meditation upon "sending and taking" serves as a method for cultivating the conventional mind of awakening. The ultimate mind of awakening, which realizes emptiness directly, will gradually arise in dependence upon the conventional mind of awakening, but the practice of "sending and taking" does not itself serve as a direct cause for the realization of emptiness.

Q: What do we see when we see the Body of Complete Resources? Do we visualize deities in order to help us to see that Body?

A: The Body of Complete Resources is seen by pure disciples. We who hold the paths of the Vajrayāna cultivate a stage of generation so that we ourselves may abandon impure appearances, enter into pure appearances, and give birth to genuine wisdom in the streams of our minds. We do not practice such meditation in order to meet with the Body of Complete Resources. There is a difference in purpose there.

Q: How do we meet with the Body of Complete Resources?
A: As we gradually complete the good qualities of abandonment and realization, we achieve the the first ground, second ground, third ground, and so forth; on those occasions, we meet the Body of Complete Resources.

Q: What is the Body of Complete Resources? I have heard that it means the realm of speech.
A: Through practicing the paths of the Great Vehicle, we achieve the Body of Truth that is the flawless and fully endowed fulfillment of our own welfare. Is that achievement the ultimate fruition? It is not. Since the capacity to benefit all sentient beings vastly is the purpose for achieving the rank of a buddha, a buddha displays bodies that enable the welfare of others to be accomplished. The Body of Complete Resources, which appears for the perspective of pure disciples, and the Supreme Emanation Body, which appears for the perspective of impure disciples, are the supports for furthering the welfare of others.

Q: What is the difference between the obstructions that are overcome as we achieve the first ground of a bodhisattva and the obstructions that are overcome as we move from the tenth ground to the ground of a buddha?
A: Generally, this involves the distinction between acquired obstructions and innate obstructions. Consider, for instance, the conception of a self. Through the force of having become accustomed to doing so from time without beginning, we naturally think "I." That conception is innate. From time to time, some other person, such as our spiritual teacher, may tell us, "You have a self" and then give reasons supporting the assertion of that self. The teacher will describe the self: "the self is of the nature of consciousness," or "the self is material in nature." Then, I myself begin to believe that, and I become certain that I have a self. This establishes tendencies in the continuum of my mind such that, even though I do not actually have a self, I am predisposed to agree with the suggestion that I do have a self. That conception of a self

is called acquired. When bodhisattvas achieve the first ground, they abandon the acquired conception of a self together with its seeds, such that it will never arise again. That is called abandoning the acquired afflictions.

From the second ground through the tenth ground, bodhisattvas abandon the innate conceptions of self. From time beyond memory, we have become accustomed to thinking that we do have a self. Now, through the power of that prior familiarization, no one needs to teach us that we have a self. It arises in us naturally. From that point of view, it is called innate.

The acquired conception of a self can be abandoned abruptly. It can be abandoned through merely seeing the truth of reality. The innate conceptions of self cannot be abandoned through merely seeing the truth. Since they arise through the power of familiarity, they must be abandoned through familiarization with selflessness on the paths of meditation.[22] Gradually, starting with its more coarse levels and proceeding through its most subtle levels, we abandon the innate conception of a self.

PART 2

*Intermediate Treatise on the Stages of Meditation
in the Middle Way School*

~

CHAPTER ONE

Compassion

I WOULD LIKE TO BEGIN by saying that I am delighted to have a chance to discuss the Buddhadharma with students of the Buddhist tradition. Thank you for giving me this opportunity.

Many highly accomplished people have appeared in India. Even among people of such distinction, Nāropa was remarkably learned. You are indeed fortunate to study the Buddhist teachings at a school that bears his name.

At the request of the Tibetan King Trisong Detsen, and while residing in Tibet itself, the Indian scholar Kamalashīla prepared three treatises that together make up his *The Stages of Meditation in the Middle Way School*. They are known as the *First*, the *Intermediate*, and the *Final* discourses on the stages of meditation. From among those three, this evening I will begin explaining the Intermediate treatise on the stages of meditation.

Due largely to the efforts of the Bodhisattva Abbot Shāntarakṣhita, the teachings of the Buddha had been introduced into Tibet and had begun to flourish there. After Shāntarakṣhita had entered nirvāṇa, a learned teacher known as Hwa Shang Mahāyāna came from China to Tibet. Generally speaking, the dharma taught by Hwa Shang Mahāyāna and the dharma taught by the Bodhisattva Abbot were the same in being the Buddhadharma. However, they differed in regard to method.

In what way did they differ? Hwa Shang Mahāyāna considered the teachings given by the Bodhisattva Abbot to be a presentation of a gradual path. He described his own teaching as the presentation of a sudden path. Some students felt that it was necessary to follow the Bodhisattva Abbot. Other students felt that it was necessary to follow Hwa Shang Mahāyāna. Doubt having arisen, students did not understand how to enter the path that leads to liberation and awakening.

In the midst of this perplexity, a few people remembered that the Bodhi-sattva Abbot himself had foretold the trouble that would arise subsequent to his own demise. In his last will and testament he had written that, in the future, when controversy had paralyzed the practice of the Buddhadharma in Tibet, the Tibetan people would do well to invite the master Kamalashīla, a student of Shāntarakṣhita, to come from India to Tibet. Shāntarakṣhita indi-cated that, if invited, Kamalashīla would be able to resolve the controversy. In accordance with Shāntarakṣhita's instructions, the Tibetan King Trisong Detsen requested Kamalashīla to come to Tibet.

Having come to Tibet, Kamalashīla wondered whether or not he and Hwa Shang Mahāyāna would be able to debate the questions troubling the Tibetans. Recognizing that this depended upon whether or not Hwa Shang Mahāyāna was both clever and knowledgeable, Kamalashīla decided to test his opponent. They proceeded to the banks of the Tsangpo River. Kamalashīla stood on the far shore while Hwa Shang Mahāyāna remained on the near shore. Kamalashīla then whirled his walking stick three times above his own head, making three circles in space. With this gesture he asked Hwa Shang Mahāyāna to identify the cause from which the three realms of cyclic existence arise. Buddhist monks in China wear robes that have long sleeves; in reply to Kamalashīla, Hwa Shang Mahāyāna withdrew his hands inside the long sleeves of his robes, thus indicating that cyclic existence arises in depend-ence upon not knowing the nature of apprehended objects and apprehend-ing consciousnesses. Kamalashīla concluded that Hwa Shang Mahāyāna was indeed a knowledgeable person and that, through discussion, the two of them would be able to settle the controversy raging in eighth-century Tibet.

Not long thereafter, King Trisong Detsen assembled all of Tibet's minis-ters, placed Kamalashīla on his right, Hwa Shang Mahāyāna on his left, and instructed the two scholars to debate. Describing himself and his ministers as householders who were not skilled in the terminology of the Buddhadharma, the king acknowledged that they would not be able to follow the discussion and would not be able to discern the outcome. Therefore, the defeated party should offer a garland of flowers to the victor and then depart to his own country, leaving the victor to hold sway in Tibet. Both Kamalashīla and Hwa Shang Mahāyāna were good scholars, but Hwa Shang Mahāyāna lost the debate, offered a garland of flowers to Kamalashīla, and left for China. Start-ing from that moment, the lineage of the dharma taught by Hwa Shang Mahāyāna seems to have evaporated and the lineage of the dharma taught by Shāntarakṣhita and Kamalashīla developed in a pure fashion.

Kamalashīla then spoke to the Tibetans about how to bring the Buddhist teachings into their experience. In so doing, he followed the pattern laid down by his teacher and theirs, Shāntarakṣhita. To guide their practice and study, he composed a treatise in three parts: the *First Treatise on the Stages of Meditation*, the *Intermediate Treatise on the Stages of Meditation*, and the *Final Treatise on the Stages of Meditation*. Because he recommended that we resolve to practice these very instructions, we regard them as important.

How does the Intermediate Treatise begin? Kamalashīla stresses that he has written this treatise for the sake of students who wish to practice by meditating upon the meanings taught in the sūtras of the Great Vehicle.

The result of accomplishing the excellent dharma ought to be the achievement of the rank of a buddha. Will the rank of a buddha be achieved casually, in the absence of its causes? No, it will not. Causes are indispensable, and the rank of a buddha will not be achieved in their absence. Why not? In the past, many religions flourished in India. Some of them have taught that things arise without dependence upon causes. They have held that a reasonable understanding requires neither former lifetimes nor later lifetimes. Other religions have taught that we achieve the result we desire through the grace of the deity Maheshvara. They have seen the kindness of the deity Maheshvara as the intervention that is necessary to our achieving the result that we desire, which is the rank of a buddha. Arguing against all of those claims, Kamalashīla writes that the causes of our achieving the rank of a buddha rest with us.

Kamalashīla argues that if the rank of a buddha could be achieved without depending upon causes, everyone would have already become a buddha. Why? No sentient being wants to suffer. Rather, everyone wants happiness and well-being. Therefore, if sentient beings did not need to rely upon causes in order to achieve the rank of a buddha, they would already have become buddhas. Similarly, if the rank of a buddha were achieved in dependence upon another, such as the deity Maheshvara, everyone would have already become a buddha. Why? Maheshvara feels loving concern for all sentient beings. Since all sentient beings want happiness and well-being, if Maheshvara were capable of bestowing the rank of a buddha upon them, why wouldn't he do so? In fact, there are causes for achieving the rank of a buddha, and the reason why we have not achieved that rank is that we either do not know how to practice them or lack the ability to practice them. Therefore, first of all, we need to know the causes of becoming a buddha.

In addition to knowing the causes, we need to accomplish them. Moreover, we need to accomplish all of them unerringly. Why? If we do not accomplish the cause, we cannot accomplish the result. Furthermore, if we lack the ability to accomplish all of them unerringly, the result will not come about perfectly. Therefore, the causes must be accomplished fully and flawlessly.

How shall we assemble the causes in full and without error? Kamalashīla describes himself as deluded and explains that, because of delusion, he cannot know the causes fully and unerringly. Therefore, in explaining the stages of meditation, he will follow and rely upon the Buddha, who understood the causes of liberation and awakening, brought them into experience, achieved the desired fruit, and then explained the way in which he had practiced. What did the Buddha teach? In speaking to Vajrapāṇi, the Lord of the Secrets, the Buddha taught that buddhahood comes about in dependence upon compassion.[23]

From that, we know compassion to be necessary. What else do we need? The mind of awakening is the second cause upon which a practitioner must rely. Will those two suffice? Not quite. Those two require the assistance of skill in method. Therefore, a practitioner needs a compassionate mind, the mind of awakening, and skill in method if he or she is to awaken fully. In dependence upon those, we can achieve the rank of a buddha. Therefore, we need to bring those three into experience.

Not suprisingly, Kamalashīla's second treatise on the stages of meditation begins by teaching the way to generate compassion, continues by teaching the way to generate the mind of awakening, and concludes with an extensive discussion of skill in method. First comes the section on compassion, and here Kamalashīla follows the Buddha's lead in emphasizing the importance of compassion. He cites an exchange between the Buddha and one of the Buddha's students in which the student asked about the principles in which a practitioner should train. The Buddha replied that it is not necessary to train in many things. In fact, one will do. Which one? Compassion. Therefore, bodhisattvas should begin by training in compassion.

What is the reason why bodhisattvas should train in great compassion? The Buddha, having destroyed the two obstructions, come into possession of all good qualities, and passed beyond the extremes of cyclic existence and peace, had thereby accomplished his own purposes perfectly. However, he had not then departed to the state of peace that is known as nirvāṇa, which would of course have been delightful for him but useless to anyone else. Rather, considering the welfare of other sentient beings, he discarded the possibility of passing into a merely peaceful state in the way that we would forego leaping into an iron cauldron that holds a roaring fire. He took no pleasure in it and had no interest in it. What gave him pleasure? It delighted him to be of benefit to sentient beings. Therefore, compassion is the cause of achieving the ultimate rank of a buddha, for, without compassion, we strive to achieve only our own liberation.

In this first section, Kamalashila presents the methods for cultivating compassion. Generally speaking, all religions consider compassion to be important. Buddhists consider compassion to be important; similarly, all other religions also consider compassion to be important. We might conclude that all religions are therefore identical in this respect. Moreover, it is not just the religions of the world that consider compassion to be important. Ordinary, worldly people think so too. In fact, everbody thinks that compassion is important, and everyone has compassion. True enough, but the Buddha gave uncommon quintessential instructions when he taught the methods for cultivating compassion, and the differences are extraordinarily important.

Generally, everyone feels compassion, but the compassion is flawed. In what way? We measure it out. For instance, some feel compassion for human beings but not for animals and other types of sentient beings. Others feel compassion for animals and some other types of sentient beings but not for humans. Others, who feel compassion for human beings, feel compassion for the human beings of their own country but not for the human beings of other countries. Then, some feel compassion for their friends but not for anyone else. Thus, it seems that we draw a line somewhere. We feel compassion for those on one side of the line but not for those on the other side of the line. We feel compassion for one group but not for another. That is where our compassion is flawed. What did the Buddha say about that? It is not necessary to draw that line. Nor is it suitable. Everyone wants compassion, and we can extend our compassion to everyone.

What fault comes from partial compassion? The story is told of catching a fish and giving it to a dog. Feeling compassion for the dog, we think, "This dog is my dog. I want to give things to it. I have to give a lot of food to this dog." To feed the dog, we catch a fish and give it to the dog. When we give the fish to the dog, our compassion helps the dog but hurts the fish. We do feel compassion for the dog but not for the fish, and because of landing outside the circle of our compassion, the fish suffers harm. When we have compassion for some but not for others, there is always the danger of the others being harmed by our efforts on behalf of those for whom we do feel concern.

Similarly, we may feel compassion for the people of our own country but not for the people of another country. We feel that they deserve to be comfortable and well. However, that entails harming anyone who threatens them. To protect the people of our own country, we fashion weapons of war. Why do we manufacture weapons? Out of compassion for the people of our own land, we make weapons that we will use to keep them safe by killing and destroying other people. Our compassion is partial. We protect our own people and we harm people who do not belong to our group.

These days, we issue visas to control the flow of people into our countries. Why? We feel that the people of our own land deserve to be comfortable and well. Were people to arrive from some other land, they would make trouble for us. Therefore, we do not permit them to come to our country. We turn them back. If they have no place to live, that's their problem. Let them suffer. The harsh treatment of others comes from restricting our compassion to some and withholding it from others.

When compassion is partial, then all that trouble will arise. For that reason, the Buddha taught that an uncommon variety of compassion is required. What is the nature of that uncommon compassion? It has two aspects. First, the compassion taught by the Buddha has no measure. That is to say, the Buddha taught that compassion is to be extended to all sentient beings. Second, compassion is a wish to free sentient beings from suffering. However, it is not possible to free others from suffering immediately. Initially, it is necessary to free others from the causes of suffering.

For example, I have diabetes. My doctor tells me that I must do something about this. What must I do? First of all, I have to avoid eating the things that cause me to feel sick: sugar and other sweet things. Why? They are the causes of my suffering. If I continue to eat sweet things, I will continue to suffer from this illness. Similarly, to overcome other types of suffering, it is necessary to stop engaging in their causes.

Given that we would like to generate a compassion that is both immeasurable and intelligent, how shall we proceed? It may surprise you to hear that we do not begin by attempting to increase compassion. Rather, we begin by cultivating equanimity. To cultivate equanimity means to consider the ways in which all sentient beings are the same. That will allow us to erase the line dividing those for whom we feel compassion from those for whom we do not feel compassion. To whatever extent we are able to see all sentient beings as similar, to that same extent we will be able gradually to generate compassion that is immeasurable. Upon what method shall we rely in order to generate compassion that excludes no one? Consider one hundred human beings.

They do not differ in wanting happiness and not wanting suffering. If ninety of them wanted happiness and the other ten wanted suffering, they would differ. In fact, all one hundred want happiness and do not want suffering. In that respect, they are the same. What need is there to feel compassion for some but not for others? If you think about it that way, you will begin to feel a little bit of compassion for everyone. Gradually, that will increase.

If we begin in this way, our compassion will increase and eventually we will be able to feel compassion even for our enemies. In the Buddhist religion, we speak of many types of sentient beings scattered throughout the Three Realms—hell beings, hungry ghosts, animals, and so on—many of whom undergo excruciating torment. In time, you will want to free all of them from suffering. Similarly, human beings suffer in various ways, and all human beings without exception suffer in many ways the pains of birth, aging, sickness, and death. It is necessary to cultivate the compassion of wanting to free all human beings from the suffering that besets them.

Subsequently, we cultivate compassion for gods. Why is it sensible to feel compassion for sentient beings who have taken birth in such privileged positions? Temporarily, gods enjoy marvelous comfort and wealth. There is no need to feel compassion for them in the way that we feel compassion for sentient beings who suffer from predators, disease, poverty, torture, and so on. However, the comfort and wealth that they enjoy now will abide only for a while. Their situations are not permanent and will change. When change comes, it will be for the worse, and the gods will then find themselves in terrible pain. Therefore, the Buddha regarded comfort and wealth as the suffering of change. Because the gods suffer the pain of change, they need the compassion that wishes to free them from the pain of change.

People such as ourselves do not see actual gods, but we do see human beings who enjoy extraordinary comfort, privilege, wealth, and knowledge. We may think that they do not need compassion from anyone at all. In fact, they do. Why? Temporarily, they enjoy comfort and wealth. In ten, twenty, thirty, forty, or fifty years, their comfort and wealth will change to something else. Now they are comfortable and wealthy; in the end, their happiness will turn to pain. Whether they are presently faring well or badly, all sentient beings deserve our compassion.

This infant compassion must grow until it extends to all sentient beings. As it grows, it will serve as the root of all other good qualities. For instance, from the compassion that wishes to free all sentient beings from suffering, the love that wishes all sentient beings to enjoy happiness will arise.

Love too must become immeasurable, and love must be intelligent. Merely thinking that sentient beings deserve to be comfortable and well will not make it so. What else will they need in addition to our good wishes? They will need the *causes* of happiness.

Results cannot come about in the absence of their causes. Suppose I were to want a flower to grow on this wooden table in front of me. I might pray for a flower to grow—"May a flower grow on this table"—but that will not make a flower appear on this table. Even if I were to pray for a month or a year, prayers alone will not cause flowers to grow on this table. What other methods will I have to employ to make that flower grow? The causes of a flower will do the trick. First, I will need to buy a flower pot. Then I will need to fill it with earth. Then I will have to plant a seed in the earth, water it, add fertilizer, and so on. If I do all those things correctly, a flower will grow here. Similarly, I may want all sentient beings to enjoy happiness, but I am not able to give that to them straightaway. They will need the causes of happiness in order to achieve it.

At its root, compassion means separating others from the causes of suffering. Similarly, at the root, love means joining others to the causes of happiness. What are the causes of suffering? Mental afflictions and bad actions. Stop accumulating those. What are the causes of happiness? Love, compassion, accumulation of virtue, and so on. Living that way, we separate from the causes of suffering and come to possess the causes of happiness. Then, in the future, sentient beings will naturally become free from suffering and will enjoy comfort and well-being.

The compassion taught by the Buddha is unusual. First we cultivate immeasurable equanimity. Then we cultivate immeasurable compassion, and following that we cultivate immeasurable love. From these three, immeasurable joy develops. Thus, the uncommon way of cultivating compassion taught by the Buddha follows the pattern of the four immeasurables.

If we do not develop ourselves in this way, compassion will become another way to suffer. For instance, suppose that someone is sick with a terrible illness. If I see this person and cannot cure the illness, then I will become discouraged. Because I lack recourse to other methods, my compassion will have become nothing more than another way to suffer. Because compassion considers not only suffering but also its causes, and because love considers not only happiness but also its causes, there is always something that I can do to help others. Something *will* come of my efforts. Because my efforts will yield results, my compassion for others does not add pain to pain. Rather, it brings pleasure and joy. Therefore, in the end, immeasurable compassion leads to immeasurable joy. If I help one person, then I have helped one person. If I help two people, then I have helped two people. If I help many people, then I have helped many people. This brings joy, and the joy increases as I am able to help more people.

As I mentioned at the outset, this treatise by Kamalashila focuses upon compassion, the mind of awakening, and skill in method. This evening I have explained the section on compassion. If you have qualms about anything I've said, please ask a question.

Q: What about compassion for yourself?
A: It *is* necessary to feel compassion for ourselves, but for the most part we already feel that. It is probably not necessary to rely much upon a special method for cultivating compassion for ourselves.

Q: Please say more about the causes of freeing others from suffering and creating happiness for them.
A: The roots of our suffering grow within our own minds, rather than externally. How so? For instance, when strong desire arises and we are able neither to quell it nor to fulfill it, we suffer. At other times, hatred arises in us. Hatred leads us to harm others, and then they will harm us in return. Sometimes we feel proud or jealous, and those afflictions bring us suffering too. Sometimes suffering comes to us because of our ignorance, which is to say, because we do not understand something. Therefore, the roots of our suffering grow within us, not outside of us. In the language of the Buddhist tradition, we say that suffering arises in dependence upon afflictions, such as desire and hatred. To put it simply and in colloquial language, we can say that our suffering comes from how we think about things. In that case, what shall we do? If we correct our mistaken way of thinking, our suffering will end.

A story from the Chinese tradition of Buddhadharma will help to illustrate this. The story tells of a bodhisattva who visited one of the hells. In that hell, he found a huge table upon which many kinds of delicious food had been arranged. Sitting around the table were the sentient beings who had taken birth in that hell. Despite sitting at a table laden with delicious food, those sentient beings were suffering terribly. Why were they suffering so? All of them had chopsticks, but the chopsticks were about six feet long. They grabbed the food with those chopsticks, but were then unable to place the food in their mouths because the chopsticks were so long. This made them miserable.

After seeing this sorry spectacle, the bodhisattva visited a buddha-field. In that buddha-field, he found a huge table upon which many kinds of delicious food had been arranged. Sitting around the table were the divine beings who had taken birth in that buddha-field, all of whom were extremely happy. What delighted them so? The chopsticks were just as long as those in the hell—six feet—but instead of trying to stuff the food into their own mouths, everyone picked up a tasty morsel and then placed it in the mouth of someone sitting on the opposite side of the table. Everyone was having a great time.

Q: What is the difference between happiness and joy? How do the first three of the four immeasurables lead to the fourth, immeasurable joy?
A: When we feel love for others, we want them to enjoy happiness. When they enjoy happiness, we feel joy.

Q: Since it is now dark, we've turned on the lights in this room. The lights have attracted insects that are flying into the lights and frying themselves. It seems that, in accomplishing something worthwhile, we have caused pain for other sentient beings. Also, in considering the comfort that the gods enjoy and the pain that they will experience later because of their attachment to that comfort, I am wondering whether or not that means that, out of compassion, we should try to put an end to their comfort.
A: In the Buddhist tradition, we consider motivation to be of great importance. We have good reason for gathering here this evening, and we have no wish or intention to harm these insects. We want to learn how to cultivate love and compassion for all sentient beings, and for that reason we have gathered here. We did not come here motivated by a wish to kill insects. I'm not sure that there is much we can do to prevent insects from dying.

Moreover, there are occasions when, if our motivation is pure, even killing is permitted. For instance, there is a story of a ship's captain named Strength-of-Heart, who, in a subsequent lifetime, became the Buddha Shākyamuni. In that era, merchants set sail from India in search of precious jewels. Their boats were not sound and would sometimes sink into the ocean. Sometimes a huge fish would destroy the boat. Sometimes a big wind would destroy the boat. It was dangerous to travel on the ocean, and one needed a good leader.

Strength-of-Heart was such a leader, and on one occasion he set sail with five hundred merchants. Among those on board, one person had an evil intention: he wanted to kill all the merchants. To accomplish his evil intention, he began drilling a hole in the bottom of the boat. Upon seeing this fellow drilling a hole in the boat, Strength-of-Heart whacked him in the head with an axe and killed him. In so doing, he protected the lives of the other merchants. He did kill someone, but he also protected five hundred others. Given the motivation and the circumstances, his action is regarded as virtuous rather than evil. Such action is permitted.

Q: How do we determine causes, in general? What is the methodology?
A: Causes are identified in relationship to their effects. If, when a thing is present, its effect arises and, when absent, its effect does not arise, the former may be identified as a cause of the latter. In the treatises on valid cognition, "when present, arising and, when absent, not arising" is given as the definition of cause. Some things have many causes; many causes and conditions must gather before they will come into being. When those causes and conditions are not complete, that thing will not come about. From that point of view, they are posited as its causes. In that sense, we speak about the causes of happiness, the causes of suffering, the causes of things, and so on.

Consider a flower. If we plant the seed of a flower, the flower will arise. If we do not have the seed for that flower, we have no method that will enable us to grow that flower. Therefore, we consider the seed to be the cause of that flower. Also, even when the seed is present, in the absence of water, fertile soil, and other elements, the flower will not grow well. We consider those other things to be conditions for the flower's growth.

Q: I have a question about intention. Sometimes we say that the road to hell is paved with good intentions. How shall we evaluate our intentions?
A: Generally speaking, if our motivation is good, then bad results will not come from our efforts. If bad things come from our actions, that indicates a flaw somewhere in our motivation. Sometimes, however, bad things come about even when our motivation is good. For instance, as we noted a few moments ago, at this place where we have gathered to discuss the Buddhadharma, bugs are flying into the hot lamps and dying. Still, it is the bugs that have flown into the lamps; we didn't make the bugs do that, did we? In this case, our action will not have an unfortunate result.

Q: I wonder whether or not we are really compassionate to ourselves. Certainly we indulge in useless and foolish things, thinking they will gratify us, but how often do we really nurture ourselves in a kind and gentle way? It seems to me that we can be extremely hard on ourselves. For instance, when students take up the practice of "sending and taking," they are willing to take on the pain of others but rarely feel that they have anything to give or share.

A: I think that what you have described is not a lack of compassion for oneself but rather a lack of courage. We tend to think, "I am bad. I am poor. I am worthless." I would call that a lack of courage rather than a lack of compassion for oneself.

Q: What are the stages of love and joy? What is the experience of those?

A: When you love someone, you want that person to have happiness and the causes of happiness, and you hope that he or she will have them. If happiness or its causes come to that person through your efforts, then you feel the joy of having helped someone. If that person is able to separate from suffering and its causes, or if that person, despite not being able to separate from suffering at that moment, is nevertheless able to abandon the causes of suffering even slightly, then too you feel the joy of having helped someone and having done something worthwhile.

Q: According to the Buddhadharma, is there any happiness other than the absence of suffering?

A: Wouldn't the abandonment of suffering be the greatest happiness?

Q: What I mean is that I don't see the difference between compassion, which means wanting others to be free from suffering, and love, which means wanting others to have happiness.

A: From one point of view, they seem to be the same. From another point of view, they are a little different. To separate from suffering, we must separate from its causes. To possess happiness, we must possess its causes. Certain causes lead to separation from suffering. Other causes lead to possession of happiness. The causes differ slightly, due to which the results differ slightly.

Q: How do we grow in courage?

A: According to the Buddhist tradition, the roots of courage are twofold. Meditation upon the difficulty of finding leisure and fortune is the first. That involves reflection upon the ways in which, among the various types of bodies that serve as supports for various types of lifetimes, the human body is unusually valuable. If you have a human body, then you can accomplish many things that animals, for instance, cannot do. Reflection upon the value of a human body leads us to regard the achievement of this body as the achievement of something precious, something that is like a jewel. In dependence upon such reflection, courage grows.

Second, we consider all sentient beings to be endowed with the essence of the Sugata. This essence serves as the root for all good qualities. It is present in us as something like a seed. As the seed grows, good qualities such as courage can grow too. If this essence were not present in us, then nothing would come of our efforts. Because this seed or cause is present in us, we can nurture it, which will enable us to accomplish whatever we would like.

CHAPTER TWO

The Mind of Awakening
and the Causes of Calm Abiding

I WOULD LIKE TO BEGIN this evening by speaking about the mind of awakening. If we had the same enthusiasm for accomplishing the welfare of others that we have for accomplishing our own welfare—the same capacity and intention to purify, train, and comprehend, and the same kindness—and if we felt that for all sentient beings, that would be the seed for the mind of awakening. Sometimes we speak of the person who has such a mind of awakening, and we call that person a warrior of the mind of awakening. We mean someone courageous, someone who does not fear anything. What, for instance, does this person not fear? When we engage in the conduct of a bodhisattva—a warrior of the mind of awakening—we must help many sentient beings. If we have only a little courage, we will think, "I can help one hundred, one thousand, ten thousand, or even one hundred thousand sentient beings, but I will not be able to help an inconceivable number of sentient beings," and we will become discouraged. To practice the way of a bodhisattva, we must not become discouraged when facing the needs of so many sentient beings. For how long must we continue to further the welfare of sentient beings? We must practice the way of a bodhisattva courageously until cyclic existence has been emptied of sentient beings. If we were to think, "For a few hundred or a few thousand years, I will be able to accomplish the activity that furthers the welfare of sentient beings, but not for the period of time that it will take to empty cyclic existence of sentient beings," that would be discouragement unbefitting a bodhisattva. Because they do not become discouraged even at the prospect of interminable labor, such people are regarded as warriors of the mind of awakening.

What are the varieties of the mind of awakening? Principally, there are two: conventional minds of awakening and ultimate minds of awakening.

Initially, a practitioner must develop a conventional mind of awakening. Generally, such a mind of awakening is a pure and vast motivation. What is the purity of this motivation? Compassion. That compassion has two characteristics. First, due to compassion, we focus upon the welfare of other sentient beings rather than upon our own welfare. Second, this compassion is not stupid. Sometimes, even though we feel compassion and want to help others, in trying to help, we harm. The compassion of the mind of awakening is accompanied by supreme knowledge. What role does supreme knowledge play? It enables us to protect others from suffering and to establish them in happiness, not just provisionally, but rather in a decisive and final manner.

The development of such an intention to achieve supreme awakening is called the mind of awakening. This motivation observes all sentient beings and wants to accomplish what is most beneficial for them. It moves internally, in our minds, yet has enormous power and potent force. Consider the way in which it has affected the unfolding of the Buddhadharma. The teachings of the Buddha have spread to many lands and, through bringing these teachings into their experience, many people have achieved the fruit of this teaching in a manner that cannot be conceived. Moreover, with the vast motivation to be of benefit to all sentient beings, they have accomplished the welfare of others in inconceivable ways. Such things have transpired during the period of approximately two thousand five hundred years since the Buddha began to teach. From what source has such activity arisen? It has arisen in dependence upon one buddha's teaching the excellent dharma. From what did the Buddha's teaching of the dharma arise? It began when, as an ordinary person, he resolved to achieve supreme awakening. Starting from there, he developed, his teachings developed, and the entire tradition developed. Had he not resolved to achieve supreme awakening, the rest of it could not have happened either.

These things tend to begin small and grow from there. For instance, in the *Sūtra of Good Fortune* the Buddha spoke of a previous lifetime in which he was poor: "Previously, when I was poor…" When the Buddha himself first developed a firm aspiration to achieve supreme awakening, inwardly he possessed great intelligence and compassion, but outwardly he was only a poor Brahmin. At that time, the Tathāgata known as Shākyamuni had come to this world. This intelligent, compassionate, but poor Brahmin felt strong faith in that Tathāgata and offered him a bowl of noodles. Because he was so poor, he had nothing else to offer. As he presented this humble offering, he made the aspirational prayer, "May I become like you. May I come to have a body like yours, activity like yours, and a name like yours." His awakening arose from that small gesture and, when our teacher came to this world, he became known as the Buddha Shākyamuni in fulfillment of the prayer that he had made many lifetimes previously.

In this way, the mind of awakening is the root both of our own ultimate happiness and of the ultimate happiness of others. We must begin to train in such ethics by coming to know the good qualities of the mind of awakening. After that, we must *generate* the intention to achieve supreme awakening, which means that we must commit ourselves to the task of leading all sentient beings to awakening. Since promising to accomplish this assists in making our intention firm, we take a vow.

Gradually, this intention to achieve supreme awakening grows and improves. In dependence upon its growth, a second variety of the mind of awakening comes into being. Called an ultimate mind of awakening, it consists in supreme knowledge and in wisdom. What serve as the causes for its appearance? Calm abiding and insight. It must arise in dependence upon those.

In the *Sūtra Unravelling the Thought*, the Buddha himself said that calm abiding and insight are extremely important. Why? When hearers achieve the result they seek, which is the state of a hearer foe destroyer, they do so in dependence upon calm abiding and insight. When bodhisattvas achieve the results they seek, which are extraordinary, they do so in dependence upon calm abiding and insight. Eventually, practitioners achieve the rank of a buddha, who has destroyed the two obstructions, come to possess all good qualities, and passed beyond the two extremes. A buddha has extraordinary wisdom, inexhaustible good qualities, and an uncommon ability to further the welfare of many other sentient beings. These endowments too are achieved in dependence upon calm abiding and insight.

In general, there are many meditative stabilizations, each different from the others. However, all of them may be included within calm abiding and insight. How must we proceed? We must cultivate both calm abiding and insight, for each has its own role. Calm abiding suppresses afflictions. That is to say, initially afflictions are powerful. In dependence upon the cultivation of calm abiding, afflictions become weak. However, calm abiding alone cannot destroy the afflictions from the root. To destroy afflictions from the root, we need insight, which may also be called supreme knowledge When the supreme knowledge of insight arises, it is able to destroy the afflictions from the root.

Therefore, both calm abiding and insight are important. Which of the two must we cultivate first? Calm abiding. Will mere calm abiding suffice? It will not. Why not? Calm abiding can suppress the afflictions slightly. However, if actual knowledge is not present, we may become proud of our calm abiding. Moreover, calm abiding alone cannot release us from having to suffer birth, aging, sickness, and death within cyclic existence.

We may wonder whether or not cultivation of insight alone will suffice. No, insight alone will not bring liberation. In the absence of calm abiding, insight will not be stable and our minds will wander. Without calm abiding, insight resembles a butter lamp in the wind. A butter lamp exposed to the wind cannot provide a steady, peaceful light because the wind causes it to tremble. Similarly, insight unaccompanied by calm abiding will not be stable and will have little capacity to illumine its object. Therefore, first we cultivate calm abiding. After that, we cultivate insight.

In dependence upon what causes do we achieve calm abiding? Generally, we need faith. Faith means knowledgeable belief together with strength of heart. In this case, knowledgeable belief describes the conviction that, in dependence upon cultivating calm abiding, we will be able to achieve good qualities. We need such faith. Similarly, we need strength of heart, which means confidence in our ability to achieve genuine calm abiding. When we have such faith and confidence, calm abiding can arise. In their absence, calm abiding cannot arise. For that reason, we mainly need faith.

Kamalashila's treatise on meditation specifies five preliminary conditions that we must fulfill in order to accomplish calm abiding. First, we must abide in a place that accords with meditation. Such a place has several aspects. Rather than remain alone, we go to a place where others who appreciate the value of calm abiding and insight have gathered. Furthermore, in a place conducive to meditation there will be a person who has the knowledge and ability to teach meditation. Moreover, that place will be free from those who would harm practitioners of meditation.

Someone who wants to achieve calm abiding must have few desires and must be content. Making meditation the main thing, we do not become involved in a great many activities because they will distract us from the task at hand. In this way, we desire very little. Also, we feel content with practicing meditation well, knowing that it will enable us to achieve calm abiding. These two qualities, which are the second and third of the five preliminary conditions for calm abiding, motivate us to practice meditation correctly.

When we cultivate meditative stabilization, we abandon a plenitude of activities. That is to say, we focus upon meditation to the exclusion of other things. If we scatter our energy among many things, our meditation will not become clear and stable. By abandoning other activities, we fulfill the fourth of the five preliminary conditions.

Purity in ethics is the fifth preliminary condition. Ethics may seem to mean that we are not permitted to do anything at all. We may see ethics as irritating, and the way of ethics may seem narrow and cramped. That is not actually the case. The Buddha, who was skilled in method, taught a way that is peaceful and relaxed. If we follow that way, there will be neither hardship nor interference, and all will go easily.

"Ethics" corresponds to the Sanskrit word *shila*. However, "cooling" would be a more literal translation of *shila*. Cooling may not compel the attention of those who live in temperate climates because they already enjoy their lands and find them to be pleasant. Were they to live in India, where this term originated, they might feel differently, for India is a land tormented by heat. To the people of India, coolness sounds sweet and pleasing. Indian poetry uses coolness to suggest the delightful and heat to suggest pain. To indicate its painful quality, an Indian poet will compare something to the sun's torment; to suggest comfort and delight, he or she will compare something to the rising of the moon. Similarly, to say that ethics brings peace and ease, Indian teachers called it *shila*, which means "cooling."

The Sanskrit term *pratimoksha* speaks directly to the point we are considering. *Pratimoksha* means "individual liberation," and the sense of the term is that each practice of ethics protects us from a particular and corresponding hardship. Thus, maintaining one practice of ethics liberates a practitioner from one hardship. Maintaining two practices of ethics liberates a practitioner from two hardships. Maintaining three practices of ethics liberates a practitioner from three hardships. That is the meaning of the term *pratimoksha*, or "individual liberation": maintaining individual practices of ethics liberates from individual hardships.

Consider the following illustration of the principles of ethics. A practitioner of the code of conduct taught by the Buddha abandons stealing. If we do not think much about this, it may seem that stealing will bring happiness, because we will then have more to use and enjoy, and that not stealing will leave us in the misery of poverty. Actually, that is not so. The person from whom we have stolen suffers because it was only through hard work that he or she acquired the things that have now been stolen. Moreover, it is unlikely that we will not be found out. Most of the time someone will know, and we will worry, "Does he know? Does she know?" If a policeman speaks with us, we will think, "Oh, he knows." We will always be afraid, and the pain of that will accompany us everywhere. If we abandon stealing, then we may waltz carefree through crowds of police, however many there may be. We have nothing to fear from them. Let them go where they will.

For this reason, to abandon stealing resembles the cool night air that offers relief from the oppressive heat of the day. It feels like liberation. By extension, I think we can understand that any aspect of Buddhist ethics feels like relief, cooling, and liberation.

We may wonder whether or not it is absolutely necessary to maintain each and every one of the practices of ethics taught by the Buddha. No, it is not. The Buddha taught two sets of ethics: one applies to the ordained, the other applies to householders. Each practitioner takes up the ethics appropriate to his or her station in life. Furthermore, the ethics of householders consist in five restraints, and a practitioner may wonder whether or not it is necessary to maintain all five of them. It is not. The Buddha understood that householders have many activities, a lot of work, and considerable hardship. In such circumstances, it would be difficult for a householder to maintain all five practices of ethics If we can maintain all five, then so much the better. If we cannot maintain all five but can maintain four, then we practice those four. If four exceeds our capacity but three does not, then we maintain three. Three may be too difficult, but two may be the right measure. Maybe we cannot maintain two but can maintain one. That's fine. Practitioners take on these practices of ethics one by one. Some adopt all five. Some adopt only one.

Suppose we cannot maintain even one of the five practices of ethics. That puts us in a tough spot. Now what? The Buddha himself arranged two ways of observing ethics: firmly and temporarily. When we take on a practice of ethics firmly, then we commit to maintaining it for a long period of time. Generally, this means throughout our lives. If we cannot maintain a practice of ethics for the entirety of our lives, we may also choose to maintain it for a specific period of time: one year, one month, one week, twenty-four hours, or just twelve hours. There is benefit in however much we can do.

Generally, we are ordinary beings who have taken birth as the result of previous actions. Because we are ordinary beings, we are not likely suddenly to find ourselves free from all faults or endowed with all good qualities. We do have faults, and we do not have a wealth of extraordinary qualities. Therefore, we train gradually. If we train gradually in ethics, gradually we achieve the coolness that is the result of ethics. In that way, our minds become peaceful and relaxed. When our minds have become peaceful and relaxed, meditative stabilization will gradually be generated. Therefore, the Buddha taught various ways of adopting and following ethics.

Such ethics is the basis for meditative stabilization. Meditative stabilization, in turn, is the basis for knowledge. The Buddha taught eighty-four thousand aggregates of dharma, but these three trainings—ethics, meditative stabilization, and knowledge—are the essence of them all. Ethics comes first and serves as the basis for the others. Meditative stabilization comes second; in dependence upon ethics, meditative stabilization arises. Knowledge follows the other two, for it arises in dependence upon meditative stabilization.

This evening I have spoken about calm abiding. Tomorrow evening I will speak about insight. If you have qualms, please ask questions.

Q: You spoke about reducing our activities. Since beginning to practice the Buddhist teachings, I've been busier than ever working for our local Buddhist center. Also, our teacher encourages us to practice the arts of tea, archery, and flowers. That keeps us busy too. Any advice?

A: Generally speaking, we are advised to abandon the busyness of plentiful activities. The reason behind that instruction is that if we are engaged solely in the furthering of our own wishes, there seems to be no limit to those. Since it is virtually impossible to satisfy them, they grow ever stronger. The advice to limit our activities is given in light of that ever expanding network of desires and ambitions.

The work done for a Buddhist group is different from the work that we do just for ourselves. As practitioners, we aspire to the path of a bodhisattva. What do bodhisattvas do? Bodhisattvas work principally to further the welfare of others. Suppose that I resolve to further others' welfare. I cannot really do all that much. If the Buddhist group grows and flourishes, then the teaching and enlightening activity of the Buddha will naturally increase. For that reason, no one is suggesting that we should not engage in activities that further the welfare of others.

When we work to further only our own welfare, desire and attachment tend to increase without limit. That doesn't happen when we aim to further the welfare of others. When we work to accomplish only our own purposes, we feel desire and attachment. A mind filled with desire and attachment will not abide anywhere. It thinks about one thing after another. When working to help others, we do so with more than usual bravery and kindness rather than out of desire and attachment. When the work is done and we set it aside, we will not be left with a lot of discursive thought. Such work will not create obstacles to meditative stabilization. There is considerable difference between the ways in which work done to further only our own aims does create obstacles to meditative stabilization and work done to further the welfare of others does not create such obstacles.

The arts of tea and archery serve as methods to enhance meditation. When we sit on our cushions, our minds will abide. Still, a little variety helps. For instance, when drinking tea, we may concentrate upon drinking tea. Or, when shooting arrows, we may concentrate upon shooting arrows. Those practices will help our minds to abide. If we eat rice for lunch day after day, that may satisfy our hunger, but after a while we will not enjoy our food. So, sometimes we have bread, sometimes we have noodles, and sometimes we have potatoes. Then our food tastes good and we enjoy it. Similarly, sometimes we meditate, sometimes we drink tea, and sometimes we shoot arrows. If we go about it that way, probably all of those practices will go well.

Flowers arise naturally. They are beautiful. They harm no one. They suggest gentleness and harmlessness. Also, when we look at beautiful flowers, we become peaceful and relaxed. It seems to me that they accord with meditation and do not conflict with it in any way.

Q: I have heard it said that we begin with a wish to liberate ourselves from suffering, and that gradually we acquire the ability to help others. I think you are saying that there will be no benefit from practicing the Buddhist teachings until we have developed the motivation to benefit others. Can you explain this?

A: Because we are ordinary beings, we are not able to take all of the Buddhadharma into our practice and experience right from the first. As beginners, we are not going to be able to take in hand everything that has been taught within the excellent dharma and accomplish it precisely. Therefore, at times there will be benefit for us, but we do not need to make our own welfare the focus of our efforts. Rather, we focus upon furthering the welfare of others. We do not need to train ourselves to accomplish our own welfare; that comes to us naturally. However, if we do not train ourselves to accomplish the welfare of others, we will not do so. Therefore, to emphasize the welfare of others is the key point.

When beginning to practice meditation, we tend to think of our own liberation as the goal of our practice. In dependence upon such practice, there will gradually be benefit for others. However, there is no need to teach ourselves to accomplish our own welfare. If we regard the welfare of others as important, then our own welfare will naturally be accomplished.

Q: I take it that our goal is to liberate other sentient beings from cyclic existence and that in order to do that we must first achieve some degree of realization. Does that mean that we should remain in retreat until we have accomplished a measure of realization?
A: Here, we may distinguish between work and motivation. We work at activities that enable us to develop good qualities. However, we consider that the furthering of our own welfare is not the reason for that work. Rather, we regard the welfare of others as the reason for our own study, meditation, and so on. Realizing that if we bring these teachings into our own experience, there will be considerable benefit for others, and that if we do not bring these teachings into our own experience, we will not be able to benefit others so deeply or pervasively, we apply ourselves to the greater task. In that way, we will not be so attached to our own welfare, and our motivation will become pure. In dependence upon purity of motivation, our activity will become pure too.

Q: Are you saying that understanding of others can lead to understanding of ourselves?
A: After speaking at great length about the advantages of generating the mind of awakening and the disadvantages of not doing so, the bodhisattva Shāntideva then said that, in fact, not much needs to be said. We need consider only that over innumerable lifetimes the Buddha devoted himself to furthering the welfare of others and that we ordinary beings have devoted ourselves to furthering our own welfare. If we look at the difference between the Buddha and ourselves, we will understand the entire matter.

Q: Please say a little more about the difference between the ultimate and the conventional minds of awakening.
A: Generally, by "mind of awakening" we understand the abandonment of faults and the mastery of good qualities. Even in a conventional context, the wish to further only our own welfare and the intention to harm others will be counted as faults. Abandoning those faults, we acquire good qualities. In particular, love and compassion increase such that, not preferring ourselves,

we are moved by the wish to help others. A mind wanting to achieve the rank of a buddha for the sake of all sentient beings is called a conventional mind of awakening.

When we realize the abiding nature of reality, the emptiness of all phenomena, precisely and accurately, inner wisdom expands. That is what we understand by final awakening. Thus, the inspiration impelling us toward the rank of a buddha is called a conventional mind of awakening and the realization of the nature that is revealed for wisdom is called an ultimate mind of awakening. The latter causes separation from all afflictions and the flourishing of wisdom.

Q: Please say more about the vow of a bodhisattva and the reason for taking it.
A: Generation of the mind of awakening and taking the restraints of the mind of awakening are distinct. When thoroughly pure motivation is born naturally in ourselves, the mind of awakening has been generated. However, we have not become familiar with it. Pure motivation is born, but later it is forgotten, or something discordant with it arises. That such pure motivation has arisen at all, even once, is excellent. But let's not stop there, for that mind can grow and become steady. That will happen only if we commit ourselves to it. How? We think, "I will not forget the mind of awakening. I will bring it to ever higher levels." In that manner, we promise to cultivate the mind of awakening. Having made such a promise, we tend not to forget the mind of awakening. Nevertheless, because our minds are not entirely stable, occasionally we do forget. Still, because we have made a commitment, later we will remember. For that reason, taking the vow of the mind of awakening is an important and meaningful step. There is great benefit in doing so.

Q: Please comment on the form of the vow. Why is a preceptor necessary? What is the importance of the liturgy?
A: Generally, we know that the mind of awakening is good. However, we have not clearly experienced that commitment in its entirety. In the liturgy, we find a clear and unambiguous statement of the commitment that adepts of former times have made. When we rely upon the liturgy, we can understand the initial motivation, the attitudes to be cultivated, and the commitment to be made. If we proceed in that way, we will be able to complete everything perfectly and authentically. If we do not rely upon the liturgy, we will have to figure this out for ourselves, through our own strength. Our own strength will not enable us to know everything that the former great

scholars and adepts knew. We may decide, "With my own mind, I will make a good promise." However, the same depth and quality of commitment will not come about. If we rely upon the liturgy, we can study it and know precisely what we have promised. That brings clarity to our minds. The clarity that comes by way of the liturgy surpasses the clarity that comes from promises that we make on our own.

Q: Now I have the idea that, by benefiting others, I will benefit myself. My motivation seems less pure because of thinking that way. Can you give me some advice?

A: Knowing that, by benefiting others, we will benefit ourselves does not need to make our motivation impure. Work that we do for the welfare of others with genuinely pure motivation will indeed further our own welfare too. However, if we think, "In dependence upon my furthering the welfare of others, things will go well for me," then things will not really go all that well for us. Because our motivation is not pure, our work will come in at about the same level. Our work will be a little phony.

Q: That's what I was afraid of.

Q: I think that, in the West, we practice compassion as morality and forget about knowledge. Can you comment on that?

A: In the Buddhist tradition, we teach compassion that is endowed with knowledge. Compassion for sentient beings is, of course, a good thing. It leads us to help others. However, in the absence of knowledge, we can help others only so much. Suppose we were to give one hundred dollars to a poor person. It is good to give that gift. The money will help him or her. However, he or she will gradually spend the money, and one day it will be gone. When it is gone, he or she will be as poor as before and will suffer just as much. Whatever we do out of compassion is compassionate work but, in the absence of knowledge, the benefit will eventually expire or change. How does knowledge help? Knowledge shows the good path. In what sense? With knowledge, we can identify the actual root of suffering, the root that must be cut. With knowledge, we can identify also the root of genuine happiness, the root that must be nourished. Then, the other person will know, "This is the root of my happiness. This is the root of my suffering." Understanding that, he or she can abandon what needs to be abandoned, accomplish what needs to be accomplished, and achieve the final fruit. Once achieved, the final fruit will never be consumed. When compassion is informed by knowledge, there will be neither degeneration nor error. Rather than harm others, we will help them. For that reason, the compassion we need is the compassion that is endowed with knowledge.

Q: Does that mean that knowledge is more important than compassion?
A: Knowledge is not more important than compassion. In the absence of compassion, knowledge alone poses a terrible threat. The exercise of knowledge always and without question requires compassion. Since, in the absence of knowledge, compassion may go astray, knowledge too is important.

Compassion has various aspects. Someone may think, "I need to kill my enemy." He may come to me and say, "I need to kill that person. Please give me some poison." If I feel compassion for him and give him the poison, he will kill his enemy and, as the result of that action, will suffer in many ways. Such compassion would be mistaken and dumb. If, as in the example I described earlier, I were to give one hundred dollars to a poor person, that would not be mistaken, but extremely vast benefit would not come from it either. If we were to teach the good path to another, vast benefit would arise. Compassion has a variety of aspects and, for that reason, compassion needs knowledge as its companion. Knowledge utterly devoid of compassion poses a terrible threat because it can lead to pride in ourselves and harm to others.

Q: But doesn't knowledge understand the causes of suffering and happiness? Doesn't knowledge see that clearly and precisely, without confusion? How could knowledge lead to pride?
A: If we have no compassion, we may think, "Others do not understand suffering and its causes. Neither do they understand happiness and its causes. I understand that. I am special." In that way, knowledge may lead to pride.

Q: You distinguished love from compassion by observing that love is the wish that others possess happiness and the causes of happiness and that compassion is the wish that others be free from suffering and the causes of suffering. You then explained that virtue is the cause of happiness and that non-virtue is the cause of suffering. How can virtue be anything other than the abandonment of non-virtue? When a particular non-virtue is abandoned, is that abandonment itself not the corresponding virtue?
A: The tradition identifies ten non-virtues and ten virtues. For each of the ten virtues, we may identify a mere virtue and a distinctive virtue. Abandoning a particular non-virtue, such as killing or stealing, equals the corresponding

mere virtue, such as not killing and not stealing. The distinctive virtues add a new element. For instance, in addition to having abandoned killing, we protect life. Some other person may try to kill a sentient being; in response, we protect the life of that sentient being. Or, in addition to having abandoned stealing, we give gifts. The ten distinctive virtues surpass mere abandonment of non-virtue. In that sense, there is a difference between compassion, the wish for others to be free from suffering and its causes, and love, the wish for others to possess happiness and its causes.

Q: I don't see the difference between the mere virtue and the distinctive virtue. Even the distinctive virtue seems to be only the abandonment of a corresponding non-virtue. For instance, how does protecting life differ from abandoning killing?

A: When we abandon killing, we merely abandon killing. Except for not killing, there is nothing that we need to do. Merely sitting there, not killing, will suffice. To protect life, we have to do some work. When we see a sentient being whose life is in danger, we think, "I must help this person," and then we have to get up and do something. Or, to abandon stealing, we need only not steal. Just sitting there, without doing anything else, will be enough. To give gifts, we have to exert ourselves and work.

CHAPTER THREE

The Causes of Insight

FROM AMONG THE THREE TOPICS that Kamalashila discusses in this treatise—compassion, the mind of awakening, and skill in method—at our previous meeting I spoke about the mind of awakening. The mind of awakening has two aspects: conventional and ultimate. Last time, I spoke about the conventional mind of awakening. To achieve an ultimate mind of awakening, we need calm abiding and insight, and Kamalashila's treatise explains the causes of calm abiding and also the causes of insight. As we have seen, calm abiding has five causes. Today, I will explain the three causes of insight.

First, we rely upon an excellent being. This refers to the need for a virtuous friend. Why do we need a virtuous friend. In general, we use our own knowledge, and sometimes, if we have knowledge, we can get along well enough without a virtuous friend. However, cultivation of insight takes us into foreign territory, which we do not know. We must meditate upon something that will abandon that ignorance. If we do not have a virtuous friend who possesses experience, we will not be able to meditate in that way. For that reason, we have no option other than to rely upon a virtuous friend, here referred to as an excellent being.

Gampopa gave us three examples that illustrate our need to rely upon a virtuous friend. First, consider a traveler. These days, even if we have not traveled on a certain road, we can follow a road to our destination by relying upon maps and signs. In the past, if we had not made the trip previously, we needed a guide who could indicate the path from one place to another. Someone who had already walked on that ground could say, "You have to go this way. If you go this way, the road is easy. If you go that way, the road is awful. If you go this other way, you will get there, but it will take a long time. If you follow this road, you will arrive quickly." In the absence of such a guide, we will probably make a mistake. Maybe we will take the long way rather than the short way. Maybe we will take the tough way rather than the easy way. If we have a guide, then we can make the journey without having to endure such hardship. Similarly, if we have a virtuous friend, the effort we make at bringing the dharma into experience will not be wasted. In the absence of a virtuous friend, we are in danger of expending our energy in vain.

Second, consider someone needing to cross a great river. To cross that river, we need a boat, and to pilot that boat, we need a good boatman. A good boatman will know from experience the eddies and currents, the depths and shallows of that river. Without such a boatman, it is likely that we will be carried away by the river. We may even drown. In the end, we will not be able to cross to the far side of the river. With a good boatman, we can cross easily and without danger. Similarly, if we have a good virtuous friend, we will be able to exert ourselves, and our exertion will be not wasted upon foolish or impossible tasks.

Third, consider a dangerous land. In such a place, we fear tigers, leopards, and other carnivores. Or, bandits and thieves may threaten our safety. When we travel across such a land, we need an heroic friend who is well-armed and who can deliver us from these dangers. In the company of such a friend, we can travel easily and comfortably amid these terrors. Without such a friend, and powerless ourselves, we may lose our possessions to bandits and thieves; we may even lose our life. That is entirely possible. In such circumstances, we need the help of a powerful and loyal guardian. The afflictions of hatred, desire, and so forth are like bandits and thieves. These afflictions deceive us; they make our heads spin. They mislead us into grave difficulty. When we have a virtuous friend, those afflictions cannot cause harm. This example and the previous two give us insight into the importance of a virtuous friend.

Kamalashila has advised us of the need to rely upon an excellent being. What are the qualities of an excellent being? Kamalashila identifies four characteristics of such a person. First, an excellent being has heard a lot. That is to say, having relied upon many virtuous friends, he or she has understood the meanings of the Buddha's speech and of the treatises composed by learned people. Second, he or she speaks clear words. When an excellent being teaches his or her students, he or she is able to explain the meaning clearly and is not someone who cannot explain the meaning clearly.

Third, an excellent being has compassion. This is extremely important. A virtuous friend may be learned, but he or she does not lord this over others in an arrogant way. Rather, a virtuous friend reflects on the meanings that his or her students have not understood but would like to understand. He or she realizes that it would help his or her students to understand those meanings and that, in the absence of such understanding, the students will experience that much more hardship. Recognizing that the conditions conducive to their understanding those meanings have yet to be completed, a virtuous friend thinks, "Definitely and without question, they need to know these things. It is my responsibility to enable them to gain the knowledge that will help them. Their lack of knowledge should be met with compassion." That is the compassion of a virtuous friend.

Fourth, a virtuous friend can bear disheartening situations. Students will not display great knowledge, exertion, and learning right from the start. They will not understand the meanings of the Buddhadharma. They will be lacking in exertion. That is just the way things are. When we explain the Buddhist teachings, our students will not understand much of what we say. That being the case, it will be necessary to say the same thing many times. Even when we do say the same thing many times, they will not be able to understand and will not be able to exert themselves. Moreover, despite not having either much knowledge or many good qualities, ordinary beings sometimes have much pride and little respect for their virtuous friend. That can happen. An excellent being can hold the view that, at the beginning, his or her students are ordinary beings, and that because they are ordinary beings, they are afflicted by delusion and suffer obscuration. Seeing things this way, he or she does not become angry and his or her intention does not wither. An excellent virtuous friend must be able to endure such difficult and disheartening situations.

Hearing a lot is the second cause of insight. What must we hear? In general, we need a teacher, someone who shows the path on which we can travel to liberation. For this tradition, the Buddha is the teacher. The Buddha said,

I teach you the methods for liberation.
Liberation depends upon oneself; make the effort.

In other words, the Buddha teaches the methods that enable us to achieve liberation. Whether we achieve liberation or not depends upon us. Therefore, exertion is necessary. In what sense did the Buddha teach the methods for liberation? He identified clearly that which is to be abandoned, that which is to be realized, and how to bring into experience that which must be brought into experience. Without relying upon the Buddha's words, we cannot know those things through the strength of our own analysis. Therefore, first we listen extensively to the words of the Buddha.

In the tradition of the Vajrayāna of Secret Mantra that has been practiced in Tibet, there are many who listen extensively to the treatises composed by Indian and Tibetan scholars. Frequently, they listen to those treatises far more than they listen to the sūtras taught by the Buddha. This worries many people, and they wonder why we do things that way, which they consider to be senseless. Actually, it does make sense. When the Buddha spoke to his students, he did not plan things in the way that we do when composing a treatise. Rather, he gave advice to a few students at a time. The collection of the Buddha's words originated in that way, and it has grown to enormous proportions. It would be difficult to know and understand everything that the Buddha said; therefore, learned people have organized his teachings into topics, clarified points that were not entirely clear, and arranged the teachings that he gave to students individually into stages. They composed treatises so that ordinary people such as ourselves can enter easily into the Buddha's teachings. Therefore, it is a little easier to listen to the treatises than to the Buddha's words. However, in listening to the treatises, we are not listening to anything other than the meaning of the Buddha's words.

Some practitioners pay even greater heed to advice and quintessential instructions. What are those? Sometimes a lama or a virtuous friend, feeling much love and tenderness for a student, will say "Here is something that you must never do. And no matter what, you must do this." In general, the lama's advice accords with the words of the Buddha and also with the treatises.. However, the lama does not present the advice as either the actual words of the Buddha or an actual citation from the treatises. The advice accords with the Buddha's words, and it accords with the instructions given in the treatises, but really it is personal advice tenderly offered with love. Usually, the teacher phrases the advice as definitive instruction to adopt or discard a particular view, practice, or mode of conduct.

Quintessential instructions originate in the lama's practice of meditation. For instance, a lama may remember, "I meditated in such-and-such a way. When I did that, this problem arose. As a method to abandon that fault, I did such-and-such, which helped. On another occasion, I tried this other technique, but that did not help." Thus, the lama speaks in accordance with personal experience. We call that quintessential instruction.

A student will need to listen to the words of the Buddha, the treatises, the advice of a virtuous friend, and quintessential instructions. If we do not hear those teachings, we will not know the path initially. Were we somehow to find the path, we might make a mistake and lose the way. Therefore, we listen to the instructions that have been given by our predecessors. If we listen, then we will find the path. Listening enables us to know the path of practice that will lead to the result we desire. For those reasons, we seek opportunities to hear the teaching.

Appropriate contemplation serves as the third cause for the birth of insight. What must we do in order to contemplate appropriately? Whether we listen to the words of the Buddha, to treatises, to the advice of a virtuous friend, or to quintessential instructions, to think, "The Buddha said this; I must do it," will not suffice. We do not place our trust in the words of the Buddha merely because they came from him. We do not practice a path merely because the Buddha taught it. First, we must contemplate well.

The Buddha instructed his students to examine his teachings in the way that a merchant tests gold for its authenticity. In a store, we might be told, "This is gold. You should buy it." To purchase the gold without examining it closely would be foolish, for we may be fooled by what looks like gold but is not. Therefore, first we place the gold in fire. If the color does not change, we may have gold. However, to purchase the gold at this point would be ill-considered, for there may be terrible flaws internally. To guard against such deception, we must carefully cut the gold and look inside for adulteration and flaws. Then, to assess the quality of the gold, we polish it. When we have examined the gold in these three ways, we can conclude that the gold is authentic, flawless, and of high quality. Then and only then should we purchase it.

Similarly, merely to believe in what the Buddha said will not do. We have to analyze the instructions that have come to us. What reasons underlie them? What purposes do they serve? We must think about all of these things well. With our own mind, knowing that the Buddha taught a particular instruction, we must identify its necessity. Through examination, we must determine the benefit that would come about through the application of that instruction. Therefore, we must contemplate extensively.

Through contemplating well, we become free from doubt. That is to say, we must contemplate until certainty arises. When doubt remains, the path may be lost at a fork in the road. Therefore, we need to contemplate appropriately.

When these three concordant conditions have been completed, which is to say, when we have relied upon a virtuous friend, heard a lot, and contemplated well, it is time to meditate. Thus, Kamalashīla then speaks of many miscellaneous methods for meditation. At first glance, they may seem to be minor and insignificant. In fact, these instructions mean quite a lot. First, Kamalashila recommends that when we sit down to meditate, we set our other concerns aside. If we continue to think about all the work that we need to accomplish, we will not be able to meditate well. Instead, we stop, and we do not worry. Then, before we go to our cushions, we visit the bathroom. Otherwise, our attention will not rest. As we begin to meditate, we set our motivation. We have come to meditate for the sake of all sentient beings. The practice of meditation will bring us to the result that, once achieved, will enable us to help sentient beings. In other words, we establish the mind of awakening as our reason for practicing meditation.

With such motivation, we prostrate with faith and devotion to all the buddhas and bodhisattvas who reside in the ten directions. We offer such prostrations "with five branches." First, we place our hands together, palms facing one another. Then, with hands joined, we touch three places on our body: the top of the head, the throat, and the heart. We consider this gesture to be an expression of faith in and respect for the Three Jewels by way of body, speech, and mind. The head, the palms of the hands, and the two knees make up the "five branches"; touching them to the ground, we prostrate. What is the reason for this? By touching the ground in this way we say, "I have abandoned pride and I respect the Three Jewels."

We will have placed a likeness of the Buddha in front of ourselves. As a sign of faith and devotion, we make offerings, sing praises, confess our ill deeds, and rejoice in the virtue that others have accomplished. Sitting down on a comfortable seat, we cross our legs, either in the vajra posture or loosely.

We do not open our eyes in an exaggerated way; neither do we shut them. Rather, we look directly ahead. Straightening our bodies, we lean neither forward nor backward. We make certain that one shoulder is not higher than the other. In this way, we sit upright and unmoving. We allow our teeth and lips to be as they usually are; there is no point in pressing our teeth together or opening our mouths widely. We breathe gently, slowly, and soundlessly. These instructions describe the body's posture in meditation.

If we are to meditate well, then we must compose not only our bodies but also our minds. Having established the conditions that promote calm abiding and insight, we begin by cultivating calm abiding. Among the many factors that promote calm abiding, longing and joy play the most important roles. For calm abiding to arise, we must take delight in it and long for it. If we long for calm abiding, then the opportunity to cultivate it will arouse great joy. Through the force of such joy, our minds will naturally abide. In dependence upon that, our minds become thoroughly refined. Longing and joy will bring a degree of independence to our minds. In their absence, our minds rudely and stubbornly refuse to heed any instruction.

When we meditate, our minds must be placed closely upon an object. Initially, we select a support for such observation, such as the aggregates of body and mind. We may observe the body's aspect, its feeling, the mind's feeling, the feeling of breathing, or something like that. Observing that, our minds are placed closely upon an object. Alternatively, we may place a pure object, such as a representation of the Buddha's body, before us. Or, we may imagine the body of the Buddha and meditate upon that. If we choose to meditate in that way, then we may follow the instruction given in the *Sūtra on the King of Meditative Stabilizations*, which directs bodhisattvas to imagine a body of the Buddha, golden in hue, and to meditate upon that image.[24]

Meditating in that way, we place our minds in equipoise. At that time, faults may occur. Sometimes, we look at our minds and ask whether or not they have stabilized in meditation. If they have, then we continue meditating in that way. If they have not, then we ask ourselves, "Am I meditating well? Are the faults of laxity and excitement present? Is the fault of distraction present, with many thoughts proliferating?"

Lethargy may overwhelm us. In lethargy, our minds become thick and unclear. Eventually, we fall asleep. What should we do when we recognize the onset of laxity and lethargy? We generate joy and delight. We meditate upon the body of a buddha or upon bright appearance, thereby making our awareness brilliant, or we aim our minds at a bright appearance. That will pacify laxity.

What is laxity? How does the mind feel when laxity arises? Kamalashila's treatise gives some examples so that beginners will be able to recognize laxity. First, laxity is like blindness. When our minds become lax, it is as if our eyes have gone blind. Second, laxity is like dwelling in darkness. When our minds become lax, it is as if we have been enveloped by darkness. Third, laxity is like eyes that have been closed. When our minds become lax, it is as if our eyes have been shut. A lax mind cannot see its intended object clearly, for laxity resembles a dark hollow. When laxity arises, first we must recognize it, and then we must apply the methods for dispelling it.

Excitement is the second fault. How does excitement arise? First, I may see something with my eyes or hear something with my ears, in dependence upon which I then think "It is good" or "It is bad." For instance, while meditating here, I may see the cord to which a lamp is attached, and then I may think about whether the cord is of good quality or poor quality. Following such thoughts, my mind has become excited. Second, seeing one thing may lead me to think about other things. What I see today may provoke me to think about what I saw yesterday or where I went at some other time. For instance, the lights shine brightly here, and seeing them may lead me to think about how dimly they shine in other places. Then I will start thinking about the machines that power the lights here, how much they cost, and so on. Again, my mind has become excited. Third, my mind may become excited by the memory of previous experience. I may have gone to a park, or to see a show, or to a delightful place. Memories dawn, I begin to feel joy and elation, I continue to think about that experience, and my mind becomes excited. For instance, I may remember a trip to New York, a picnic in Central Park, the wonderful view from the top of tall buildings, and so on.

That describes three ways in which our minds may become excited. Sometimes, even though excitement has yet to arise, when I examine my mind, I can see that there is the danger of excitement arising. At such times, it is necessary to rely upon the antidotes that prevent excitement.

When we see that our minds have become excited or are becoming excited, what shall we cultivate as antidotes for excitement? Meditation upon impermanence helps our minds to relax. Similarly, we may meditate upon suffering. For instance, we may contemplate the suffering of suffering, the suffering of change, and the pervasive suffering of conditioning. This helps us to remember that cyclic existence does not have much essence. When we contemplate suffering and the futility of cyclic existence, we become a little sad. Things that sadden the mind pacify distraction.

Mindfulness and introspection play a central role in the pacification of laxity and excitement. Mindfulness and introspection resemble a rope, and our minds resemble elephants. Just as a rope ties an elephant to the trunk of a large tree, so mindfulness and introspection must restrain our minds.

As we learn to apply these techniques, laxity and excitement subside, meditation goes well, and our minds enter into their natural states. When our minds are neither lax nor excited, and our meditation is going well, we loosen our minds a little. Initially, it is necessary to bind the mind well with mindfulness and introspection. Then, when mindfulness and introspection are operating well, we relax a little within equanimity, which is natural to the mind. If we tighten too much, that will create problems. We allow our minds to relax within equanimity for as long as they will remain there.

Meditating in that way, we cultivate calm abiding until we become accustomed to it. When such familiarity evolves, a sense of well-being arises in our bodies, for they have become thoroughly refined. Our minds remain at ease no matter how long we abide in meditation, for they too have become thoroughly refined. That body and mind become thoroughly refined indicates that the mind actually achieves calm abiding. Calm abiding is the name given to the the mind becoming independent. Within the environment of calm abiding, we must cultivate insight, about which I will speak tonight. If you have questions now, please ask them.

Q: Is there a remedy for pride other than offering prostrations?
A: There are many antidotes for pride, just as there are for all afflictions. We may contemplate the faults of pride, the disadvantages of pride, and the advantages of abandoning pride. Also, if we hear the stories of liberation of the buddhas, the bodhisattvas, and the learned great ones, and then look at our own qualities, we will think, "I do not have the same measure of good qualities, do I?" That will undermine our pride. In the practice of offering prostrations, pride is abandoned in dependence upon a physical gesture, which makes it beneficial to the mind too.

Q: You have talked about the importance of caring for others. As a child, that was taught to me in ways that involved abuse. Sometimes I just want to take care of myself. I have a hard time thinking about taking care of others, and I have a hard time when I realize that I want to care for myself.
A: First we have to train our own minds. Some say, "I *must* further the welfare of others. That is what we Buddhists *do*. Therefore, I *will* cultivate love and I *will* cultivate compassion." Then we go to the temple to meditate, but this is pointless. "We must place others first." Such is said, but if assumption of altruism precedes development of love and compassion, the situation is perilous. Altruism must be sown in our minds through training in love and compassion. If we immediately embark upon altruistic tasks, we will come to grief. What must we do? First, through cultivating love and compassion, cut the ropes that bind you. The force of love and compassion will lead you to altruism. Then there will be neither danger nor hardship.

Q: When we are engaged in daily activities, how can we transform strong desire or irritation into compassion on the spot?

A: We Buddhists regard causes as extremely important. It is difficult to suppress strong afflictions, such as hatred, in the moment. First, we must rely upon mindfulness and introspection. That is to say, from the first, when hatred has yet to arise, rely upon mindfulness and introspection. Also, on a daily basis, consider well the faults of hatred and other afflictions. If we have a strong intention to be mindful of and careful about afflictions, then gradually they will recede into the distance. When afflictions such as hatred have already arisen in full force, it is a little difficult to suppress them abruptly.

For this reason, I examine myself constantly. I may know that, in relation to a certain situation, I am in danger of becoming terribly angry. I may know that I am a little angry about something, and that if I am not careful, my anger will gradually increase until I am furious. Or, I may know that I feel desire for something and that gradually the desire will grow. I may see such afflictions coming long before they arrive. If I rely upon mindfulness and introspection from the first, the afflictions will not increase or become greater. If we rely upon mindfulness and introspection from the first, we can purify the afflictions and protect ourselves.

Gampopa had something to say about this. Beginners such as ourselves, he said, must flee from the afflictions rather than fight with them. When we sense that afflictions are rising in us, that is the time to rely upon mindfulness and introspection so that afflictions will not arise. When they have actually arisen, it is already too late for beginners such as ourselves to do battle with them. At that point, fighting will not help.

Q: Is there a way to steal the energy of the afflictions and infuse it into compassion without suppressing the afflictions?
A: I am not sure that I understand your question. Afflictions and compassion are different natures. When we understand the faults of afflictions, their strength diminishes. When we understand clearly the good qualities of compassion, compassion increases in strength. I do not really understand the meaning of taking something from the afflictions and moving it to some other thing.

Q: Within "other" there are so many gradations: those to whom we feel extremely close, such as our children and grandchildren; those to whom we feel close but not as close, such as our friends; and the many others whom we do not even know. How shall we decide whom to help and whom not to help? Will fathers and mothers answer this question differently? Will men and women answer this question differently?

A: I think we have to consider the occasion. Speaking for myself, I think that children need the best we can give them. Others who are close to us can take care of themselves. Small children do not have sufficient knowledge or experience to take care of themselves. In a sense, that leaves them without refuge or protection. Who will protect and care for them? Their fathers and mothers must do so. If their parents do not protect and care for them, will there be anyone to whom they can turn? For those reasons, it is terribly important that fathers and mothers care for their children lovingly.

The time of childhood is extremely important. This is because childhood is the root of the entire life. If childhood goes well, which is to say, if the child acquires education and good conduct, then his or her entire life will go well. If something goes wrong in childhood, then the rest of his or her life will be difficult. Therefore, it is terribly important that fathers and mothers care for their children lovingly. As for the responsibility of the parents, I think that the father and mother share that equally.

Q: You have mentioned that there are various ways in which to cultivate calm abiding. I would like to know how to cultivate calm abiding without relying upon an object of observation.

A: There is calm abiding that does not employ an object of observation. However, we should begin to cultivate calm abiding by directing the mind to an object such as the breath. When we have grown well accustomed to that way of practicing, we will sometimes be able to practice calm abiding without observing an object. When meditation without an object of observation becomes difficult, we return to observation of an object. Gradually, we grow accustomed to the mind's abiding calmly without any object.

Q: How *do* we practice calm abiding without an object?

A: It is like calm abiding directed toward an object of observation. In the absence of an observed object, the mind rests naturally and in a relaxed way. We say, "Do not review the past or invite the future." In other words, do not think about what you have done in the past or will do in the future. That brings you to the consciousness of the present moment, the extremely brief present moment. Rest there, directly, with clear knowledge and recognition. If mindfulness and introspection are present, our minds will not move.

Q: Could the unmoving quality become a problem?

A: There is the danger of the mind becoming lethargic, and sometimes it does. As advised by Kamalashīla, we must watch for the mind turning toward lethargy. If it does, then we must use the appropriate methods to dispel it.

CHAPTER FOUR

The Selflessness of Persons

WE HAVE ALREADY DISCUSSED the causes of calm abiding, the causes of insight, and the ways in which to cultivate calm abiding. Now it is time to consider the way in which to cultivate insight.

What is insight? Insight adds knowledge to calm abiding. That knowledge sees the abiding nature of phenomena, their genuine and actual way of abiding. At its best, knowledge knows the abiding nature in direct perception. Prior to achieving that, we investigate and analyze with reasoning, so that we come to a good understanding of that abiding nature. Gradually, we arrive at direct perception. When the sun shines, darkness vanishes. Similarly, when insight dawns, ignorance and obscuration vanish. That is the importance of insight.

Calm abiding stabilizes the mind, but calm abiding alone does not generate wisdom. Only wisdom can dispel obscuration, and wisdom takes birth only in the presence of insight. Therefore, it is important to cultivate insight. We may think, "Now I have accomplished calm abiding nicely. That will suffice." In fact, calm abiding alone will not suffice. For that reason, having accomplished a refined practice of calm abiding, we go on to seek knowledge and insight.

How do we cultivate insight? Generally, there are two methods, one that is taught within Sūtra and another that is taught within Secret Mantra. In the context of Sūtra, we cultivate insight by taking inference as the path. First, we investigate and analyze well, for which reason this approach is also called analytical meditation. Through investigation, we give rise to certainty, which thinks, "It is like this." That certainty, which is knowledge, serves as the platform or medium for meditation. The paths of Secret Mantra operate differently. In that context, we rest in meditative equipoise and meditate as we look directly at the mind's abiding nature, for which reason this approach is called placement meditation. For the most part, we practice meditation in the style of Secret Mantra. However, Kamalashila's treatise gives instructions for meditation in the style of Sūtra. For that reason, it emphasizes analytical meditation.

There are two stages to such analytical meditation: meditation upon the selflessness of the person and meditation upon the selflessness of phenomena. This is because selflessness is the principal Buddhist view. Buddhists consider that to be extremely important.

In the Buddhist view, it is said that there were births prior to this one, that there will be births subsequent to this one, and that there is this birth now. It is also said that there is no self of the person. For beginners, it seems that these two statements contradict one another. If there is no self, who came here from a former birth? If there is no self, who will go from here to a later birth? If, on the other hand, there were births prior to this one, how can we say that there is no self? For beginners, selflessness seems to be in contradiction with a continuity of previous and later births. Due to the power of familiarization from time without beginning, we think, "Of course there is a self. I am here, am I not?" We feel that way naturally. Therefore, the doctrine of selflessness is extremely important.

What is the importance of selflessness? To achieve the rank of liberation and omniscience, we will need to abandon the mental afflictions. What are mental afflictions? Desire, hatred, bewilderment, pride, and envy, which constitute the five poisons, are the principal ones. If it is necessary to abandon such mental afflictions, then what will enable us to abandon them? We may decide, "I will not hate. I will give up hatred," but that alone will not enable anyone to abandon hatred. Also, even though we decide, "I will give up desire. I will not desire," that intention alone will not suffice to eradicate desire. What are we to do? The Buddha considered this and asked, "What are the roots of the mental afflictions such as hatred and desire?" In the case of hatred, we think, "This harms me." Thus, hatred grows from the conception of a self, which is its root. In the case of desire, we think, "I need this." Desire also grows from the conception of a self, which is its root. Similarly, in the case of pride, we think, "I am superior to others." Pride too grows from the conception of a self. In the case of envy, we think, "This one surpasses me." Envy also grows from the conception of a self. In the case of bewilderment, we think, "I do not know this"; such doubt grows from the conception of a self. Therefore, to abandon the mental afflictions, we must first demolish the conception of a self, which is the root of all the mental afflictions. It will not be possible to abandon the mental afflictions without destroying the conception of a self that is their root.

The mental afflictions grow from the conception of a self. If the conception of a self can be abandoned, then all the mental afflictions will naturally be abandoned. If the conception of a self cannot be abandoned, then the mental afflictions cannot be abandoned either. What do we need as a method for abandoning the conception of a self? Merely thinking, "I will not conceive of a self; I will not apprehend the five aggregates as a self," will not enable us to abandon the conception of a self. We are fortunate in this regard. If we look for the root of the conception of a self, the object that it observes, there is not much of one.

The conception of a self has two aspects: the conception of something as a self, and the conception of something as mine. To think, "I," is, for the most part, to conceive of something as a self. To think, "mine," is, similarly, to conceive of something as belonging to that self: for instance, "my clothes," or "my house." To start with, we can recognize that the object of the conception of something as mine does not exist. We do conceive of things as belonging to ourselves, and we generate fierce attachment to those things. However, if we look for the object that is conceived to be mine, it is not there, not at all. For instance, I may consider this watch to be "my watch." There is a watch, but as for "*my* watch," where is it?

Suppose that I go into a store. While I am there, some other person drops a watch, and the watch breaks when it hits the floor. When I see that, I think, "Someone dropped a watch, and the watch has broken," but I do not feel any special pain about this accident. However, if someone were to drop my watch to the ground, then I would think, "Oh! My watch has broken!," and I would feel miserable. Or, if I thought that this person had thrown my watch to the ground, I would feel angry. Why? What is the reason? From what would my feeling grow? My unhappiness would grow from considering the watch to be mine. In dependence upon that, hatred grows. In dependence upon conceiving something to be mine, suffering grows.

Where is the "mine" that serves as the cause of that suffering? Look for it. Is "mine" one entity with the watch? Is "mine" present as an entity different from that of the watch? Is "mine" present inside the watch? Is "mine" present outside of the watch? No. Mine is not present anywhere inside the watch, outside the watch, or somewhere in between inside and outside. Having become confused, I just think that some watch is mine.

We tend to think that "mine" is present with external things. For instance, we say, "My glass, my clothes, my watch." We add "mine" to all sorts of things. In fact, there is just a glass, but not "my glass," and there are clothes, but not "my clothes." As for this abstract "mine," where is that?

That is not so difficult to realize, but what about "I"? Now that really exists, doesn't it? We tend to think, "My body exists, and my mind exists, so that must mean that I exist." It does seem that way, but when we really investigate and analyze, "I" cannot be found to exist. Why not? The Buddha spoke of the five aggregates, the aggregates of form, feeling, discrimination, compositional factors, and consciousness. The term "aggregate" indicates a gathering of many things that, taken together, look like something they are not. In that sense, "aggregate" indicates a fiction that lacks any pith. There isn't really anything there.

The aggregate of form is the first from among the five aggregates. What is the aggregate of form? We tend to think, "My body exists, and that means that I exist." However, these bodies of ours are aggregations of other things. The head is the head. The arms are the arms. The legs are the legs. The body is a bundle of many things gathered together. It is not truly one thing, not in any way. Is the head me? Are the arms me? Are the legs me? Which one is me? None of them. The arms are the arms. The legs are the legs. The head is the head. They are not me. There is no object that can be considered to be me.

Of course, it seems to me that I have been around since my birth and will remain until my death. However, even the aggregate of form does not remain over time without change. For instance, how much does a baby weigh at birth? A few pounds, right? I don't know exactly, but it cannot be much; infants are tiny. Gradually, the body changes, and the way of moving around changes too. The child of a few years differs considerably from the infant; the two are not identical, not at all. When the child becomes a young man or a young woman, then his or her body differs in aspect, shape, size, and posture from the body of the child. We tend to think, "I was the child, I was the youth, I have now become old, and all of those are one and the same." They are not at all the same. We may think they are the same, but they differ from one another in shape, aspect, size, and color. We lump the baby, the child, the youth, the adult, and the old person all together, and we consider that continuity over time to be the aggregate of form. If you were to look at photographs of the baby, the youth, the adult, and the old person, and if someone were then to ask you, "Who is that?," what could you say except, "Beats me, how would I know?"

Therefore, a self is not present in the aggregate of form. The aggregate of form is not a self, but we have minds as well as bodies, and we may think that the mind is probably the self. However, the mind doesn't fit the bill any better than the body does. Sometimes feeling is present in the mind: a feeling of pleasure, a feeling of pain, or a neutral feeling. Such feeling is the second of the five aggregates; discrimination and compositional factors are the third and fourth of the five aggregates. As for feeling, pleasure changes to pain, pain changes to a neutral feeling, neutral feelings change back into pain, and so on. Feeling changes over the course of a year, a month, a day, and even within an hour. How could feeling be a self? Similarly, discrimination and compositional factors also change.

What about the aggregate of consciousness? There are many consciousnesses within the aggregate of consciousness: eye consciousnesses, ear consciousnesses, nose consciousnesses, tongue consciousnesses, body consciousnesses, and mental consciousnesses. Which one of those is the self? It is not possible to identify a self there. Moreover, consciousnesses arise suddenly and disintegrate just as suddenly. A thought appears before our minds, and in the same instant it vanishes. Then another thought appears. If that is what we mean by self, then we will have to say that the self changes continually, and that there is no self that goes from a previous lifetime to a later lifetime. There may be a mere continuum of consciousness, but there can be no self.

Examine also the quality of mind over the span of a lifetime. How much does an infant know? Do infants know how to eat food or drink tea? Most do not. They know how to nurse, but that is about all. As they grow older, they learn to play. However, they do not then know how to read aloud or to write the letters of the alphabet. Later, they learn to read and write, and gradually they become knowledgeable. These moments in a life differ strongly from one another. We may think, "My mind is always itself, and that is me," but our minds do not remain the same. The minds of the infant, the child, the youth, and so on differ from one another. Their characteristics differ. They differ in knowledge and intelligence. They differ in levels of exertion. We tend to think that something in us has remained constant throughout our lives, and we identify that as "me." We think of some moment in our lives and we say, "Yeah, that was me," but nothing actually survives the changes that have occurred subsequently.

There is no self anywhere within either body or mind. When we know that a self does not exist, then the conception of a self will naturally be driven back. When the conception of a self has been driven back, then the mental afflictions will naturally cease. Why? All mental afflictions are rooted in the conception of a self. Some people will wonder, "When I investigate and analyze the self, I understand that there is no self. Even so, I am not able to repel the conception of a self. I understand selflessness, but I am not able to repel the conception of a self, and I am not able to repel the mental afflictions." Why is that? We have grown accustomed to the conception of a self. From time without beginning, we have imagined that we have such a self. Because we are so accustomed to thinking that way, a little understanding of selflessness will not suffice to repel the conception of a self immediately. Therefore, after we understand the meaning of selflessness, we must grow accustomed to it in meditation. We have grown well accustomed to imagining the existence of a self; now we must grow accustomed to understanding the nonexistence of a self.

Buddhists say that other lifetimes have preceded this one and that other lifetimes will follow this one. If there is no self, then who came from a previous lifetime to this one? If there is no self, then who will go from this lifetime to a subsequent one? In fact, other lifetimes *have* preceded this one and other lifetimes *will* follow this one. And, of course, we see this lifetime right in front of our eyes. However, there is no *self* present in any of these lifetimes. In fact, if there were a self, there could never have been a lifetime previous to this one. Rather, in the absence of a self, the stream of the five aggregates changes gradually. Does the change from infancy to the prime of life involve change in a self? No. The aggregate of form grows larger. The mind's experience increases. In that way, a child grows into the prime of life, but there is no self that goes from its childhood to its prime. Similarly, has a self come from a previous lifetime to this one? No. Rather, the mere continuity of the aggregates of consciousness have come from a previous lifetime, and the mere continuity of the aggregates of consciousness will go to a subsequent lifetime.

Consider a great river. From where does this great river come down? It comes down from snow mountains. To where will this great river go? It will go down to the ocean. Between the snow mountains and the ocean there are so many miles. The river running from the mountains to the ocean cannot be just one thing. Many drops of water come down separately. However, we consider all those drops of water to be one river, and we say that *the river* came down from the snow mountains and that *the river* will go down to the ocean. In fact, each drop of water comes down individually. They do not all come down together or at one time. Nevertheless, we say that there is a river that comes down from snow mountains and goes down to the ocean. In fact, many things meeting and gathering come down from the mountain. Similarly, in the case of our aggregates, many things meeting and gathering come from a previous lifetime to the present lifetime and go from the present lifetime to a subsequent lifetime.

Initially, we analyze the selflessness of the person with reasoning. After that, with understanding of the selflessness of the person, we meditate upon it. When the selflessness of the person becomes manifest, the conception of the aggregates as a self will be abandoned. When the conception of the aggregates as a self has been abandoned, then all the mental afflictions will naturally be repelled. Why? All the mental afflictions are rooted in the conception of a self of persons. Having seen that the self of the person does not exist, and having seen also the purpose of realizing its nonexistence, the Buddha taught the selflessness of persons.

How do we come to realize the selflessness of the person? The master Chandrakīrti demonstrated this using a reasoning that involves a chariot. We apprehend chariots. We think that there are such things as chariots. Supported by a chariot, we can go from place to place. However, if we really look, where is the chariot? Are the wheels the chariot? Is the axle the chariot? Is the place where the driver stands the chariot? No. The wheels are the wheels. The axle is the axle. The place where someone stands is just that and nothing more. Each part of the chariot is, individually, just that part of the chariot and, individually, none of them are the chariot. Is there a chariot that is separate from those individual elements? Not at all. What about the shape of those elements? Is that the chariot? The shape is formed by the gathering together of many things; how could it be a chariot? Well, what is going on? We apprehend the gathering of many things as a chariot when, in fact, there is no chariot. Similarly, we apprehend the gathering of the aggregates of form, feeling, discrimination, compositional factors, and consciousness as "I," and we consider the aggregation of those many things all piled up together to be "I." In fact, there is no "I."

That gives you a glimpse into the selflessness of the person. Tomorrow I will talk about the selflessness of phenomena. If you have any questions, either about the selflessness of persons or about any other topic we have discussed, please ask them.

Q: What does it mean to flee from the mental afflictions?
A: When we know that an affliction will arise in a particular situation, then

we use methods to prevent their arising. For instance, we may know that we will become angry if we meet a certain person. Instead, for the time being, we go out of our way not to meet him or her. Or, we may know that, in dependence upon some particular thing, desire will arise. Instead, for the time being, we avoid it. Sometimes it is necessary to do such things.

Q: I understand that the five aggregates are not a self, but I do not understand what goes from lifetime to lifetime.

A: Consider this example. I came from Nepal to Boulder, and I will return from Boulder to Nepal. Who goes? If a self does not go, then who goes? A self does not go. My body goes. Legs, arms, head, intestines, heart, and so on. Those go from place to place. A self does not go. Similarly, if you ask, "Who goes to a subsequent lifetime?," the answer is that the five aggregates—the aggregates of form, feeling, discrimination, compositional factors, and consciousness—go to a subsequent lifetime. A self does not go.

Q: In what sense does the aggregate of form go to a subsequent lifetime?

A: It changes. The aggregate of form of this lifetime dies. Then another aggregate of form is taken up. In that sense, the aggregate of form goes from lifetime to lifetime. It is the same way with the aggregates of mind. In the case of someone like me, at the end of this lifetime, the consciousnesses of a human being will be thrown away and the consciousnesses of a bear will be taken up. Then, when the bear dies, the consciousnesses of a bear will be thrown away and the consciousnesses of a dog will be taken up. As for the body, first the body of a human being will be thrown away and the body of a bear will be taken up. Then, when the bear dies, the body of a bear will be thrown away and the body of a dog will be taken up.

Q: Why is it impossible to remember past lives?

A: Such radical change occurs in the transition from one lifetime to another. Even within this lifetime, the changes that occur make it difficult to remember what has happened. For instance, we do not remember being inside the wombs of our mothers. Nor do we remember coming out from the wombs of our mothers. Not only that, but most of us also do not remember much from the first few years of our lives. Why not? At such tender ages, our minds have yet to experience much. When we come from previous lifetimes to subsequent lifetimes, so much changes. Because of the change, we do not remember much.

Q: What is the force that keeps the five aggregates rolling on from day to day and lifetime to lifetime?

A: In the tradition of the Buddhadharma, we speak not of "force" but of "continuum." For instance, we will say that certain things are of the same continuum. Consider the river that flows south from Tibet through Vietnam to the ocean. In Tibet proper, this river is called *Dza Chu*. Near the border between Tibet and China, the river is called *Da Chu*. Further along, the river is called the *Mekong*. The *Dza Chu* becomes the *Da Chu*, and the *Da Chu* becomes the *Mekong*. Are the *Dza Chu* and the *Da Chu* identical? No, they are not exactly the same. They are different. Nevertheless, they are of the same continuum. We may take that kind of change within continuity as an example for the change within continuity that we experience in passing from one lifetime to another or from an earlier stage of a particular lifetime to a later stage within that same lifetime. For instance, we move from childhood to adulthood, from adulthood to old age, and from old age to a subsequent lifetime. We describe that motion as a continuum and say that the distinct phenomena included within it are of the same continuum.

Q: What is the difference, then, between the notion of a continuum and the notion of a self?

A: A self would always be the same. If there were a self, then the "me" of this lifetime, the "me" of the previous lifetime, and the "me" of the lifetime that will follow this one would be identical. We tend to think of things as being like that, but that is not how things are in fact. Over time things change radically. For example, are the *Dza Chu* and the *Mekong* the same? No, they are not. If a man jumps into the *Dza Chu*, has he jumped into the *Mekong*? Of course not. Are the *Mekong* and the *Dza Chu* unrelatedly different? No, they are a single river flowing from Tibet to Vietnam. Along the way, the shape, aspect, and other qualities of that river vary quite a lot.

Suppose that, after this lifetime as a human being, I take birth as a bear. Are the human being and the bear identical? Not at all. The human being is a human being and the bear is a bear. The mind has the mind of a human being, the body of a human being, and the other qualities of a human being. The bear has the mind of a bear, the body of a bear, the other qualities of a bear. They cannot be regarded as identical with one another. Nevertheless, gradually, one follows the other. From that point of view, they are said to be merely of the same continuum. There is no semblance of a self in that.

What is the reason for calling that mere continuum "selfless"? We conceive the self to be single and permanent. There is no such self. "Continuum" refers to one thing arising in dependence upon another. Consider the seed of a flower. The seed develops gradually and becomes a flower. The flower grows old and becomes seeds. Placed in the ground and moistened by water, the seeds become flowers. Thus, these transitions occur gradually and sequentially. Are the seed and the flower identical? Not at all. They are distinct. The mere continuum of seed, flower, seed, and flower comes about through the dependence of one thing upon another. We may call that a continuum; we may call that a relationship of dependence. Why do we say that this mere continuum of dependence does not amount to a self? This continuum does not resemble the self that we conceive. The way in which we conceive the self does not fit with mere continuity through a dependent relationship. Therefore, this continuum is not said to be a self. Rather, it is said that it is not a self.

Q: Are you saying that we do not conceive of the self as changing and that, for that reason, we must consider a continuum to be lacking a self?
A: Radical change should arouse our suspicion that something is amiss with our notion of a self. For instance, in dependence upon a seed, a flower arises. That describes the extent of their relationship. In every other way, they differ considerably and must be counted as distinct in entity and nature. In light of that, consider previous and subsequent lifetimes. In dependence upon a previous lifetime, a subsequent lifetime arises. That describes the extent of their relationship. For instance, a human being—the previous lifetime—and a bear—the subsequent lifetime—cannot be said to be the same. Like the seed and the flower, they differ considerably. The self that we conceive to exist would not change. A self, if there were such a thing, would always be the same.

Q: When we realize that we are nothing more than aggregates of form, feeling, and so on, and the mental afflictions of desire, hatred, and so on fall away, what happens to compassion?
A: When selflessness has been realized, compassion develops to surpassing levels. Why? We do not generate compassion in dependence upon a self. Consider someone suffering a painful feeling. While suffering, he or she may generate many mental afflictions. Is there a self that causes those mental afflictions? No. Nevertheless, conceiving what is not a self to be a self, he or she has become confused.

We feel compassion for such a person. We know that, in fact, there is no self. We also recognize that he or she has not realized selflessness. In dependence upon not realizing selflessness, people become terribly confused. Once confused, they hate what they do not need to hate, and they desire what what they do not need to desire, and they feel bewildered by what need not bewilder them. In dependence upon generating those mental afflictions, they suffer needlessly. They are terribly confused, and we feel compassion for them.

Suppose that a man falls asleep and begins to dream a bad dream. For instance, he may dream of being chased by a hungry tiger. He feels afraid, but he does not need to fear the tiger because the tiger is not really there. Nevertheless, thinking that the tiger will eat him, he feels terribly afraid. Along comes someone who has clairvoyant abilities. The clairvoyant sees the bad dream and feels compassion for the dreamer. "This person is dreaming a terrible dream! He fears that a tiger will eat him!" Out of compassion for the dreamer, the clairvoyant shakes him, saying, "Wake up! Wake up!"

Q: Something wakes up from the dream. Something realizes "not me" and "not mine." What is that? It would seem to be the real self.
A: Earlier and later moments of mind are different entities. Nevertheless, there is a mere continuum of mind, and that mere continuum realizes selflessness. Even though there is no permanent, unchanging self, there is the continuum of mind, in dependence upon which selflessness is realized.

Q: What unifies those moments? What holds them together?
A: Nothing. There is no force holding them together. After one moment, another moment comes. Then, after that one, another one comes. Moments come along sequentially, but there is no energy that fastens them together. For instance, a thought arises in our minds, and it ceases. It vanishes. A new thought arises. The continuum of that new thought is cut also. Another thought arises. In that way, stage by stage, a continuum of thoughts comes about. However, nothing unifies them. We may say that, in dependence upon a previous consciousness, a subsequent one arises; except for that, there is nothing at all.

When the earlier thought is present, the later one is not present. When the later thought is present, the earlier one is not present. There is nothing whatsoever joining them. Consider a flower and a seed. When the flower is present, the seed is not. When the seed is present, the flower is not. There is nothing fastening them together. In dependence upon a seed, a flower arises, but there is no potent force that joins them. If the seed and the flower were present at the same time, it would be possible to join them. Since they are not present at the same time, how could they be joined?

Q: Is there a relationship between an action of compassion and its effect, which continues after the action has ceased? May we say that the effects of a person's actions continue, and that those effects extend beyond death to the creation of a new lifetime by those actions?

A: Whether we speak about actions and their effects or about causes and their effects, it comes to the same point: in dependence upon something, something arises. The dependent relationship allows us to speak of a continuum. In dependence upon accumulation of a good action, a good result arises. In dependence upon accumulation of a bad action, a bad result arises. For instance, in dependence upon planting the seed for a yellow flower, a yellow flower arises. In dependence upon planting the seed for a red flower, a red flower arises. However, the seed and the flower appear each in their own time, which are not the same time. Similarly, an action and the ripened result of that action appear separately.

Q: Does that mean that the result of a compassionate action reflects the compassion in some way?

A: There are various types of relationships between causes and their effects. Let's identify two: some effects come about as the ripened effects of their causes, and other effects come about through the force of familiarization with their causes. For instance, if we familiarize with compassion in this lifetime, in a later lifetime compassion will arise with great force. Such strong compassion will come about in dependence upon predispositions that were established by prior familiarization with compassion. In the case of ripened effects, in dependence upon generating in our continuum a pure and compassionate motivation to help others, in a later lifetime, we will experience well-being and comfort in various ways as the result of our actions. Such results are called ripened effects. These two patterns differ slightly.

Does compassion lead to compassion as its result? Yes, it does, but such compassion is not the ripened result of an action. Rather, it comes about in dependence upon predispositions established by familiarization with compassion. Ripened results are always experienced in the aspect of either pleasure or pain. Such is said in Vasubandhu's *Treasury of Knowledge*.

Q: I have a question about rebirth, and I would like to phrase it in terms of the examples you gave, those of a river and a flower. When the river that flows from Tibet into China and then through Vietnam finally reaches the ocean, it joins the ocean. Later, its molecules evaporate, fall to the earth again as rain, and eventually become pieces of various other rivers, streams, and lakes. They do not necessarily return to Tibet and become part of the same river again. Second, a seed becomes a flower, but that flower then bears many seeds, and those seeds can create many different flowers. When the flower itself dies, its molecules can become parts not only of flowers but also of all sorts of animate or inanimate objects. Why, then, after death, does a human become a single entity rather than pieces of many entities?

A: Exactly. Well done. It is just as you have said: many different effects come from the life and death of even just one sentient being. From that, we can understand that there is no self. Suppose that, after I die, I then take birth as a bear. For me, the appearances become those of a bear. However, the corpse, the continuum of my previous body, will be carried off to the charnel-house and burned. Then the ashes, blown this way and that by the wind, will scatter in every direction. Thus, the body has its various, individual effects. The appearances established by my mind's predispositions change and I take birth as a bear. From where does the bear's body arise? It is born in its bear mother's womb, isn't it? The body I have now will not go into the bear, will it? As for the mind, much change will strike the mind. Various appearances will dawn for the mind. As you have said, there will be many causes, each of which will have its own, numerous effects. This illuminates the meaning of selflessness both clearly and beautifully.

Q: I have heard that there are a number of questions that the Buddha declined to answer, presumably because no answer could be proven by experience. Why, then, does the notion of rebirth play such an important role in the Buddha's teaching?

A: The instructions on previous and subsequent births are important because, even though we are not able to see previous and subsequent births, the continuum of our minds cannot be cut. In dependence upon the continuity of mind, the appearances of later lifetimes will dawn. As those appearances dawn, we will experience pleasure and pain that will arise in dependence upon the actions that we have accumulated in previous lifetimes. Serious problems would come from not understanding that later lifetimes follow former lifetimes. Understanding that lifetimes follow one another in an unbroken continuum allows us to prepare in ways that will enable those future lifetimes to go well. For that reason, the Buddha taught the doctrine of previous and subsequent lifetimes widely.

The Buddha declined to answer fourteen questions that were posed to him. Generally, they were asked as a challenge to his knowledge and to his teaching. That is to say, the questioner wished to debate with the Buddha and defeat him. For instance, the Buddha was asked, "Is the self permanent or impermanent?" The Buddha did not give an answer. Why not? Had the Buddha answered straightforwardly, he would have said that the self does not even exist and for that reason cannot be either permanent or impermanent. To answer in that way would have been to say, "Your question is the question of an idiot," and the questioner would then have become angry. The fourteen questions to which you have referred were of that nature. Since the answer would not have been of help to the questioner, the Buddha did not reply to the questions when they were asked.

CHAPTER FIVE

The Selflessness of Phenomena

I N OUR STUDY of the master Kamalashīla's *Intermediate Treatise on the Stages of Meditation in the Middle Way School*, we are considering his presentation of the mind turned toward supreme awakening. That mind has two aspects: conventional and ultimate. We are now considering the ultimate mind of awakening. Generally, that consists in the way to meditate upon the selflessness of persons and the way to meditate upon the selflessness of phenomena. Yesterday, I spoke about the selflessness of persons. Today, I will talk about the selflessness of phenomena.

As for the selflessness of phenomena, it is said that all phenomena are not inherently established and are emptiness. Generally, those who do not hold the tenets of Buddhists see the Buddhadharma as depressing. They feel that the Buddhadharma does not strengthen the hearts of human beings. Rather, by speaking of the impermanent, the selfless, and the empty, it saddens human beings and thus weakens their hearts. They cannot find in the Buddhadharma any capacity to strengthen the hearts or increase the good qualities of human beings. Thus, they will regard this teaching of the selflessness of phenomena as a dreary matter.

They are mistaken, because the recognition of selflessness does not diminish the strength of our heart. We need peace and gentleness in our lives. In the absence of mental afflictions such as extraordinarily strong desire and hatred, our lives naturally become peaceful and gentle. If we meditate that all phenomena naturally lack an essence and are empty, then attachment and aversion naturally dissipate. In dependence upon that, we naturally enjoy a sense of peace and leisure.

Those of you who have heard many of the Buddha's teachings and have practiced a lot understand the meaning of emptiness quite well. Nevertheless, beginners will be shocked upon first hearing of emptiness. When told that all phenomena are emptiness, they will think that such is probably not the case. For instance, when I was young and began to study texts, I read about self-lessness and thought, "No, it is not so, I am pretty sure that there is a self." Then I studied the *Treasury of Higher Knowledge*, composed by the master Vasubandhu, and I decided, "Okay, probably there is no self, but as for empti-ness, no way! That is just not possible." That is how I saw it. Later, the rea-sonings of the Middle Way School were taught to me, and I came to feel differently. "Probably these phenomena are emptiness. Yes, most likely they are emptiness." That is how it goes when you begin to consider these teachings.

I will be talking about emptiness today, and when we talk about emptiness, we find ourselves speaking about elevated reasonings and high views. How-ever, many beginners have come here today, and for that reason I want to make the meaning accessible and the reasonings less forbidding. Those of you who have studied extensively and practiced a lot may find this explana-tion to be weak and pathetic. You may feel that I have not explained the depth and the height of this view. You may wonder, with some dismay, why I have given such a low and easy presentation of emptiness. Please do not look at it that way. If I explain the height and the depth, beginners will not under-stand. I will tune this explanation of emptiness to beginners, and I will explain it in a simple way that is relatively easy to understand.

It is said that "dharmas have no self." This means that individual dharmas have no essence and are not inherently established. What, then, are "dhar-mas?" This Sanskrit term, "dharma," has ten meanings. Sometimes, "dharma" refers to the dharma that we practice. Sometimes, "dharma" refers to medi-tative stabilization. Sometimes, "dharma" refers to all things. In the state-ment, "A self of dharmas does not exist," "dharma" refers to all things. Thus, that statement is to be understood as meaning that all phenomena have no essence.

How is the way in which phenomena lack a self taught in Kamalashīla's *Intermediate Treatise on the Stages of Meditation in the Middle Way School?* First, external things, which are composed of particles and have form, are not inherently established. Nevertheless, appearances do dawn for us. If they are not established by way of their own nature, then how do they dawn? They dawn as appearances for the internal mind; they dawn in dependence upon the internal mind. Here, Kamalashīla presents a view that accords with that of the Mind Only School, which is one of the four schools of Buddhist tenets. After that, Kamalashīla demonstrates that the internal, mere mind, is also not inherently established. Mind has no true establishment whatsoever;

it is emptiness. In this, Kamalashīla settles the lack of inherent establishment in all phenomena—external, apprehended objects and internal, apprehending minds—in a manner that accords with the tenets of the Middle Way School.

Science has progressed remarkably in its ability to investigate external things. This has enabled all of us to understand that external things are not truly established. Scientists have already settled that, and we are already familiar with their findings: when they look with reasoning and with instruments, they see that all phenomena are not inherently established. Still, they do not come right out and say that phenomena are emptiness, and who would blame them for that? From time without beginning they have grown accustomed to believing in the existence of things. The force of that leads them to feel that they need those things, and they cannot say that things are emptiness despite seeing that things are emptiness. We tend to think, "For some time, I have seen these things, and it will not do to say that they are emptiness." Even these brilliant scientists cannot quite relinquish their grip upon things. After all, they say, "There may not be things, but there is energy." That seems to be where they wind up. Apparently, they are not able to toss away the predispositions to which they have become accustomed from time without beginning. They are held back by the nagging doubt that if they say that things are emptiness, that will not agree with what they experience. "We're not sure what, but something exists." Buddhists teach that things do not exist. Rather, things are emptiness. In general, that much difference divides the two points of view.

To us, all these appearances look like they exist. I'll use a simple example to challenge that appearance and our agreement with it. Take a look at the pieces of paper that I'm holding.[25] This piece of paper is large, and this one is small. It really does look that way. Ask anyone. "Is this one large?"[26] "No, no, not at all; it is small." "Is this one small?"[27] "No, no, not at all; it is large." Show these pieces of paper to anyone and they will agree: this one is large, and this one is small. When I look at them, that is what I see, and when other people look at them, that is what they see.

Things do appear that way, but what happens when I change the mix?[28] If I ask, "Is this one large?," I will be told, "No, it is small."[29] It does not matter who looks at it. Anybody would say that this one is large and this one is small, and that is the way it looks to me too. So why does our sense of the size of things change? Because things are neither large nor small. Neither of those properties abides with the thing in question.

Someone may respond that even though large and small do not abide with things, nevertheless other properties do. For instance, how about long and short?[30] If I were to ask, "Is this long?," everyone would say that it is long, and no one would say that it is short. If I then add another stick to the group,[31] then everyone will say that this one is long and that the other one, which seemed long a moment ago, is short. If we extend this line of reasoning, we can understand that all things are like this. Large, small, long, short, good, bad, and other qualities that appear to reside in objects do not really dwell there.

Furthermore, even though I consider myself to be "I," no one else does. If I ask someone, "Do you think of me as 'I'?," then that person will reply, "Of course not. I think of you as 'you.'" Suppose I ask about a third person. "No, that's 'him.'" From my point of view, another person is "you," but from that person's point of view, he or she is "I." I, you, he—they all lack stability. Sometimes my mind thinks "I," sometimes "you," sometimes "he"—not much stays put.

Places are like that too. For instance, when I stay here, I call this place "here" and that place "there." When I go "there," I call it "here" and refer to this place as "there." "Here" does not always remain here. Similarly, standing here, we say "that mountain" and "this mountain." Then we go to the far mountain and look back from there: "this mountain" has become "that mountain" and "that mountain" has become "this mountain." They really seem to be that way, but it is my mind that makes them so. There is no far mountain or near mountain, here or there, I, you, he, or she. Mind makes all of these to suit the occasion.

The master Nāgārjuna applied the reasoning of dependent relationship to these properties. All things arise individually in dependence upon other things. When we investigate and analyze with reasoning, such properties disappear. Therefore, ultimately, they are emptiness. Nevertheless, as mere conventions, they are present. In what manner are they present? Through the power of dependent relationship. In dependence upon something large, some other thing is small. In dependence upon something small, some other thing is large. For instance, in relation to one another, this stick of incense is large, and this one is small.[32] In dependence upon one another, is one of them large? Yes. Is the other one small? Yes. As mere conventions and for the perspective of my mind, some things are large and others are small. Are they actually and ultimately large or small? No. Ultimately, nothing is either large or small.

For that reason, external appearances are internal mind. Externally there is neither large nor small. Large and small are made in the internal mind. Internal mind declares that this is large and that in relation to it, that is small. Internal mind makes it so. Who makes good and bad, I and you, and all the other categories? They are not external. Those properties are not present with things. Internal mind makes them. Therefore, all appearances are mind. They are not appearances of an external; they are the mind that is internal. Therefore, there are no external things; they are internal mind. Kamalashīla explains the matter that way; this is also the view of the Mind Only School.

Having shown external things to be emptiness, Kamalashīla then demonstrates that internal mind is emptiness also. When we investigate and analyze with reasoning, we see that external things do not exist. However, we may think that internal mind really does exist. In fact, internal mind is not established by way of its own nature. When we actually investigate and analyze, it is not present. How is the internal mind's lack of establishment demonstrated? Kamalashīla cites a passage from the *Sūtra of the Heap of Jewels*. In this passage, the Buddha addresses Mahākashyapa: "Kashyapa, when mind is sought thoroughly, it is not found."[33] Looking for the mind and asking "Where is it?," there is nothing to be found. When we do not investigate and analyze, we think that mind does exist. However, if we look for the mind and ask "Where is it?," it is not present. Similarly, in his *Ornament for Precious Liberation*, Gampopa writes that mind does not exist. Why not? "I have not seen mind. Others have not seen mind. In fact, no one has seen mind. Therefore, mind does not exist."

How is it that no one has seen mind? Generally, we have six collections of consciousnesses. Consider the eye consciousness, which is one of the six. An eye consciousness sees forms. What happens when we look for the eye consciousness and ask, "Where is it?" Is it in the eye? No. There are various things in the eye, but consciousness is not one of them. Suppose that I see a glass; is my eye consciousness with the glass? No. Is my eye consciousness somewhere in between my eye and the glass? No. Nothing at all. Through the power of dependent relationship, an eye consciousness sees a glass. However, if we look for the consciousness that sees, nothing turns up.

The same holds for the other sense consciousnesses—those of the ear, nose, tongue, and body. What about the mental consciousness? Sometimes the mental consciousness generates coarse thoughts. For instance, sometimes hatred accompanies the mental consciousness. At other times, compassion accompanies the mental consciousness. At still other times, pride accompanies the mental consciousness. In that manner, the mental consciousness generates coarse thoughts. How does that come about? Other causes and conditions play their roles, but ignorance lies at the root of the matter. From the start, our consciousnesses face outwards. What is the internal mind? We have never looked there. Have we ever seen it? "I do have a mind!" We think so; after all, our minds generate our thoughts, right? But have we ever looked for our minds? Where are they? Where are our thoughts born? Suppose we become really angry. Now we have a chance to inquire: "Now I'm furious! Okay, what is that hatred? Where is that hatred born?" We look, but we do not find anything. We may imagine that hatred is born in a particular place and travels along a certain path to some other place. Except for knowing that it has vanished as suddenly and inexplicably as it arose, we cannot find it anywhere. We are sure that we feel hatred, but no matter where we look—outside, inside, or somewhere in between—we do not find anything at all. Desire and other thoughts, whatever they may be, are like that too. Look wherever we will, nothing turns up.

If I were to ask someone, "Do you ever feel hatred?," he or she would certainly respond, "I have felt hatred many times." If I were then to ask, "When you feel hatred, what is it like?," he or she would probably answer, "I don't really know." Why would someone not understand his or her own feeling of hatred? Because the very entity of hatred itself, like the entity of other consciousnesses, is not established. To realize the emptiness of external things, we have to analyze with reasoning. To realize the internal mind's lack of inherent establishment, we can dispense with reasoning and look directly. There is nothing to be seen; and nothing will be found. Therefore, the noble Gampopa wrote, "Because no one has seen mind." Mind is not present. Why not? Because no one has seen it. We have not seen our own minds, and we have not seen others' minds.

In that way, we ascertain that both internal mind and external things are not inherently established. Then we must familiarize with what we have ascertained. When we investigate and analyze with knowledge, ascertain that all phenomena are not inherently established, and then meditate upon, which is to say familiarize with, what we have understood, we are practicing the analytical meditation of the sūtras, which is called the analytical meditation of learned persons.

When we meditate, investigating and analyzing in stages, flaws may assail our practice. What flaws? Many thoughts will dawn. On one occasion, we meditate well, and on another occasion, many thoughts will dawn. What should we do when many thoughts dawn? First, we investigate and analyze.

That is to say, we ask ourselves, "What thoughts are dawning for me?" Sometimes, the mental affliction of hatred will arise. That may begin as a barely noticeable thought. If we follow thoughts of hatred, more of them will arise. We may discard them repeatedly, and yet they may continue to arise. In that fashion, such thoughts interrupt meditative stabilization. At other times, a barely noticeable thought of desire will arise. We attempt to meditate, but such thoughts return again and again, interrupting meditative stabilization. At still other times, we do not enjoy meditative stabilization and we have no wish to meditate; we feel lazy. The first step toward stability in meditation will be to identify the thoughts that are interrupting our practice of meditative stabilization during a particular session of practice. That identification will spur us to recognize the good qualities of meditative stabilization, which will enable us to remedy the flaw.

Similarly, if we gain insight into emptiness and meditate strongly upon the emptiness that we have discovered, insight will become more clear. In dependence upon insight becoming more clear, however, calm abiding will diminish. As the factor of stability diminishes, insight then worsens. Therefore, we inspect our own practice and, noticing that calm abiding has weakened, we strengthen it. To meditate well, we must be able to balance calm abiding and insight evenly.

Investigating and analyzing our minds, we look for mental afflictions, the motion of thought, laxity, or excitement. When, free from those factors, the mind rests relaxed, leave it that way. Were we then to investigate and analyze a lot, our minds would become disturbed again. So, when our minds abide in a balanced way, we leave them that way. If thoughts appear, we identify them as such and continue to meditate.

When practice of such a meditative stabilization becomes difficult or feels uncomfortable, we set it aside for awhile. All phenomena lack inherent establishment, for that is their abiding nature. However, not all sentient beings have realized this to be so. Not all sentient beings have generated such meditative stabilization. In brief, not all sentient beings know the abiding nature of phenomena. Reflecting in this way, we cultivate compassion. Having refreshed ourselves, we again place the mind in meditative stabilization upon the emptiness that is the abiding nature of phenomena. The alternation helps us to persist in the practice of meditative stabilization.

Having finished the session of cultivating meditative stabilization, we allow our minds to rise from meditative stabilization but hold our bodies upon the cushion in the posture of meditation. Then, we must consider our own situation and the situations of others in the following way: "I understand how to meditate, and I am able to meditate well. Other sentient beings do not realize the abiding nature of phenomena, and they are not able to meditate well or generate meditative stabilization. Therefore, having meditated well, in the future I must enable all sentient beings to realize the abiding nature of phenomena, to bring the excellent dharma into their experience, and to achieve the rank of a buddha." Having made that resolution and established that motivation, we slowly unfold our legs, stand up, prostrate to all the buddhas and bodhisattvas in the ten directions, make offerings to them, and conclude with a good prayer of aspiration.

Kamalashīla's intermediate treatise on the stages of meditation contains three sections. In the first of those three he discusses compassion. In the second he considers the mind of awakening, and in particular he presents the methods for cultivating a conventional mind of awakening and an ultimate mind of awakening. We have now heard the explanations of those two sections. In the third and final section, Kamalashīla writes about skill in method. This morning I will stop here; this afternoon and again tomorrow morning I will speak about skill in method. If you have questions, please ask them.

Q: Is there an individuation of internal mind? That is to say, is one person's internal mind different from another person's internal mind?
A: Yes, they are different. Individual people have individual minds, and individual appearances dawn for their minds.

Q: If mind cannot be found anywhere, then how can we work with our own individual minds, and how can everything be based on the internal mind? This seems like a contradiction.
A: Whether we are considering internal minds or external things, we may say that appearances dawn. However, those appearances are not established as the things they appear to be. For instance, various appearances dawn in our dreams. When appearances dawn in dreams, sometimes the dream will be wonderful. We may see magnificent houses, visit delightful countries, and feel extremely well. At other times, our dreams will be terrible. We may dream of horrible places, wretched buildings, and bad feelings. If asked, "Do these appearances dawn for your mind?," we would have to reply that they do. For instance, I may dream of an elephant. If asked, "Do you see an elephant?

Does an elephant appear to your mind?," I would have to respond that, yes, in that dream I certainly do see an elephant. In fact, the elephant that appears before my mind in that dream looks exactly like an elephant. If asked, "Is an elephant present there?," I would have to admit that an elephant had not crept into my bedroom. Nevertheless, I am most definitely seeing and looking at an elephant. Ultimately, elephants are not established; conventionally, elephants are seen. We may apply this to external things too. For instance, if asked whether or not, conventionally, this stick of incense is long, I would say that it is long. I, you, and everyone else would agree that it is long. However, when analyzed carefully, it turns out not to be long. Ultimately, nothing is either long or short but, conventionally, some things are long and others are short. These two perspectives do not contradict one another.

Q: You recommended visualizing a golden buddha as an antidote to depression. Should we visualize ourselves as that buddha, or should we visualize that buddha in the space before ourselves, or on the top of our head, or where?

A: In the tradition of Secret Mantra, and particularly in Unsurpassed Secret Mantra, we consider ourselves and the Buddha to be the same, and from that point of view we meditate upon the body of a deity, regarding it as our own. That is to say, we visualize ourselves as a buddha. This meditation upon the form of a golden buddha belongs to the tradition of Sūtra, and the sūtras do not teach meditation upon ourselves as having the body and qualities of a buddha. They teach meditations in which we consider the Buddha to be outstanding and ourselves to be ordinary. Also, we do not meditate that this buddha rests upon the top of our head. Rather, we imagine the Buddha to be sitting in front of ourselves. When we meditate upon a figure who sits upon the top of our head, we meditate upon the image of a deity. When we meditate upon a figure who sits before ourselves, we meditate upon the image of a human being. We consider ourselves to be in the presence of the Buddha, who is remarkable but nevertheless human. We consider him to be present in this place. That imagination gives rise to joy and delight, which dispel laxity and lethargy.

Q: I am beginning to understand that things are empty of our concepts of them in that we may name them according to our wish, such that a table becomes firewood if we change our idea about it. Still, it does seem that things have a nature of their own. For instance, fire has the nature of burning, and if we stick our hands into a fire, our hands will be burned. Then we hear stories of highly accomplished practitioners whom fire cannot burn and walls cannot obstruct. That suggests another level of emptiness, one that I have not even begun to touch. Are we moving in that direction?

A: People such as ourselves may understand emptiness, but we are not able to realize emptiness directly. At present, we think about emptiness, using the sixth consciousness, which is the mental consciousness. That leads to inferential understanding of emptiness. Inference enables us to think, "Probaby that is so. Yes, that is how it is," but does not amount to direct realization of emptiness. Because of not having realized emptiness directly, we must meditate upon emptiness. That is to say, we must become accustomed to emptiness. From time without beginning we have become accustomed to regarding phenomena as not being emptiness. Now we must become accustomed to phenomena being emptiness. The highly accomplished practitioners of whom you spoke have become accustomed to emptiness and have realized it directly. Because they have realized directly that, for instance, a wall is emptiness, they can put their hands through a wall without changing or damaging either their hands or the wall. By way of reasoning, we understand that wall to be emptiness, but we have not realized it as such. Therefore, it continues seeming to be a real thing. For that reason, it is necessary to meditate upon emptiness.

Q: When I practice analytical meditation in the way you have instructed, I look into my body and mind and I find that they are not localized anywhere. I then conclude that I am confused, and I rest in that confusion. Then, some strange things begin to happen. For instance, instead of seeing the rug on the floor in front of me, I may see infrared colors, or I may not really feel that I'm sitting in my body. Am I practicing this incorrectly? Will you comment on this?

A: When we meditate, we look at the mind's abiding nature. Contemplating the abiding nature of mind, we investigate that. Since the mind's abiding nature receives our focused attention, we do not put much energy into our eyes. Were we to concentrate upon our eyes, we would see a variety of things; we may not see the rug in front of us, and so on. When meditating, instead of following our eyes, we attend to our mind. Whether we see something with our eyes or not, we let that go and pay attention to the course of our mind. We turn inward.

Q: It seems to me that, when I turn inward and analyze the nature of mind, things should get very clear and stable. My experience of what you are calling meditative stabilization is very unstable. I am assuming that in trying to become very clear, things would become normal and mundane, and I would be there quite clearly. When I really let go of everything, what happens is not like that.

A: The clarity of which this tradition speaks does not involve an extraordinarily strong experience of vivid presence. Rather, clarity means the continuity of awareness; the mind does not stop. Mind does not resemble stone, and nothing severs the continuity of mind. Clarity is the very entity of mind. If we place our attention there without forgetfulness, that will probably do. As for the absence of stability, if we cultivate calm abiding, that will help. That is to say, if we set the practice of insight aside temporarily and focus upon developing calm abiding, holding our minds to the breath and sustaining the mindfulness of breathing, that will help our minds to stabilize.

Q: You illustrated the selflessness of phenomena by showing the relativity of long and short, large and small, and so on. It seems to me that some qualities exist in and of themselves without reference to other things. For instance, a certain color may be yellow or a certain substance may be gold, and that does not seem to shift in dependence upon its relationship to other things.

A: At first I had intended to speak about this aspect of the selflessness of phenomena, but later it seemed unnecessary because scientists have already shown all things to be composed of tiny particles that are themselves composed of even smaller particles. For that reason, I thought it would be all right if I did not say anything about that. I spoke about dependent relationship rather than about individual things. Since you have asked, let's consider the way in which we analyze discrete things.

This is a hand, isn't it?[34] It does not rely upon something else in the way that long and short obviously rely upon the other things to which they are being compared. By its nature, it is a hand. However, let us investigate this carefully. A hand is a coarse thing. Look more closely. Is this the hand?[35] No, this is a thumb. Is this the hand?[36] No, this is a finger: the first finger, the second finger, the third finger, and so on. Is this the hand?[37] No, this is skin. What about the things inside the skin? Are they the hand? No, there we find flesh, bone, blood, and so on. So, what is a hand? A hand is made by our minds, isn't it? Put fingers, flesh, skin, and many other things together, and we think "This is my hand." Except for that, actually there is no hand.

Maybe we will accept the absence of a hand, but we will insist that fingers are present. In that case, is the first joint the finger? The second? The third?

The nail? Our minds designate finger to the assembly of many things. There is no finger present with those things.

We may analyze ever more finely. At last, we reach the most subtle particles. Do we ever come to something that has no parts, something that cannot be divided further? We may think so. We may imagine a particle so tiny that it will not admit of further division, but even that tiniest of particles will have dimensions. If a second particle, equally tiny, touches the first one at a particular point, it will not touch it at other points. The two particles touch at one point, but they do not touch at other points. That means that they have parts. We may imagine particles so small as to lack parts, but this is not supported by reasoning and they are not truly established.

In the absence of such truly established things, how do all these appearances dawn? They dawn with mind. When we follow such a path of reasoned analysis, we are employing the methods set forth by the Middle Way School. Here, we have considered briefly the mode of investigation known as the freedom from being either one or many set forth by the master Shāntarakṣhita in his *Ornament for the Middle Way*.

Q: I think that I follow that, but I am asking more about qualities than about things. It seems to me that there are qualities that have an inherent existence; for instance, color.
A: Consider the color of this book, which is yellow. It depends upon the book itself, does it not? The yellow of this book comes by way of many small particles of yellow gathering together. Since the particles themselves are not established, neither is the yellow.

Q: When a person loses a limb, such as a hand, he or she still has the sensation of having that limb. What is the difference between the absence of the limb and absence of the experience of that limb?
A: Those emptinesses differ in kind. Ultimately, appearances such as hands are not established, but various conventional appearances can nevertheless dawn. The absence of inherent establishment is one kind of emptiness, and nonexistence is another. The emptiness we are considering here lives happily right with appearances: while empty of inherent establishment, appearances dawn.

Feeling the presence of a hand even when that hand has been lost comes, I think, from the predispositions to which our minds have grown accustomed over a long period of time. I have had hands for many thousands of years. If I were suddenly to lose one of my hands, due to the predispositions to which I have become accustomed over time I would probably still have the sensation of that hand's presence.

In fact, I can relate something from my own experience that resembles the situation you have described. I wear eyeglasses all the time, and I have been doing so for many years. At night, I remove my eyeglasses when I go to sleep, but when I wake up in the middle of the night, it seems to me that I am still wearing eyeglasses. Even though I am not wearing eyeglasses, I have the feeling of wearing them due to the predispositions to which I have grown accustomed.

When something is absent even conventionally, that absence is solely an absence and solely an emptiness. It cannot become something else. Emptiness of inherent existence—that's another matter altogether. Though empty ultimately, various appearances may dawn. Our texts describe that sort of emptiness as the emptiness that possesses the supreme of all aspects. In that emptiness anything may dawn. In dependence upon being emptiness, we may change in many ways: we may achieve the rank of a buddha, we may wander in cyclic existence, and so on. For instance, if a seed were not emptiness, it would always remain a seed and could never become a flower. Gradually, a seed does become a flower. How can that be? By the power of being an empty entity, sometimes it is a seed, at other times it becomes a flower, and at other times it becomes nothing. All these various aspects may dawn in dependence upon being emptiness. In dependence upon being emptiness, things may depend upon one another. Through dependent relationship, all appearances may dawn.

You have asked good questions, and that is a source of joy for me. Thank you. You have great interest in Dharma, great interest in meditation, a serious wish to realize the meaning of emptiness, and because of that you have asked extremely good questions. That gives me real joy, and I thank you for your genuine wish to learn and understand.

CHAPTER SIX

The Six Transcendent Actions

Wawakening in its two aspects, conventional and ultimate. In the context of the ultimate mind of awakening, we have considered the way to meditate upon the selflessness of persons and the selflessness of phenomena. This morning we will turn our attention to the conduct that skillfully furthers the welfare of others. That refers mainly to the way in which we practice the six transcendent actions.

In meditative equipoise we meditate upon the emptiness that is the selflessness of persons and of phenomena. In dependence upon our own realization of emptiness, great compassion for all sentient beings who have not realized emptiness is born in us. Thus, initially compassion is born in dependence upon emptiness. In dependence upon compassion, we engage in the six transcendent actions of giving gifts, guarding ethics, developing constancy, and so forth. All of these practices may be included within the collection of merit and the collection of wisdom. How shall we accumulate merit and wisdom? In meditative equipoise we realize emptiness; in subsequent attainment we must exert ourselves to practice in accordance with such realization.

In dependence upon realization of emptiness, we become able to exert ourselves at the practices of compassion and the transcendent actions. Also, in dependence upon exerting ourselves at the six transcendent actions, both meditative stabilization and the knowledge that realizes emptiness increase to higher levels. Thus, in dependence upon meditative equipoise, subsequent attainment increases, and in dependence upon subsequent attainment, meditative equipoise increases. Such exertion at the six transcendent actions is called skill in method. In dependence upon those methods, meditative stabilization increases to a higher level. In dependence upon meditative stabilization increasing to a higher level, the six transcendent actions increase to a higher level. This serves as a cause for coming to the end of the path; therefore, it is called skill in method.

In the *Sūtra of the Jewel On the Crown*, speaking to Maitreya about the six transcendent actions, the Buddha said, "Maitreya, wear the armor." In order to accomplish the paths that lead to liberation and omniscience, we need great strength of heart. That strength of heart arms us for the journey. Along with such great strength of heart, we need compassion that considers all sentient beings with tender love. Abiding in compassion, we must realize emptiness. What kind of emptiness must we realize? We must realize the emptiness that possesses the supreme of all aspects. To accomplish that, we will need to cultivate the appropriate stable contemplation.

What is the emptiness that possesses the supreme of all aspects? Having realized emptiness directly in periods of meditative equipoise, in periods of subsequent attainment we practice the transcendent actions. The emptiness that we have realized does not require us to dispense with everything else. Realization of emptiness does not separate us from generosity; we realize emptiness, and we also give gifts. Similarly, we realize emptiness, and we also guard ethics. We realize emptiness, and we also do not separate from developing constancy. Having realized emptiness, we initiate exertion. Having realized emptiness, we do not separate from stable contemplation. Having realized emptiness, we do not separate from knowledge. Having realized emptiness, we do not separate from method. The emptiness that possesses the supreme of all aspects does not lead us to separate from the transcendent actions. Rather, in dependence upon realization of emptiness, we can engage in any appropriate and beneficial actions. Emptiness does not lead us to quietude and inactivity.

This emptiness is not an emptiness that is a nothingness. The Buddha said that in dependence upon realization of an emptiness that is the suitability of all things to arise, we must perfect generosity and the other transcendent actions. Therefore, a bodhisattva must give gifts, guard ethics, and so forth. We must rely upon method; were we to think that realization of emptiness alone will bring us to the rank of a buddha, we would be mistaken. Speaking in this way, the Buddha taught that a bodhisattva's meditation upon emptiness will not, by itself, become the conduct of a bodhisattva.

The Buddha himself said that we become buddhas in dependence upon the accomplishment of all six of the transcendent actions. Nevertheless, some people have said that we need to train only in transcendent knowledge and do not need to train in the other transcendent actions. Not considering the other transcendent actions to be of much importance, they have found fault with the practices of transcendent generosity, transcendent ethics, and so on. The Buddha spoke to Maitreya about this very point when he recalled a lifetime in which he had taken birth as a king.[38] To protect the life of a pigeon, he had cut flesh from his own body and given it to a hawk stalking the pigeon. The Buddha asked Maitreya, "Was that an ignorant, mistaken, and stupid thing to do?" Maitreya replied, "That was not mistaken. That was good. It was the work of great compassion." The Buddha then said, "Similarly, it is important that bodhisattvas engage in the six transcendent actions."

Here it is said that training in the six transcendent actions is very important. For what reason is that said? Generally, Hwa Shang Mahāyāna's coming to Tibet and teaching the excellent dharma was a good thing. In particular, he taught meditative stabilization extremely well. However, Hwa Shang Mahāyāna did not consider exertion at the six transcendent actions to be important. Mainly, he said, we must cultivate meditative stabilization. That is why it became necessary for Kamalashīla to come to Tibet and debate with Hwa Shang Mahāyāna. Only to meditate upon emptiness will not do. In saying that we must without fail make effort at the six transcendent actions, Kamalashīla accorded them a great importance.

When we make effort at the six transcendent actions, where does the emphasis land? The emphasis lands upon mind. We begin with generosity, and when we practice the transcendent action of generosity, of course we give food, clothing and other resources to those who are impoverished and bereft of food, clothing, and so on. Even so, the emphasis does not land upon external things. The emphasis lands upon internal mind. For instance, out of compassion, we think, "I will give to others, I must give to others." In the words of Shantideva, who was an heir to the Victorious Ones,

> In order to achieve a charitable mind
> Engage in transcendent generosity.

We may think that if we have resources, then we can give vastly to others, and that if we do not have resources, then we cannot give vastly to others. We would be mistaken. Generosity does not depend mainly upon resources; generosity depends mainly upon our minds. We would do better to think, "Whether I have resources or not, I will give to others. In order to benefit sentient beings, I will give." Such an impulse to give is called generosity.

The Fifth Gyalwang Karmapa, Teshin Shekpa, received an invitation from the Emperor of China. He accepted the invitation, traveled from Tibet to China, and later returned from China to Tibet. As he returned to Tibet, an old woman offered him a goat with a broken leg. In response, Karmapa Teshin Shekpa said, "During the entire course of the journey that I have made from Tibet to China and from China to Tibet I have not met with generosity greater than hers." When they heard this, others thought, "How strange! The Emperor of China has offered remarkable, precious jewels and many other wonderful gifts. How can this gift of a goat with a broken leg surpass the Emperor's generosity?" This deserves careful examination. The old woman had few resources and yet offered whatever she had. The Emperor of China possessed inconceivable resources but did not offer even one percent of what he owned. Generosity is not measured by the things given. Generosity depends upon our own intention and motivation.

When we give gifts, what is most important? We must give intelligently rather than foolishly. Giving compulsively and heedlessly, we will give some gifts that help and others that harm. We may give impure things. For instance, we may give poison or weapons. Eventually, they will fall into the hands of someone who will use them to cause harm. Someone may offer something to us and say, "I will give this to you; please use it to kill so-and-so." Or, our reasons for giving may be impure. We may be motivated by envy or competitiveness. We may calculate that if we give something now, in the future we will receive a good return. Or we may intend to deceive others. Nothing meaningful will come of that. Also, those to whom we give may be impure. That is to say, we may give to people who have bad intentions and who want to harm others. Or, if we were to give something of great value to a crazy person, he or she would probably misuse it. In those ways, we would give foolishly rather than intelligently. If we give stupidly, then harm will come about in dependence upon our gifts. It would be better not to make such gifts. If we give wisely, then benefit will arise, the recipient's wishes will be fulfilled, and, in dependence upon that, no one—neither ourselves nor others—will be harmed. That is the way in which to give.

In the context of ethics, there are the seven nonvirtuous actions of body and speech—killing, stealing, sexual misconduct, and so on—that we must abandon. Still, we must apply these principles knowledgeably. When the seven nonvirtuous actions of body and speech benefit others, they have become virtue and are permitted. For instance, when the Buddha took birth as the leader known as Strength-of-Heart, he killed an evil person who intended to take the lives of five hundred bodhisattvas. He did kill, but the intention made his action a virtuous one. For that reason, his action did not contradict the practice of ethics. To understand ethical practice, we have to understand that ethics requires us to abandon harming others.

Generally, constancy means not hating. However, mere display of hatred does not contradict constancy in any way. For instance, the dharmapālas such as Mahākāla and the deities such as Vajrakīlaya look wrathful, and some people ask me why this is so. After all, we are to abandon hatred, and they show wrath. What's going on? It's a good question, for it allows doubt to be dispelled. Compassion does not always have to be delivered with a smile, and smiles are not always backed up by compassion. Some people smile in order to deceive. Others display anger while feeling kindness. In that case, the appearance of anger is rooted in compassion. Consider a mother who loves her child dearly: when the child tries to jump into fire or leap into a chasm, the mother will become furious! What is that anger? Does she feel anger for her own sake? No, she feels angry because she loves her child so much, and that love expresses itself outwardly as fury, but the display of anger does not mean that she hates her child. It is not necessary always to show a patient face.

When protecting others from harm and helping them, it does not matter if we merely express anger within developing constancy. For instance, when a mother protects her child from harm, she does not really hate her child. She may well display anger with a fierce expression, strong words, and so on, but that is not real anger. The mere display of anger or expression of anger does not contradict constancy.

Generally, we consider hard work to be exertion. That may be exertion, but it does not qualify as transcendent exertion. Shantideva, who was an heir to the Victorious Ones, described exertion as taking delight in virtue. Taking delight in nonvirtue and working hard at nonvirtue—for instance, working hard at killing, at doing bad things to other people, and at waging war—such actions would not be regarded as exertion that is taught in the Great Vehicle. Why not? Exertion refers to actions that benefit ourselves and others, and nonvirtue does not benefit either ourselves or others. There is a name for working hard at nonvirtue: the laziness of attachment to bad activity. Strong attachment to bad activity is not exertion. It is necessary to examine closely and identify what exertion is and what it is not.

To practice transcendent stable contemplation, we must actually cultivate meditative stabilization. To practice transcendent knowledge, we must develop extraordinary knowledge that accords with the excellent dharma. That is to say, our knowledge must be of benefit both to ourselves and to others. Cleverness and arrogance that harm others will not be called transcendent knowledge; such misuse of intelligence will be regarded as degenerate knowledge. Not having used our knowledge well, we have instead misused that talent to harm both ourselves and others.

It is necessary to have both method and knowledge. Knowledge alone will not suffice. Knowledge devoid of method and great compassion leads one to the paths of hearers, on which we strive earnestly at accomplishing only our own welfare. Because bodhisattvas must achieve an extraordinary nirvāṇa that benefits everyone, they need both method and knowledge. Method prevents their falling into nirvāṇa; knowledge prevents their falling into saṃsāra. Thus, method and knowledge enable bodhisattvas to achieve the rank of a buddha, who dwells neither in peace nor in existence.

For that reason, the Buddha said, knowledge endowed with method serves as a cause for achieving liberation, and knowledge devoid of method serves as a cause of bondage in saṃsāra. Similarly, method endowed with knowledge makes a path that releases us from saṃsāra, and method devoid of knowledge causes further bondage in saṃsāra.

Therefore, in dependence upon method, great bodhisattvas do not strive earnestly to achieve nirvāṇa. What is the reason? The Buddha gave an example for this. A fire burning within a home will heat the home well, and we enjoy the fire. However, we do not like it so much that we put our hands into the fire. Similarly, in order to benefit ourselves and others, we do need to gain nirvāṇa. However, we do not strive so earnestly for the welfare of ourselves alone that we then enter nirvāṇa. Rather, we must conduct ourselves as bodhisattvas.

This evening I have spoken about the methods for bringing the six transcendent actions into experience. I will stop here tonight. Tomorrow, I will speak about the benefit that comes from such practice. If you have questions, please ask them.

Q: What is the relationship between compassion and emptiness?
A: Suppose that I were to realize all phenomena to be emptiness. Having done so, I would not need to fear illness, death, mental afflictions, enemies, or anything else. After all, I would have realized everything to be emptiness. I would not fear anything or agonize over anything. Instead, I would enjoy a remarkable and flawless peace. Meanwhile, others would continue to suffer

greatly. Not having realized emptiness, they would fear illness, enemies, death, and many other types of suffering. Things would continue to be terribly difficult and painful for them.

Would there really be any need for them to suffer? Of course not. There would be no reason for others not to realize emptiness in just the same way that I had. Having realized emptiness, I would no longer suffer; not having realized emptiness, they would suffer incessantly. Unable to realize emptiness, they suffer horribly but to no purpose.

When we see this spectacle, compassion arises naturally and effortlessly. It is as if we could not stop compassion from arising. Generally, people such as ourselves have to be urged to feel compassion for others. Someone who has realized emptiness requires no urging; compassion arises naturally. We cannot bear to stand by idly while others suffer. Thus, we speak of "emptiness having compassion as its essence." When we realize emptiness, compassion arises with tremendous force.

Q: How does entering nirvāṇa resemble putting our hands in a fire?
A: At first, we must strive earnestly for liberation. Liberation is something worth striving for. However, if we desire liberation excessively, the welfare of others will not be served. If I further only my own welfare, then I will not do much for others. In that sense, entering nirvāṇa resembles putting our hands in a fire. That does not mean that entering nirvāṇa will bring pain; it means that others will not flourish and that we should refrain from liking nirvāṇa so much that we abandon others and care only for ourselves.

Q: In the tradition of Vajrayāna it is said that method is an expression of the masculine principle and that supreme knowledge is an expression of the feminine principle. Can you explain the way in which method expresses the masculine principle?
A: In speaking of method as the father and supreme knowledge as the mother, we are joining purity to impurity. From what do we achieve the ultimate result? Mainly, in dependence upon supreme knowledge. Supreme knowledge increases to higher and higher levels, and in dependence upon that increase, the rank of a buddha, which is the supreme accomplishment, is achieved. Is this achieved solely by knowledge? No. What else do we need? Method, the companion to knowledge. This describes purity, the accomplishment of the ultimate result. We can join this to the way in which a human being takes birth in cyclic existence. We take birth in these human

bodies that serve as our supports. What really serves as the cause of these bodies? Our mothers, for we must take birth in dependence upon our mothers. Therefore, we envision knowledge in the aspect of a mother. Do we take birth solely in dependence upon our mother? No, of course not. Another method or condition is necessary: a father. Thus, method appears in the aspect of a father.

To describe the path leading to a buddha's complete awakening, we speak about method and knowledge. A woman serves as the image of supreme knowledge and a man serves as the image of method. When the fruit is achieved, it is achieved mainly in dependence upon knowledge. In the impure state, our bodies are born mainly in dependence upon our mothers. Therefore, the mother is joined to knowledge. Method serves as the companion and aid to knowledge. A father accompanies and assists the birth of the body. Therefore, the father is joined to method

In the impure state, the body is established in dependence upon the father and the mother. In the pure state, Chakrasaṃvara serves as an image of method and Vajravārāhī serves as an image of knowledge. They are spoken of as father and mother. In Secret Mantra, impurity systematically indicates purity.

Q: How do we join knowledge with the transcendent actions? If we do not have much knowledge, will we be unable to practice the transcendent actions? A: We can practice the six transcendent actions. Although some people have more knowledge and some have less, things change during the course of a lifetime. Knowledge may increase, and it may decrease. Both occur. Those with great knowledge may fail to cherish it and thereby lose it. Those with little knowledge may seek and obtain great knowledge. Knowledge can change, and it depends upon our own interest and practice. If we have interest and bring what we learn into our experience, then our knowledge will increase. If we have no interest and do not bring the learning into experience, then knowledge probably cannot increase. We cannot say decisively either that those with little knowledge cannot practice the six transcendent actions or that they can. It depends upon the individual's exertion and interest.

Q: How do we determine whether or not another person has knowledge and compassion? How do we know whether to rely upon another person or not? A: We cannot see another person's knowledge and compassion directly. What we *can* do is see how another person applies the teachings. We *can* observe another person's conduct. When we examine another person's conduct, we will see whether or not a wish to help others and a pure intention to be of benefit directs that person's work. If so, then we have come upon purity of knowledge and we may expect to see that knowledge increase stage by stage. That is to say, if kindness and altruism accompany someone's knowledge, then the knowledge will be firm and will increase. If, however, someone's knowledge seems mixed with pride or hatred, or if pride, hatred, and other mental afflictions accompany someone's compassion, then his or her knowledge will gradually sink to lower and lower levels. Nothing favorable will come of such degenerate knowledge.

Q: If a bodhisattva abides neither in cyclic existence nor in nirvāṇa, then where does a bodhisattva dwell?
A: Due to compassion, bodhisattvas do not abide in peace. If we ask a bodhisattva, "Will you achieve liberation from cyclic existence and then go to nirvāṇa alone?," he or she will say, "No." If we then ask, "Why not?," a bodhisattva will reply, "Because of the power of compassion." Bodhisattvas come back to cyclic existence, and bodhisattvas abide in cyclic existence. When bodhisattvas abide in cyclic existence, do they experience suffering, hardship, and the pain of bad migrations in the way that we do? No. Due to supreme knowledge, bodhisattvas do not abide in existence either. Because such knowledge has realized the abiding nature of all phenomena, bodhisattvas do no evil and generate no mental afflictions. In dependence upon having realized all phenomena to be emptiness, bodhisattvas do not suffer. Therefore, due to supreme knowledge, bodhisattvas do not abide in cyclic existence. If bodhisattvas do not abide in cyclic existence, do they pass into liberation? No. Due to compassion, bodhisattvas further the welfare of sentient beings. Bodhisattvas do not seek their own welfare to the exclusion of others. Rather, to further the welfare of sentient beings, bodhisattvas return to cyclic existence. Therefore, it is said that bodhisattvas dwell neither in cyclic existence nor in nirvāṇa.

Q: It seems that if we had knowledge, our actions would be informed by that knowledge. How is it possible for someone to have knowledge but not method?
A: If we were to cultivate meditative stabilization only, meditate always upon emptiness, and not practice generosity, ethics, constancy, and so forth, we would have knowledge that lacks method. Knowledge alone cannot achieve the rank of a buddha. Why not? Knowledge alone does not further the wel-

fare of sentient beings. Falling into solitary peace, we enter upon the paths of hearers. That would be knowledge devoid of method.

Q: We would like to become more skillful in our activity. Can study help us to do that?
A: Delusion tends to dominate ordinary beings such as ourselves. When we think about a place that we have never visited, its shapes, colors, and features do not appear clearly to our minds. Similarly, in regard to dharma, we do not clearly know the way in which to proceed, the result that will come of our actions, or the method for achieving the result we desire. Moreover, we cannot know such things through our own power. Nevertheless, we do have the speech of the Buddha and the commentary given by greatly learned teachers. In their writings, we find clear explanations of the results of actions and the necessity for particular conduct, as well as clear identification of the suffering that sentient beings endure and the consequent need to feel compassion. They have not written such things casually. Rather, they have found such things to be true, and they write with both knowledge and conviction: "If you do that, this is what will come of it." Because they have spelled it out so clearly, when we study, we can recognize the truth in their words: "That is true, isn't it? I had not thought about that before. What's taught here, it's actually the truth, isn't it?" These writings enable us to know how sentient beings suffer and the reasons why they suffer. On that basis, we come to feel compassion, and compassion causes us to study the ways in which to achieve liberation from suffering and the ways in which to further the welfare of others. In dependence upon knowing that, we become more skillful in the methods of helping others.

Q: Should ordinary people such as ourselves try to use wrath in a skillful way?
A: Hatred will not help in any way; sometimes a wrathful appearance will help. For instance, if a friend of yours is doing poor work, you may say, very sweetly, "Please don't do that; it's not good." Your friend will probably not listen. So, one day you come in and holler, "What's the matter with you! Why are you doing things this way!" Maybe that will help.

Q: Is there a difference between nirvāṇa and liberation?
A: There is not much difference between them. The Tibetan word for nirvāṇa is *nya ngen lay day ba*. It means "passed beyond misery." *Nya ngen*, which

means "misery," is to be understood as referring to suffering. The second part of the word, *lay day ba*, means "to have passed beyond." Beyond what? Beyond suffering. As for liberation, from what do we become liberated? From suffering. The words do not differ much in their meaning.

We can nevertheless distinguish two types of liberation and two types of nirvāṇa. If we enter the path of hearers, focus merely on temporarily not having to suffer, abandon mental afflictions related to various states, cultivate only meditative stabilization, further only our own welfare, do not do much to further the welfare of other sentient beings, and merely become liberated from cyclic existence, we achieve what may be called "liberation." It is the liberation of a hearer and the nirvāṇa of a hearer. Such people are called hearer foe destroyers. That liberation is regarded as a lesser liberation. Alternatively, we may enter the paths of bodhisattvas, further the welfare of sentient beings, and accomplish great benefit for others while, in the end, achieving the rank of a buddha ourselves. That complete purification and mastery can also be called nirvāṇa. Both the greater nirvāṇa and the lesser nirvāṇa are called nirvāṇa, but they differ radically. Similarly, we may speak of a greater liberation and a lesser liberation. Both are called liberation, but they are not the same. Still, in general, "nirvāṇa" and "liberation" mean more or less the same thing.

Q:When you spoke about selflessness, you observed that, for instance, an eye consciousness seeing a glass cannot be found in the glass, in the eye sense power, or somewhere between the two of them. What about the sixth consciousness, which is the mental consciousness? Why can that consciousness not be located in the brain?
A: Suppose that the mental consciousness resides in the brain. If so, and if the legs were to hurt, the mental consciousness would not know anything of their pain.

Q: Does the Buddhist tradition recognize life and sentience in plants, rocks, trees, and mountains? Do Buddhists regard the earth as a living being?
A: I have not looked into that much, and I cannot answer the question based on my own study and knowledge. In questions of this nature, I rely on the Buddha's teachings. Prior to the Buddha's appearance in this world, the Naked Ones asserted that trees, grass, and so on have life. They held that if we were to cut trees and grass, we would be killing a living being and would have to suffer the consequences. The Buddha appeared in this world after the

Naked Ones had given those teachings. He must have disagreed with them, for he taught that although we would have to suffer painful consequences if we were to kill a living being, we would not suffer them due to having cut grass and so on. He taught that even small sentient beings such as bugs have life, and that from that point of view there was not much difference between killing a large sentient being and killing a small sentient being. He did not instruct his students to avoid cutting grass and trees as a way to avoid killing sentient beings. Because I have confidence in the Buddha, I think that grass, flowers, and such things do not have life.

There are stories of the hells in which we hear of trees and so forth that experience sensation and think "I." They suffer terribly. There are such stories, told by sublime people of what they have seen in environments other than our own. However, generally, I do not think that trees, grass, and so on have life.

Q: In that case, how would somone choose to establish a monastery in a particular place or choose a particular mountain as a place to make offerings?
A: Shrines are placed upon mountains and near trees not because we regard the mountain or the tree as a living being, but because gods and spirits have chosen those places as their residence. The god thinks, "I will live here." Just as human beings have houses, so the god thinks, "This mountain is my home. This is where I live." Some gods or spirits may choose a particular tree: "I will live near this tree. This will be my home." The god or spirit will not remain there all the time. Rather, he or she will think, "I will stay here for awhile. Then I will go to another place. Then I will come back to my home." We place a shrine there not because of the mountain or the tree, but because of the god or spirit who lives there.

Q: If I were to take birth as a bear, the body of my mother—a bear's body—would be the cause of my body, which would be the body of a bear. Does that mean that, in subsequent lives, we experience the results of actions that we have not accumulated ourselves?
A: In the Buddha's tradition, we speak of actions and their results. In dependence upon virtuous and nonvirtuous actions that we have performed in previous lifetimes, in a later lifetime we experience results that are either pleasurable or painful. The results that ripen stem from actions that we have accumulated ourselves rather than from the actions that others have accumulated. We do not meet with the results of what we have not done—not at all.

However, the force of that to which our minds have grown accustomed does not arise in dependence upon actions. That arises in dependence upon familiarization. The strength of mental afflictions, the strength of tender love, and so on. Some people are so loving. Some people naturally feel great compassion. Others feel no compassion whatsoever. Some people are full of hatred. Others have hardly any; they rarely become angry. In dependence upon what does that come about? Not in dependence upon actions. Such dispositions come about in dependence upon predispositions that have been established in former lifetimes. Some people like virtue. Others like to accumulate evil deeds. We may ask, "Does that come about in dependence upon actions?" No. That comes about in dependence upon the predispositions with which we have become familiar.

Therefore, we cannot explain everything solely in terms of actions, which is to say, causes and their results. Pleasure and pain come about in dependence upon actions, which serve as causes. The rest—our own mental afflictions and so on—come about in dependence upon the greater or lesser force of states of mind to which we have grown accustomed.

Q: You spoke about the emptiness of persons and things; in what way do spirits and deities exist?

A: Results ripen in different ways in dependence upon the actions that different sentient beings have accumulated. We human beings are able to see the forms of other human beings, but we are not able to see the forms of deities and spirits. The difference in the actions that impel these different types of lifetimes render their forms invisible to us. They are able to see one another's forms, but we are unable to see their forms. Their minds are present, as are their bodies, but their bodies cannot become objects for our eyes. Now and then, through the power of the predispositions established by actions, it happens that we see them. Sometimes, some people see them. But not everyone, and not always. As for emptiness, their situation does not differ from ours. Conventionally, we see what we see, and they see what they see. Ultimately, neither human beings, nor gods, nor spirits truly exist.

Q:If I cannot perceive them, and therefore do not acknowledge their existence, then in what context do they exist?

A: Suppose that I go to sleep and dream of going to a lovely place. In my dream, I may ride horses, lead elephants, and do all sorts of things. If you were to look at me, you would see me sleeping, but you would not see me riding horses and directing elephants. You would not be able to see those appearances. They *would* appear to me. I would see myself traveling to a wonderful place, riding horses, playing with elephants, and having a grand time. Those appearances would dawn for me, but not for others. Similarly, gods and spirits perceive gods and spirits. We cannot see them.

Q: Since phenomena do not exist independently of mind, what will become of them when all sentient beings have awakened fully?
A: Suppose that I fall asleep and dream of an elephant. Someone may ask, "Where is that elephant's mother?" Then, when I wake up, someone may ask, "Who is leading that elephant now?" The elephant did not have a mother, and when I wake up the elephant will no longer be present. They appeared for me. These appearances of the external appear for sentient beings. When all sentient beings have become buddhas, these appearances will no longer be present.

Q: You described desire as an affliction. It seems to me that some desire is beneficial. What is the problem with desire?
A: When desire is minimal, it tends to bind us in cyclic existence but is not a great fault. However, it is the nature of desire to increase without limit. It grows boundlessly. It overflows every container. At that point, desire has become terribly dangerous. For that reason, however much we can subdue desire, so much the better.

For instance, consider Adolph Hitler. Initially, he may have had a good intention. Perhaps he wanted to help people. Gradually, he came to feel that he must become a leader. Then, he wanted to become the leader of Germany. Next, he wanted to become the leader of all of Europe. Finally, he wanted to become the leader of the entire world. His desire had exceeded all limits. In the end, he had to be destroyed.

Q: Does every kind of desire lead to pain?
A: Not all desire leads directly to pain. However, the very word expresses the sense of sticking to something. It does not permit freedom. It binds. When attached and fastened to something, we cannot move far away. It is as if the desired object pulls us back, and we cannot free ourselves from it. For this kind of desire we use a term meaning attachment. So long as we are attached, we stick there and cannot achieve liberation. However, this does not necessarily entail chaos and pain.

Q: Does that mean that some desire is actually beneficial?

A: In the Tibetan language, desire names an attachment that harms ourselves and others. The source of benefit for ourselves and others receives a different name; we call that "longing."[39]

CHAPTER SEVEN

The Fruit of Realization

THE MASTER KAMALASHĪLA presents the Middle Way School's style of meditation in terms of three topics. First, he discusses the need for compassion to increase. Then he explains the main practice: the methods for cultivating a conventional mind of awakening and the methods for cultivating an ultimate mind of awakening. After that, he portrays the way in which to bring the six transcendences, generosity and so forth, into experience, which we do in periods of subsequent attainment. We have finished that much. Now, he turns his attention to describing the benefit that will come to us in dependence upon having brought such instructions into experience.

Kamalashīla explains this in terms of temporary signs and ultimate results. As for the first, temporary signs, initially we need the thoroughly pure motivation of compassion; along the way, we need thoroughly pure practice of the Great Vehicle; ultimately, we come to thoroughly pure results, the conduct of the six transcendences. Where does this lead? The inner mind becomes thoroughly pure.

Generally speaking, our minds are not thoroughly pure. Why not? From time without beginning we have grown accustomed to the conception of a self and to powerful afflictions of the mind. In dependence upon bringing the excellent dharma into our experience, the mental afflictions will gradually be pacified and our minds will gradually become thoroughly pure. As signs of this gradual purification and through the strength of the mind's purity, we will begin to dream good dreams of encountering buddhas and bodhisattvas, of receiving dharma from them, and of benefit arising both for ourselves and for others in dependence upon receiving that dharma.

Such signs of the gradual purification of our minds will arise internally. Externally, deities will rejoice in our practice and will offer their help and protection. There are many deities; they did not create this world, but deities reside in various places, and most of you know something about *drala*. Many deities have faith and confidence in the Buddha and the Dharma, and some of them have actually met with the Buddha and received instruction from him. That has enabled many deities to develop love, compassion, and the mind of awakening. The development of such good qualities has, in many cases, provided the foundation for knowledge of things normally hidden from view. When they look with such clairvoyant eyes, they may see someone who has developed good meditative stabilization and who also practices compassion and the mind of awakening. Of course, they will feel overjoyed and, in dependence upon their delight in sincere practice, they will protect that practitioner. When we practice, we do not hope for such protection. However, even though we do not hope to receive their protection, in dependence upon our success in cultivating meditative stabilization, developing pure motivation, and bringing these teachings into our experience, deities rejoice in our practice, protect us from obstacles, and help us to gather the conditions that are conducive to further practice.

Kamalashīla writes that, for such a bodhisattva, vast collections of merit and wisdom are completed in every moment. How does this come about? Whenever compassion and the mind of awakening are present, vast merit arises. Why? Ordinarily, compassion arises when we observe one sentient being who is suffering. "This one is suffering," we think, and compassion arises. Or, we see a hundred people who are suffering, and we feel compassion for them. Generally, this does help, and not merely in a small way. Still, to accord with the compassion taught by the Buddha, we generate compassion not for only one hundred sentient beings, or only one thousand, or only ten thousand, but for each and every sentient being throughout limitless space. Consider the benefit that will arise from compassion for one sentient being, multiply that by an inconceivable number of sentient beings, and that will give you a sense of the virtue and merit that arise when we develop compassion for all sentient beings. Such vast virtue and merit elevate our practice of meditative stabilization. Since that remarkable path does not err, our collection of wisdom also becomes vast.

Kamalashīla writes also that the afflictive obstructions and the adoption of bad states will be refined. How so? We have many mental afflictions. What is their root? They come about in dependence upon conceiving the aggregation of body and mind to be a self. To destroy that root, we meditate upon the selflessness of persons and phenomena. That attacks the very root of mental afflictions. If we do not see ourselves as the most important person—if compassion leads us to see furthering the welfare of other sentient beings as more important than furthering our own welfare—the conception of a self and the mental afflictions that arise in dependence upon that conception will be suppressed.

This presents both the provisional antidote and the final one. Thereby, the afflictive obstructions will gradually be refined. When afflictive obstructions are refined, bad actions will also be refined. In the absence of mental afflictions, bad actions will not be accumulated newly. Moreover, bad actions that have been accumulated previously will be weakened by the application of their antidote because mental afflictions no longer support them. Therefore, bad actions will be refined also.

Similarly, it is said that happiness and well-being of body and mind will increase at all times. If we have love, compassion, the mind of awakening, and the good qualities of meditative stabilization, we will only help others and we will not harm them. In dependence upon not harming others, we will be well in body and also in mind, for we will be free from hatred, discouragement, and so on. Similarly, it is said that there will be beauty in many lifetimes. This means that in dependence upon our own pure motivation and pure conduct, others will not harm us and many will bring help.

Also, it is said that our bodies will not be struck by illness. When our minds are disturbed by mental afflictions, the internal channels and winds do not function well. When they do not function well, we become sick. If we bring the excellent dharma into our experience and develop love and compassion, then our internal motivation will be transformed, we will have few mental afflictions, and meditative stabilization will increase. This causes the internal channels and winds to function well. When they work well, fewer illnesses come to the body.

Furthermore, our minds become pliable. Having cultivated meditative stabilization and grown accustomed to it, when we decide to stop certain faults or increase good qualities, we will have the power to master such provisional good qualities. In the context of the ultimate, outstanding meditative stabilization enables us gradually to achieve remarkable clairvoyance and magical abilities.

Having achieved great magical abilities, we meet all buddhas, make offerings to them, listen to the excellent dharma in their presence, and in successive lifetimes we take birth in the pure fields of all buddhas and bodhisattvas. Also, in each of those births we naturally delight in furthering the welfare of others and in practicing the excellent dharma ourselves. These favorable external and internal circumstances come about through the power of predispositions that have been established previously and to which we have become accustomed. These circumstances enable our roots of virtue gradually to increase to higher levels, due to which we quickly achieve the final result.

Thus far, Kamalashila has indicated the benefit that accrues principally for ourselves. Now he considers the benefit that accrues principally to others. In dependence upon the increase of our own meditative stabilization, our knowledge increases also. When we have such knowledge, we become skilled in method. Because we have both knowledge and skill in method, we further not only our own welfare but also the welfare of other sentient beings in far ranging ways.

Such benefits arise for ourselves and for others when we cultivate love, compassion, good motivation, and meditative stabilization. Additionally, it is said that many people will rejoice when someone practices the dharma well. To that I can attest from my own experience. Some years ago I had to flee from the Chinese Communists. When I fled, soldiers pursued me. They had no choice other than to pursue me, for their commanders had ordered them to chase me. One day the soldiers had caught up with me, and there was nothing for me to do but cross right before them. There I was, well within their range, and with two or three hundred soldiers firing automatic weapons at me. Could all of those soldiers, shooting freely for a long time, fail to hit just one person? Had they wanted to kill me, I would have died right then and there. Is it possible that a couple of hundred soldiers shooting right at me from close range could have failed to kill me? Clearly, they did not want to kill me, for they liked me. Their commanders had ordered them to fire directly at me, which left them little choice, but the soldiers did not want to kill me. Had they wanted to kill me, they had all the permission they required. And yet they allowed me to live. Why? As is said, many will rejoice in our practice of dharma. I had done nothing else to please them. I had made some effort to bring the Buddhist teachings into my own experience and to develop a little bit of kindness. That is all. They liked me for that, and they spared me.

If we develop kindness and refrain from harming others, in return others will not harm us. Even soldiers with guns will feel affection for us. Moreover, familiarizing with this repeatedly over a long period of time enables kindness to grow in our minds. Thus, we can give birth to an ultimate mind of awakening, realize the abiding nature of the sphere of reality, become able to further the welfare of many sentient beings, and achieve a buddha's wisdom.

In that way, until we achieve the final rank of a completely perfected buddha, abandoning the afflictions present in our own minds and generating good qualities, we progress gradually over the grounds of a bodhisattva from the first and second grounds to the tenth and eleventh grounds. In dependence upon the view generated in meditative equipoise, the wisdom attained subsequently increases to ever higher levels, and in dependence upon the wisdom attained subsequently, meditative equipoise also increases to ever higher levels. For example, in prior ages, rubbing one stick against another led initially to warmth and eventually to fire; the fire would then burn the two sticks. Similarly, through the steady development of meditative equipoise and subsequent attainment, the two mix indistinguishably, at which point the rank of a buddha has been achieved.

What happens after we become buddhas? Until cyclic existence has been emptied of sentient beings, a buddha's activities arise unceasingly. Why do such activities arise? Previously we heard of the emptiness having compassion as its essence. When we have found a good path ourselves and achieved a good result, it is only natural that to feel compassion for those who have not realized the nature of reality and achieved the results of such realization. Once such strong compassion arises, the actions of a buddha cannot help but arise, and they will not cease until cyclic existence has been emptied of sentient beings. Does that mean that a buddha must endure hardship? No, a buddha does not find such work to be difficult. Why not? A buddha feels great tenderness and love for all sentient beings. That causes a buddha to engage in the lives of sentient beings, to help them in any way possible, however many there may be. Unlike us, a buddha does not feel helpless before the vast suffering of cyclic existence. Buddhas establish hundreds of thousands of sentient beings in dharma and help them to achieve the results that the dharma can provide. Such meaningful activity gives them great joy and happiness. They never weary of it.

Having completed his exposition of the stages of meditation, Kamalashīla now offers advice in the form of verse.[40] This advice is not really part of the main text; rather, it is presented as a poetic conclusion to the treatise. Kamalashīla remarks that excellent beings do not envy others or exhibit pride. What do the excellent desire? Great learning. They will accept instruction from anyone who has such learning, and they will listen to anyone who has acquired great learning. Whatever they find of value, they hold in their minds. In so doing, they resemble swans. How so? If we pour water into milk and give the mixture to swans, the swans know how to separate the water from the milk, discard the water, and drink the milk. Similarly, excellent beings go everywhere to acquire learning and they will listen to everyone. Sometimes they meet with excellent beings. Sometimes they meet with inferior beings. From excellent beings they obtain dharma and remarkable advice. From inferior beings they hear bad words and poor counsel. Like swans separating milk from water, an excellent being will embrace that which has value and will naturally discard the remainder without feeling any need to criticize it.

The verse expresses the matter in a metaphor. What does the metaphor mean? All of us ought to rid ourselves of bias, the stubborn adherence to our own point of view and rejection of others' points of view. We tend to think, "This is our position, and that is their position." We would do well if we were to abandon such bias, listen carefully to the advice given by others, place the good advice into our own minds, and then use it to help both ourselves and others. Excellent beings conduct themselves in that manner; we should emulate them. That is the message that Kamalashila offers as his parting advice.

Kamalashila then offers a prayer of aspiration: by the power of whatever virtue may have arisen in dependence upon having composed this treatise, may many sentient beings be able to enter into and cultivate these paths. Having offered this prayer, Kamalashila then says that he has completed the composition of this text.

The colophon that follows this prayer identifies the Indian scholar who taught the text and the Tibetan translator who translated it. It is customary to append such a colophon to all Tibetan treatises. Why has this custom arisen? Identifying the Indian scholar who taught the text shows that the translator himself did not compose it newly. It shows that the treatise originated and flourished in India, the land to which the Buddha had come. Thus, it shows the text to be worthy of respect. Why does the colophon mention the translator also? Had the translator not rendered the Sanskrit text into Tibetan, then we Tibetans would not be able to read it, chant it, explain it to others, contemplate it ourselves, meditate upon it, or bring it into our experience. Such opportunities have arisen in dependence upon the translator's kindness; the colophon reminds us of that kindness.

When the Buddhadharma spread from India to Tibet, there were about one hundred and eight translators. The dharma of the Secret Mantra has begun to spread to the West, but there are not many translators. In their absence, it has not been possible to translate many books; without translations, the dharma taught in those books cannot easily spread to other lands and be practiced by other people. For instance, Kalu Rinpoche has asked that Jamgön Kongtrül Lodrö Thaye's *Treasury of Knowledge* be translated into English; because there are so few people who can help with that task, the work is proceeding slowly and with considerable difficulty. In the past, the entire Kanjur and Tenjur were translated in a relatively brief period of time and without overly much hardship. To put it simply: we need more translators, as many as possible. Please think about that, and join in if you can.

If you have questions, please ask them.

Q: Please discuss the practice of "sending and taking."
A: Kamalashīla has not written about the practice of "sending and taking" in this treatise, but the practice is an important one. In this treatise, Kamalashīla has written in a general manner about the methods for cultivating compassion and the methods for meditating upon emptiness, but he has not written specifically about the practice of "sending and taking." However, the methods for meditation upon "sending and taking" have been discussed in other texts that present the stages of meditation, and it is extremely important that we understand and know how to practice this meditation.

People like us want happiness for ourselves and do not particularly care whether or not other people have happiness. Generally, that outlook characterizes ordinary beings. In order to change that underlying disposition and give rise to great compassion, we familiarize with the attitude of desiring happiness for others and suffering for ourselves. When we have become accustomed to that, great compassion will arise naturally. We have to make the effort to become familiar with this radically different way of regarding ourselves and others; in order to do that, we cultivate the practice of "sending and taking."

Some people hope that, in dependence upon this contemplative practice, they will be able to take on the suffering of others in fact. They may come upon a sick person, feel tenderness toward him or her, think to themselves, "Now I will take this upon myself," inhale strongly, and afterwards think, "Probably this person will become well now." Then, the other person does not get any better at all, and the would-be benefactor feels dismayed. Others feel afraid. They think, "I have already suffered a lot. What if I get sick? It will be so difficult when the suffering of others actually does land on me! I do not dare to practice this meditation."

Rather than hope or fear that we will indeed take the suffering of others upon ourselves, we practice "sending and taking" within understanding that our happiness and misery depend upon our own previous actions. We cannot actually take the suffering of others upon ourselves or give them our well-being.

If we are not able to help others directly and immediately through "sending and taking," does that mean that nothing beneficial comes of it at all? No. This will help. For instance, were I to think, "I will give my happiness to this other person and take his suffering upon myself," that good motivation would cause the roots that virtue has established in me to grow ever higher. In the future, I would then become able to give happiness to others through giving them the excellent dharma. I would be able to explain the dharma to them; they would then be able to bring the dharma into their experience; and through practicing the dharma, they would achieve happiness. In that way, I would be able to give happiness to them in fact. In a similar fashion, I would be doing something like taking their suffering from them: giving happiness amounts to taking suffering away. It would be a mistake to say that the contemplative practice of "sending and taking" bears no fruit. Taking a longer view, we may say that we can indeed take suffering from others without fear, and we can give happiness to others without hesitation.

Q: Will you say more about how we can replenish the earth?
A: Some years ago I had a conversation about this with Trungpa Rinpoche. At that time, he was living here, and I had come from India. Because he had been living here, he was able to explain some aspects of life in North America that puzzled me. Generally, America has prospered and grown. As one part of that prosperity, Americans have removed many valuable substances from under the earth: gold, silver, jewels, iron, copper, and so forth. Whatever can be extracted from the earth has been extracted enthusiastically. Trungpa Rinpoche explained that in dependence upon many precious metals and other precious substances having been taken from the earth, the energy of the earth has declined. Because of that decline, people do not want to remain where they are. Maybe they want to move to New York. Then, after living in New York for awhile, they want to move to California. Then, from California they go to some other place. The continual movement, he said, suggests that the energy of the earth has declined.

When the earth has suffered such depletion, the deities depart from the places where they have lived, and human beings no longer enjoy living there.

When people practice *lha sang*, wear good clothes, treat one another decently and with honor, shout *ki ki* and *so so*, and engage in other rituals that please the deities, the *drala* return to their former abodes. When the *drala* return, then brilliance and dignity are restored to the body and courage is restored to the mind.

Q: If someone has taken his or her own life, what will happen in the intermediate state? Is there anything that we can do to help those people?
A: If we will practice the dharma, dedicate ourselves to furthering the welfare of others, give generously, live with good ethics, and explicitly dedicate the roots of virtue established by such actions to the welfare of someone who has taken his or her own life, that virtue will help him or her to separate from suffering and achieve happiness.

Q: We seem to be so fickle. Sometimes we want one thing; then we want another. A lot of pain comes from that. Do you have any advice?
A: In the midst of mental afflictions such as desire and hatred, ignorance is always present. Ignorance itself comes in two varieties: mixed and unmixed. Unmixed ignorance stands alone; it merely does not know anything at all. Mixed ignorance, by contrast, accompanies other mental afflictions: when they arise, so does ignorance. Those mental afflictions do not know whether their objects are good or bad, for ignorance makes them stupid. For instance, desire does not know whether the thing it desires is good or bad. Why not? Because ignorance is present. Similarly, when hatred arises, we become dumb, and we misunderstand everything. Why? Because of ignorance. What should we do? When desire arises, we can avoid falling entirely under its spell. Desire thinks that what it wants is good, but we can set that aside. We can rely instead upon knowledge, investigate and analyze with knowledge, and determine whether we have become enamored of something worthwhile or something noxious. If we can avoid slipping into the spell cast by desire, not follow its lead, and rely instead upon knowledge, we will see clearly, and we will be able to determine what to undertake and when to desist.

Q: Please tell us something of your own activities: Thrangu Monastery in Tibet, the nunnery in Nepal, spreading the dharma, and so on.
A: This has been a difficult era for Buddhists generally and especially for the dharma of the Vajrayāna of Secret Mantra. There have been major obstacles and interruptions. For instance, in 1959 the Chinese came to Tibet and began

to destroy texts and monasteries, require the ordained to give up their vows, and disrupt study and meditation. Would I say that they damaged the Buddhadharma to an extreme degree? No, I would not say that because Gyalwa Rinpoche,[41] Gyalwang Karmapa,[42] Trungpa Rinpoche,[43] and other remarkable lamas have prevented the utter destruction of the Buddhadharma by a variety of methods. They have accomplished extraordinary deeds, but of course there is more to be done. In Tibet, the learning and accomplishment of many practitioners has been lost to us, and therefore many lineages of instruction have also been lost. Many teachers came to India, but the elder among them have now passed on. Moreover, the younger practitioners often have difficulty obtaining sufficient livelihood to sustain their study and practice. That creates an obstacle to the survival and propagation of the Buddhadharma. Inspired by the example of the great lamas, I have felt strongly that I must do something to help.

Some of you already know about the projects that I have initiated, and you know that I have not done anything vast or magnificent. I have gathered many young monks and tried to make it possible for them to train in the instructions that have been passed down through many generations in Tibet. First, they need to listen to the teachings. Then, they need to contemplate what they have heard. Finally, they need to bring those teachings into their own experience. I have done what I can to enable them to study and practice in those ways. Also, since the Buddhadharma has now spread to many parts of the world, I have tried to make it possible for these young people to study the English language. So that a few young people can study and practice, I built a monastery and a retreat center in Nepal. Afterwards, seeing that the situation in Tibet had improved slightly, and thinking of the way in which the dharma had flourished there for many generations, I felt it important that I do something to help restore the Buddhadharma in Tibet. The time seemed auspicious, so I made two trips to Tibet. While there I was able construct a temple and gather a group of the ordained for the purpose of practice; I hope that will help in the restoration of the Buddhadharma in Tibet.

Many people both in the West and in the East have helped me in this work. Their kindness has made it possible to build a monastery in Nepal and rebuild some parts of the monastery in Tibet. This helps a lot because it enables people there to study and practice. I have not been able to accomplish anything on a vast scale; there are, for instance, one hundred and seven monks at the monastery in Nepal. Many people have given money, and that has enabled these projects to go forward without interruption. I feel grateful to all the kind people who have helped in any way.

Many women from the West have come to me and said with a certain vehemence, "You have built a monastery for men but you have not built a monastery for women. What's that about!" What they say is true. There's no denying it. Still, when I set about building the monastery for men, many people offered their help. Almost no one has come forward and said, "If you build a monastery for women, I will help you." When I reply to my questioners, I promise that I will definitely build a monastery for women if they will help me. I am preparing to go forward with that intention, and some people have begun to help. I think that this will go well.

The only other thing is the school. In Nepal, there are many Tibetan children who do not learn to read or write their own language. That hurts Tibet all the more. So I've established a small elementary school for very young children.

That's about it. I have not done a lot.

Q: We too are looking for ways to introduce our children to the Buddhist teachings; do you have any suggestions for us?

A: Children need a good foundation. I think that the way of life presented by the Buddhist teachings would serve them well. Give them a good way of conducting themselves, a peaceful and well tamed disposition, the confidence and ability to succeed, and, as Trungpa Rinpoche taught you, good clothes to wear and a radiant bearing. Wouldn't we all be delighted to see our children looking like that? Also, in my own way of thinking about this, it makes such a difference when the children's fathers and mothers are friendly, warm, and loving toward one another, do not fight a lot, and also extend that same warmth and love to their children. Then, gradually, the children will follow in the same way of life. When children see their parents living a good life, they will want to do the same. When their parents act badly and fight a lot, the children come to feel that their parents are no good, and then the children often become even worse than their parents. For the dharma to flourish, we will have to live well and make the effort to bring these teachings into our experience. For things to go well for our children in the future, we have to live decently ourselves and offer them something both lovely and worthy of respect.

A doctor of homeopathy gave me some advice. He said that we must take care of our bodies by curing our illnesses and promoting our health in every way possible. Our children will then inherit our strength and health, and their bodies will be strong and healthy. Their children will then flourish and be well, and so on in each succeeding generation. If, on the other hand, we do not care for our own bodies—if we contract many illnesses and do not cure those illnesses with medicine—then our children will not be healthy either. Rather, they will suffer from illness, and each subsequent generation will become more sick than the previous one. Therefore, he said, it is our responsibility to take good care of our bodies.

Similarly, we must also take good care of our treasury of knowledge and conduct. If we do, then our children and their children will become better and better. If we do not, then our children and grandchildren will become worse and worse.

I feel fortunate to have had this opportunity to talk with you about the Buddhadharma. You may wonder why I have come here. I have not come to the West imagining that I would be able to propagate the Buddhadharma vastly. What have I hoped to do? In the past, I was able to meet many remarkable lamas, and I did receive extraordinary instructions from them, some of which I have been able to remember. I have thought that explaining those teachings to other people will help them. Some things you may not like, but those can be set aside, and what you like will surely help you. Thinking along those lines, I have traveled to this place. A lot of people have come to the lectures, and no one could miss the joy in your expressions. You have shown ardent interest, and you have asked good questions. Nāropa Institute is not like other schools, and the difference has given me much joy. Thank you.

Notes

1 Kamalashīla, *Bhāvanākramaḥ of Ācārya Kamalaśīla: Tibetan Version, Sanskrit Restoration, and Hindi Translation*, ed. & trans. Ācārya Gyaltsen Namdol (Sarnath, Varanasi: Central Institute of Higher Tibetan Studies, 1985). Hereinafter cited as "Kamalaśīla."

2 Thrangu Rinpoche is referring to the practice of *jö (gcod)*. *jö* means "cut" and, in this context, "cut" means cut attachment. "The pacifier" *(zhi byed)* is another name for this practice. For a discussion of it, see Khetsun Sangpo Rinbochay, *Tantric Practice in Nyingma*, trans. Jeffrey Hopkins, ed. Jeffrey Hopkins and Anne Klein (Ithaca, New York: Gabriel/Snow Lion, 1982), 161-166.

3 *bzod pa, kṣānti*. In departing from the usual translation of *bzod pa* as "patience," I have followed Shunryu Suzuki's lead: "The usual translation of the Japanese word *nin* is 'patience,' but perhaps 'constancy' is a better word. You must force yourself to be patient, but in constancy there is no particular effort involved—there is only the unchanging ability to accept things as they are." Shunryu Suzuki, *Zen Mind, Beginner's Mind*, ed. Trudy Dixon (New York and Tokyo: John Weatherhill, Inc., 1970), 86.

4 *bsam gtan, dhyāna*. In translating *bsam gtan* as "stable contemplation," I have sought consistency with the translation of *bsam pa* as "contemplation" elsewhere. For instance, I have translated *thos pa bsam pa sgom pa gsum* as "hearing, contemplation, and meditation," and I have translated *bsam pa la brten nas 'byung ba'i shes rab* as "knowledge that arises in dependence upon contemplation." Stable contemplation need not be conceptual (*rtog bcas kyi blo*), even though the term may suggest otherwise. In dependence upon the fourth stable contemplation of the Form Realm, bodhisattvas of the Vehicle of Transcendence (*phar phyin theg pa, pāramitāyāna*) realize emptiness in direct perception, and they bring the

practice of transcendent stable contemplation to a surpassing completion on the fifth ground as "the stable contemplation that pleases the mind of the Tathāgata" (*de bzhin gshegs pa'i thugs dgyes pa'i bsam gtan*), a nonconceptual and nondual entrance into the emptiness that is the reality of all phenomena.

5 In this discussion, "permanent" *(rtag pa, nitya)* means unchanging. For an explanation of the meaning of permanence, see Jeffrey Hopkins, *Meditation on Emptiness* (London: Wisdom Publications, 1983), 215–219.

6 In this discussion, "thing" *(dngos po, bhāva)* means that which can perform a function. For an explanation of the meaning of "thing," see Hopkins, 219–220.

7 Thrangu Rinpoche holds up two sticks of incense, one of which is longer than the other.

8 Thrangu Rinpoche now holds up a third stick of incense, longer than either of the other two, and pairs it with the stick that was the long one in the previous pair.

9 Thrangu Rinpoche holds up the stick of incense that was the larger of two in the first pairing and the shorter of two in the second pairing.

10 Thrangu Rinpoche holds up his hand for all to see.

11 In the last four sentences of this paragraph, Thrangu Rinpoche is making use of the similarity between the Tibetan word *kom (goms)*, which means "become accustomed to, become familiar with, get used to," and the Tibetan word *gom (sgom)*, which means "meditate." The two words sound similar to the ear, and by explicitly associating them with one another in the way that he structures his sentence and inflects his voice, Thrangu Rinpoche highlights one of the significant characteristics of meditation in the Buddhist tradition: Buddhist meditation is, among other things, a matter of getting used to initially unfamiliar states. Since the corresponding English words do not resemble one another in the way that the Tibetan words do, I have noted the resemblance here.

12 Kamalashīla, 35

13 Kamalashīla, 35

14 Thrangu Rinpoche indicates the book from which he is teaching.

15 Thrangu Rinpoche indicates a glass of water resting on the table at his side, in which the lights overhead are reflected.

16 *snang ba'i 'du shes sgom.* Kamalashīla, 37

17 In the following discussion of these twelve branches, I have marked the first occurrence of the names of the twelve branches with *italic* type.

18 Thrangu Rinpoche refers to the building where he resided during the course of his lectures. It is located a few miles from the hall where he gave the lectures.

19 More literally, one would have to say something like "individually born being." In deference to the meaning of the Tibetan term and out of concern for the strange implications of the more literal English translation, I have used the more conventional translation, "ordinary being." Unfortunately, the close relationship between the etymology and the term itself gets lost in the translation.

20 The final syllable, *pa*, indicates a person of masculine gender. To indicate a person of feminine gender, *ma* would be affixed to *rnal 'byor*, yielding *rnal 'byor ma; yoginī* would be the corresponding Sanskrit.

21 *skye mched, āyatana.* Sometimes there are six, and sometimes there are twelve. Six sense fields refers to the six sense powers, i.e., those of eye, ear, nose, tongue, body, and mind. Adding the six kinds of objects—visible forms, sounds, smells, tastes, tangible objects, and objects for a mental consciousness—to the six sense powers makes twelve.

22 Here, as elsewhere, Thrangu Rinpoche uses the similarity of two Tibetan words to reinforce his point. He has said something like "Through familiarizing on paths of familiarization."

23 Kamalashīla, 74

24 The body that resembles gold in color,
The entirely beautified protector of the world:
The bodhisattva's mind placed on that object for observation
Is called "meditative equipoise."

Cited in Kamalashīla, 91

25 Thrangu Rinpoche shows two pieces of paper to the students. One of the pieces is considerably larger than the other.

26 Thrangu Rinpoche holds up the smaller of the two pieces of paper.

27 Thrangu Rinpoche holds up the larger of the two pieces of paper.

28 Thrangu Rinpoche now holds up a piece of paper that is much larger than either of the other two.

29 Thrangu Rinpoche holds up the piece of paper that, a moment ago, looked large.

30 Thrangu Rinpoche now holds up two sticks of incense, one of which is much longer than the other.

31 Thrangu Rinpoche holds up a third stick of incense, much longer than either of the other two.

32 Thrangu Rinpoche holds up two sticks of incense, one longer than the other.

33 Kamalashīla, 96

34 Thrangu Rinpoche holds his hand up for everyone to see.

35 Thrangu Rinpoche points to his thumb.

36 Thrangu Rinpoche points to his index finger.

37 Thrangu Rinpoche pulls at the flesh on the back of his hand.

38 In the *Sūtra of the Extensive Collection of All Qualities*, cited in Kamala-shīla, 104.

39 *mos pa*. This word may be translated in many ways: admiration, interest, inspiration, imagination, aspiration, and so on.

40 The verses have been translated in The Dalai Lama, *Stages of Meditation*, trans.Geshe Lobsang Jordhen, Losang Choephel Ganchenpa, and Jeremy Russell (Ithaca, New York: Snow Lion Publications, 2001), 157:

The wise distance themselves from jealousy and other stains;
Their thirst for knowledge is unquenchable like an ocean.
They retain only what is proper through discrimination,
Just like swans extracting milk from water.

Thus, scholars should distance themselves
From divisive attitudes and bigotry.
Even from a child
Good words are received.

41 This is the name by which many Tibetans refer to Tenzin Gyatso, the Fourteenth Dalai Lama.

42 Rangjung Rikpe Dorje (1923-1982), the Sixteenth Gyalwang Karmapa

43 Chökyi Gyatso (1940-1987), the Eleventh Trungpa Tulku

Glossary

English	Tibetan	Sanskrit
accomplished person	grub thob	siddha
accomplishment	dngos grub	siddhi
advice	gdams ngag	
afflictions	nyon mongs	klesha
afflictive obstructions	nyon mongs pa'i sgrib pa	kleshāvaraṇa
aggregate	phung po	skandha
aggregate of form	gzugs kyi phung po	rūpaskandha
aging and death	rga shi	jarāmaraṇa
analytical meditation of the scholar	paṇḍita'i dpyad sgom	
appropriate contemplation	tshul bzhin du bsam pa	
attachment	chags pa	
bewilderment	gti mug	moha
birth	skye ba	jāti
bodhisattva	byang chub sems dpa'	bodhisattva
Body of Complete Resources	longs spyod rdzogs pa'i sku	sambhogakāya
Body of Truth	chos kyi sku	dharmakāya
buddha	sangs rgyas	buddha
calm abiding	zhi gnas	shamatha
close placement	nye bar 'jog pa	

close placement of mindfulness	dran pa nye bar bzhag pa	smṛtyupasthāna
Cloud of Dharma	chos kyi sprin	dharmamegha
collection of merit	bsod nams kyi tshogs	puṇyasaṃbhāra
collection of wisdom	ye shes kyi tshogs	jñānasaṃbhāra
compassion	snying rje	karuṇā
compositional factors	'du byed	saṃskāra
conditioned action	'du byed kyi las	saṃskārakarma
conscientiousness	bag yod	
consciousness	rnam shes	vijñāna
consciousness that is the basis of all	kun gzhi rnam par shes pa	ālayavijñāna
constancy	bzod pa	kṣānti
contact	reg pa	sparsha
continually placing	rgyun du 'jog pa	
conventional	kun rdzob	saṃvṛti
courage	spobs pa	
craving	sred pa	tṛṣṇa
degenerate knowledge	shes rab 'chal ba	
dependent relationship	rten 'brel	pratītya-samutpāda
deprecation	skur ba 'debs pa	apavāda
desire	'dod chags	
Desire Realm	'dod khams	kāmadhātu
dharma	chos	dharma
Difficult Training	sbyang dka' ba	sudurjayā
discrimination	'du shes	saṃjñā
element	khams	dhātu
emptiness having compassion as its essence	stong nyid snying rje snying po can	

essence of the one gone to bliss	bde bar gshegs pa'i snying po	sugatagarbha
evenly placing	mnyam par 'jog pa	
excellent being	skye bu dam pa	
exertion	brtson 'grus	vīrya
existence	srid pa	bhava
feeling	tshor ba	vedanā
Forders	mu stegs pa	tīrthika
Form Realm	gzugs khams	rūpadhātu
Formless Realm	gzugs med khams	ārūpyadhātu
four genuine abandonments	yang dag par spong ba bzhi	
four individual correct knowledges	so so yang dag par rig pa bzhi	
god	lha	deva
Gone Afar	ring du song ba	dūraṃgama
Good Intelligence	legs pa'i blo gros	sādhumatī
grasping	len pa	upādāna
Great Completeness	rdzogs chen	mahāsaṃdhi
ground	sa	bhūmi
ground of a sublime person	'phags pa'i sa	āryabhūmi
grounds of conduct through admiration	mos pas spyod pa'i sa	adhimukti charyā bhûmi
hearer	nyan thos	shravaka
Heat	drod	uṣmagata
higher knowledge	mngon pa	abhidharma
ignorance	ma rig pa	avidyā
Immovable	mi g.yo ba	acalā
individual liberation	so sor thar pa	pratimokṣha
insight	lhag mthong	vipashyanā
intermediate state	bar do	

knowledge arisen from contemplation	bsam pa las 'byung ba'i shes rab	
knowledge arisen from meditation	sgom pa las 'byung ba'i shes rab	
knowledge arisen from hearing	thos pa las 'byung ba'i shes rab	
knowledge of the modes	ji lta ba rtogs pa'i mkhyen pa	
knowledge of the varieties	ji snyed pa rtogs pa'i mkhyen pa	
laziness of attachment to bad activity	bya ba ngan zhen gyi le lo	
legs of magical emanation	rdzu 'phrul gyi rkang pa	ṛddhipāda
liberation	thar pa	
life	srog	jīva
Luminous	'od byed pa	prabhākarī
making one-pointed	rtse gcig tu byed pa	
manifest	mngon du gyur pa	abhimukhī
manner of appearance	snang tshul	
meaning generality	don spyi	sāmānya
meditative equipoise	mnyam bzhag	samāhita
method	thabs	upāya
Middle Way School	dbu ma	mādhyamaka
mind of awakening	byang chub kyi sems	bodhichitta
Mind Only School	sems tsam	chittamātra
mistaken	'khrul pa	bhrānti
mode of abiding	gnas tshul	
name and form	ming gzugs	nāmarūpa
nirvāṇa	mya ngan las 'das pa	nirvāṇa
obstructions to omniscience	shes bya'i sgrib pa	jñeyāvaraṇa

ordinary being	so sor skye bu	pṛthagjana
pacifying	zhi bar byed pa	
path of accumulation	tshogs lam	saṃbhāramārga
path of preparation	sbyor lam	prayogamārga
path of seeing	mthong lam	darshanamārga
peak	rtse mo	mūrdhan
placement meditation of a simple person	ku sā li'i 'jog sgom	
placing the mind	sems 'jog pa	
predisposition	bag chags	vāsanā
proximate afflictions	nye ba'i nyon mongs	upaklesha
quintessential instructions	man ngag	
Radiant	'od 'phro ba	arcishmatī
repeatedly placing	bslan te 'jog pa	
ripened effects	rnam smin gyi 'bras bu	
sending and taking	gtong len	
six sense fields	skyed mched drug	shadāyatana
six types of wanderers	'gro ba rigs drug	
skill in method	thabs la mkhas pa	upāyakaushala
solitary realizer	rang sangs rgyas	pratyekabuddha
spiritual friend	dge ba'i bshes gnyen	kalyānamitra
stable contemplation	bsam gtan	dhyāna
stage of generation	bskyed rim	utpattikrama
Stainless	dri ma med pa	vimalā
strength of heart	snying stobs	
sublime person	'phags pa	ārya
subsequent attainment	rjes thob	pṛṣṭhalabdha
suffering	sdug bsngal	duḥkha
superimposition	sgro 'dogs	samāropa

Supreme Emanation Body	mchog gi sprul pa'i sku	nirmāṇakāya
supreme mundane quality	'jig rten pa'i chos kyi mchog	laukikā-gryadharma
taming	dul bar byed pa	
thing	dngos po	bhāva/vastu
thoroughly pacifying	rnam par zhi bar byed pa	
thoroughly refined	shin sbyang	
transcendence	pha rol tu phyin pa	pāramitā
transcendent aspirational prayer	smon lam gyi pha rol tu phyin pa	praṇidhāna-pāramitā
transcendent constancy	bzod pa'i pha rol tu phyin pa	kṣāntipāramitā
transcendent ethics	tshul khrims kyi pha rol tu phyin pa	shīlapāramitā
transcendent exertion	brtson 'grus kyi pha rol tu phyin pa	vīryapāramitā
transcendent generosity	sbyin pa'i pha rol tu phyin pa	dānapāramitā
transcendent knowledge	shes rab kyi pha rol tu phyin pa	prajñāpāramitā
transcendent method	thabs kyi pha rol tu phyin pa	upāyapāramitā
transcendent power	stobs kyi pha upāyapāramitā	balapāramitā
transcendent stable contemplation	bsam gtan kyi pha rol tu phyin pa	dhyāna-pāramitā
transcendent wisdom	ye shes kyi pha rol tu phyin pa	jñānapāramitā
treatise	bstan bcos	shāstra
twelve branches of dependent relationship	rten 'brel yan lag bcu gnyis	
ultimate	don dam pa	paramārtha
vajra-like meditative stabilization	rdo rje lta bu'i ting nge 'dzin	vajropama-samādhi

valid cognition	tshad ma	pramāṇa
Vehicle of Secret Mantra	gsnang sngags kyi theg pa	gūhyamantra-yāna
Very Joyful	rab tu dga' ba	pramuditā
warrior	dpa' bo	vīra
wisdom	ye shes	jñāna
yogin	rnal 'byor pa	yogin

List of Works Cited

Sūtras

Sūtra Compiling the Dharma Correctly
dharmasaṃgītisūtra
chos yang dag par sdud pa'i mdo

Sūtra of Good Fortune
bhadrakalpikāsūtra
mdo sde bskal ba bzang po

Sūtra of the Descent into Laṅka
laṅkāvatārasūtra
lang kar gshegs pa'i mdo

Sūtra of the Extensive Collection of All Qualities
sarvadharmasaṃgrahavaipulyasūtra
chos thams cad shin tu rgyas par bsdus pa

Sūtra of the Heap of Jewels
mahāratnakūṭadharmaparyāyashatasāhasrikagranthasūtra
dkon mchog brtsegs pa'i mdo

Sūtra of the Hill of the Gayā Head
gayāshīrṣasūtra
ga yā mgo'i ri'i mdo

Sūtra of the Jewel On the Crown
ratnachūḍasūtra
gtsug na rin po che'i mdo

Sūtra of the King of Meditative Stabilizations
samādhirājasūtra
mdo ting nge 'dzin rgyal po

Sūtra of Transcendent Knowledge
prajñāpāramitāsūtra
shes rab kyi pha rol tu phyin pa'i mdo

Sūtra Taught by Akshayamati
akṣhayamatinirdeshasūtra
blo gros mi zad pas bstan pa'i mdo

Sūtra Unravelling the Thought
saṃdhinirmochanasūtra
dgongs pa nges par 'grel pa'i mdo

Shāstras

Chandrakīrti. *Entrance to the Middle Way* (madhyamakāvatāra, dbu ma la 'jug pa). P5261, P5262, Vol. 98. Edition of the Tibetan by Louis de La Vallée Poussin in *Madhyamakāvatāra par Candrakīrti*. Bibliotheca Buddhica IX (Osnabrück: Biblio Verlag, 1970). English translation of Chapters I-V by Jeffrey Hopkins within *Compassion in Tibetan Buddhism* (Valois, NY: Gabriel/ Snow Lion, 1980). English translation of Chapter VI by Stephen Batchelor in Geshé Rabten's *Echoes of Voidness*. London: Wisdom Publications, 1983), p. 47-92.

Kamalashīla. *Bhāvanākramaḥ of Ācārya Kamalaśīla: Tibetan Version, Sanskrit Restoration, and Hindi Translation*. Ed. & trans. Ācārya Gyaltsen Namdol. Sarnath, Varanasi: Central Institute of Higher Tibetan Studies, 1985.

Shāntarakṣhita. *Ornament for the Middle Way* (madhyamakālaṃkāra, dbu ma rgyan gyi tshig le'ur byas pa). P5284, Vol. 101.

Shāntideva. *Engaging in the Conduct of a Bodhisattva* (bodhisattvacharyāvatāra, byang chub sems dpa'i spyod pa la 'jug pa). P5272, Vol. 99.

Vasubandhu. *Treasury of Higher Knowledge (abhidharmakosha, chos mngon pa mdzod)*. Translation by Louis de La Vallée Poussin, *L'Abhidharmakośa de Vasubandhu* (Paris: Geuthner, 1923-1931)

Tibetan Treatises

Gampopa (sgam po pa, 1079-1153). *Explanation of the Stages of the Paths of the Great Vehicle Called "The Excellent Dharma, the Wish-Fulfilling Jewel, the Ornament for Precious Liberation"* (dam chos yid bzhin gyi nor bu thar pa rin po che'i rgyan zhes bya ba theg pa chen po'i lam rim gyi bshad pa). Thimphu, Bhutan: National Library of Bhutan, 1985.

Wangchuk Dorje, Karmapa IX (karma pa dbang phyug rdo rje, 1555-1603). *Pointing a Finger at the Dharmakāya* (phyag rgya chen po lhan cig skyes sbyor gyi khrid zin bris snying po gsal ba'i sgron me bdud rtsi'i snying khu chos sku mdzub tshugs su ngo sprod pa). Included within *The Treasury of Precious Instructions* (gdams ngag rin po che'i mdzod), volume *ta*, pages 71-106.

_____. *Mahāmudrā: Eliminating the Darkness of Ignorance* (phyag rgya chen po ma rig mun sel). English translation by Alexander Berzin (Dharamsala, India: Library of Tibetan Works and Archives, 1978).

_____. *The Ocean of Definitive Meaning* (lhan cig skyes sbyor gyi zab khrid nges don rgya mtsho'i snying po phrin las 'od 'phro). English translation by Elizabeth M. Callahan (Seattle, WA: Nitartha *international*, 2001).

Other Works

Hopkins, Jeffrey. *Meditation on Emptiness*. London: Wisdom Publications, 1983.

Kamalashila. *Bhāvanākramaḥ of Ācārya Kamalaśīla: Tibetan Version, Sanskrit Restoration, and Hindi Translation*. Ed. & trans. Ācārya Gyaltsen Namdol. Sarnath, Varanasi: Central Institute of Higher Tibetan Studies, 1985.

Khetsun Sangpo Rinbochay. *Tantric Practice in Nying-ma.* Trans. Jeffrey Hopkins. Ed. Jeffrey Hopkins and Anne Klein. Ithaca, New York: Gabriel/ Snow Lion, 1982.

Suzuki, Shunryu. *Zen Mind, Beginner's Mind.* ed. Trudy Dixon. New York and Tokyo: John Weatherhill, Inc., 1970

The Dalai Lama. *Stages of Meditation.* trans. Geshe Lobsang Jordhen, Losang Choephel Ganchenpa, and Jeremy Russell. Ithaca, New York: Snow Lion Publications, 2001.